Apocalypse of Truth

Apocalypse of Truth

Heideggerian Meditations

Jean Vioulac

With a foreword by Jean-Luc Marion

Translated by Matthew J. Peterson

THE UNIVERSITY OF CHICAGO PRESS | *Chicago and London*

The University of Chicago Press, Chicago 60637
The University of Chicago Press, Ltd., London

Published 2021
Printed in the United States of America

30 29 28 27 26 25 24 23 22 21   1 2 3 4 5

ISBN-13: 978-0-226-76673-7 (cloth)
ISBN-13: 978-0-226-76687-4 (e-book)
DOI: https://doi.org/10.7208/chicago/9780226766874.001.0001

Original title in French : *Apocalypse de la vérité*

Solari éditions SàRL
Ruelle du Carroz 2b
1168 Villars-sous-Yens
Switzerland

Library of Congress Cataloging-in-Publication Data

Names: Vioulac, Jean, author. | Peterson, Matthew J., translator. | Marion, Jean-Luc, 1946– writer of foreword.
Title: Apocalypse of truth : Heideggerian meditations / Jean Vioulac ; with a foreword by Jean-Luc Marion ; translated by Matthew J. Peterson.
Other titles: Apocalypse de la vérité. English
Description: Chicago : The University of Chicago Press, 2021. | Includes bibliographical references and index.
Identifiers: LCCN 2020042356 | ISBN 9780226766737 (cloth) | ISBN 9780226766874 (ebook)
Subjects: LCSH: Heidegger, Martin, 1889–1976. | Truth. | Logos (Philosophy) Ontology.
Classification: LCC BD171 .V5513 2021 | DDC 193—dc23
LC record available at https://lccn.loc.gov/2020042356.

⊗ This paper meets the requirements of ANSI/NISO Z39.48-1992 (Permanence of Paper).

To Timothée

Τιμοθέῳ ἀγαπητῷ τέκνῳ

2 Tm 1:2

My wisdom is as spurned as chaos.
What is my nothingness, compared
to the amazement that awaits you?

RIMBAUD | *"Lives," trans. John Ashbery*

Contents

Foreword

JEAN-LUC MARION | *Académie Française*

Although irreducibly distinguished by their uses of language, the poet (who composes from words), the prose writer (who proceeds by metaphors), and the philosopher (who works with concepts) are all recognizable by the same obviousness and the same strangeness: certainly, what they say takes hold as if the reader had always understood and known it, with an evident tone and the authority of one who is familiar with the great texts because he knew how to go back to them; but what they compel to be thought also contradicts and troubles what the same reader previously took for granted. By this criterion, Jean Vioulac, who works with concepts, establishes himself as a new and distinguished philosopher, indeed. He masters the textual tradition as a scholar, but he controls it and puts it to work, because he does not speak so much of philosophers as—a difficult and rare thing—of that about which philosophers speak. About things, about what we make of them, and especially about what they demand of us.

Therefore, we must read him and listen to him. In fact, the pages we are about to open take on their brilliance only in view of the two works of this already attested beginning. In the first, perfectly academic in tone and intent, at least on first reading, *L'époque de la technique. Marx, Heidegger et l'accomplissement de la métaphysique* (Paris: PUF, 2009) (The Epoch of Technology: Marx, Heidegger, and the Consummation of Metaphysics), it was a matter of taking up the question of technology. Not as it might be treated by a historian or theoretician of technology, as if it could be understood on its own terms, but as the effect and even the consummation of what metaphysics established and released (as one releases a wild animal, a mob, or a flood) under the heading of rationality. Taking up the effort that perhaps Kostas Axelos and Michel Henry alone had attempted, he conjoined, in a singular interpretation, the arguments of Marx, Nietzsche, and Heidegger: what we hear under the name "technology" does not "apply" anything (science) to anything else (nature), but deploys a *machine* (machination as much as machinery), such as the *mathesis universalis* made not only possible but inevitable because ultra-powerful, ever since Descartes (or rather *one* of Descartes's postulates) allowed for the object alone to be considered real. The object, *namely*, what remains of the thing when one only retains of the phenomenon that which is constituted by model and parameters, by *ordo et mensura*. The machine deploys the ultimate interpretation of beings allowed and demanded by metaphysical reason, which radicalizes the question, "Why is there something rather than nothing?" into this other one, which governs us, the users of the machine, as well as the objects it produces: "How does it work?" Knowing how to answer this question now suffices to fulfill the "great metaphysical principle," that of sufficient reason. Capital and the will to power then appear as the presuppositions of the machine. Together, they define a process that decides itself, without our having to will it, direct it, decide it, or even understand it.

It is at this stage that the second work, *La logique totalitaire. Essai sur la crise de l'Occident* (Paris: PUF, 2013) (Totalitarian Logic: An Essay on the Crisis of the West), takes up the question. How does the machine's mechanical machination not only determine the state of contemporary rationality, but also inscribe itself within universal history and politics? Tacitly taking up the implicit but uncompromising struggle against Hegel made by Levinas (and, more explicitly, by Rosenzweig and Kierkegaard, even better than by Arendt), this essay traces a genealogy of totalitarianism, which, by way of its indisputably realized historical figures, leads it back to its unique condition of possibility—the consummation of rationality, understood according to the logic of the concept, in the philosophical figure of totality. The totalitarianisms of the twentieth and twenty-first centuries could not have been deployed if they had not fulfilled and achieved the program of totalizing beings announced, inaugurated, and *consummated* by the logical totalization of knowledge, such as it is established by Hegel's philosophy in the name of metaphysics as a whole. The demonstration carried out in these pages is all the more impressive given that each actual figure of totalitarianism (Bolshevism, Nazism, so-called liberal economics) is led back to Hegel through the intermediary of the thinkers who described them in advance, and above all Marx, Nietzsche, Hobbes, and Tocqueville. Henceforth, it becomes possible to read, as a *confirmatur* to the letter, certain decisive (terrifying and often nearly comical) texts by the ideologues of these totalitarian movements: but the soundness of the scholarship here depends on the rigor of the conceptual analyses. However, by granting these figures of totalitarianism the logical coherence of a singular consummation of the totalization of beings by the metaphysics of machinery, Jean Vioulac's demonstration could itself appear to become aporetic: if totality governs not only imperialist totalitarianisms (Bolshevism and Nazism), but also the liberal totalitarianism of economic and financial technologies, if therefore supposed "democracy" is also inscribed within totality (all the more effectively as it does not need to resort to an external military or police constraint in order to come about, but simply relies on the implacable immanence of the desire to consume), what way out of the crisis remains possible? The end of history has indeed taken place—not, as announced by kind souls, because democracy would be its crowning achievement, but rather because it consecrates once and again the metaphysical totality of machinery. Whence the evocation (at that time too brief to convince in a short epilogue) of eschatology.

It is up to the pages we are about to read to face this aporia head on, with a radicality that deserves all of our attention. The hypothesis could, very briefly, be summarized in this way. First, we must get out of metaphysics, not because it would be dead, finished, destroyed, but, on the contrary, because it prevails and now carries out unchecked over the whole world, like a cancer without end or limit, the totalization of beings by machinery. Second, metaphysics unfolds in this way because in it, thought began from the outset by masking the difference between Being and beings under the tautology that ὄν (Being/beings) is equal only to itself and that every other way had to remain unfollowed, anonymous, and abandoned. Henceforth, the uncovering performed by ἀλήθεια (understood as ἀ-λήθεια, withdrawn from λήθη) could only discover beings, the only *things* an uncovering could make visible, and kept secret Being itself, buried under the tautology of λόγος with νοῦς (let us say spirit). The forgetting of the ontological difference comes from the *ontic* interpretation of the uncovering, itself based on the tautology (the Parmenidean τὸ γὰρ αὐτό) that λόγος would return (in every sense of the word)[1] to the spirit—of men, or of the world, of course. But there remains another way than the Greek tautology, for there remains an uncovering other than ἀλήθεια. What is called, in biblical Greek, ἀποκάλυψις, in fact also names an uncovering (ἀπο-κάλυψις, to un-cover, to remove a veil, to bring to light). But it is not a matter, in *this* uncovering, first (or even at all) of discovering things as beings taken out of darkness (and which, at the same time, leave non-being, the Being from which they arise, unquestioned and unsuspected), of discovering worldly beings on the basis of the world. It is a matter of bringing the world itself to light on the basis of a λόγος other than the one that returns to the same (τὸ αὐτό), than the spirit of the world (of men), on the basis of the λόγος τοῦ θεοῦ. (Biblical) apocalypse unveils, over and against the uncovering of (Greek) truth, that which escapes the ontological difference itself and the tautology of spirit with Being: the world seen, no longer on the basis of what it unveils of itself (in the double sense of illuminating itself and illuminating on the basis of itself), but on the basis of what God uncovers of it in and through his own λόγος. This reversal (this catastrophe, this revolution) of one uncovering by another revelation, of ἀλήθεια by ἀποκάλυψις, indeed constitutes the last word of the New Testament, a large-scale commentary on an astonishing recommendation from the Epistle to the Hebrews: "what is seen was not made from phenomena [or: was made from non-phenomena], μὴ ἐκ φαινομένων" (Heb 11:3).

We will not go any further into introducing, which would inevitably be too brief, the daring of this confrontation—that, the honest reader must be left to face directly. Several remarks, however, are necessary. First, the undertaking is justified if one endeavors, as achieved scrupulously by Jean Vioulac, to read the New Testament (but also the Old according to the Septuagint) in Greek, with the same literal care and the same openness to the evidence that Heidegger brought to his reading of the Greeks (and by guiding this reading, as he did, through the commentaries of Hölderlin or Eckhart, of Nietzsche and Augustine). That demands more than knowing a little Greek, and more than having made exegetical studies: it demands not denying the evidence when it is glaringly obvious. Next, this confrontation takes up, with an unaffected and more positive candor, the question of Heidegger's unthought debt to the biblical text discussed many times before (by Paul Ricoeur, Marlène Zarader, and Didier Franck, to name only the major French interpreters who have ventured down this path). In any event, this trial remains before us as an inevitable task, failing which, the future of philosophy will remain hindered and compromised. It is about time to undertake it, without excuses, precautions, or hesitations, since the urgency is pressing. Finally, such a confrontation confirms what myriad symptoms have indicated for years even to the most recalcitrant public (French or otherwise): if there is an "end of metaphysics" (and there is one, blinding, threatening), we will not be able to—I would not say respond to it, or even confront it (we have certainly not yet reached this point), but simply—face it head on without also mobilizing the aid of theology coming from the Bible. We must recall that, for a long time, from Justin to Augustine, from Saint Bernard to Erasmus, Christians too have claimed the title of philosophers as disciples of the Logos. And therefore that, when it comes to λόγος, they have, along with the Prologue of John and the Epistles of Paul, something to think and something to say.

The pages of Jean Vioulac will surprise. But there are good surprises, and firstly that of the sudden appearance of a thought.

Translator's Note

MATTHEW J. PETERSON | *University of Chicago*

Jean Vioulac's book is not so much a commentary on the work of Martin Heidegger as it is an original work of philosophy in its own right. With such works, when the author translates the philosophical tradition into his own idiom and voice, fidelity to this same tradition can appear as a betrayal. Yet in such cases, the particular exigency of the translator is fidelity to the idiom of the author. Accordingly, I offer the following notes on the translation.

Although Heidegger's central notion of *Dasein* is often left untranslated, Vioulac renders it with two different terms, depending on the context. He writes *existant* to refer to the kinds of beings that we are, and *existance* (with an *a*) to name the existant's fundamental ontological structure, its being-in-the-world and temporality. I have retained the French spelling of "existant" to preserve this correspondence and follow Vioulac's own translations of *Dasein* as either "existant" or "existance." Throughout the text, Vioulac also writes *essance* with an *a*, following the spelling proposed by Emmanuel Levinas to translate Heidegger's *Wesen*. This is meant to capture Heidegger's understanding of "essence" as occurring temporally and historically (in French, the letter *a* often marks the gerund verb form). Vioulac highlights any other significant or idiosyncratic translations of Heideggerian terms in the endnotes. Quotations from preexisting English translations have been altered to reflect these and the following decisions, which I hope are justified by the consistency and readability they afford.

I have translated the infinitival *l'être* and the participial *l'étant*, which render the German *das Sein* and *das Seiende*, respectively, as "Being" and "beings." *L'Être*, which Vioulac uses to express the archaic German *Seyn*, is translated as

"Beyng." The adjectives *historial* and *historique*, which render the Heideggerian distinction between *geschichtlich* and *historisch*, have been translated as "historical" and "historiological," following convention.

Défaillance is a central term for Vioulac that proved resistant to translation. In French, *défaillance* can mean "weakness, failure, defect," or it can be used figuratively to mean "a misstep or error." Vioulac uses *défaillance* to describe phenomena that express the experience of intentionality before a lack or absence of intuition, as well as to name the condition of being hollowed out by an inner *faille*, the "crack" or "fault" (in the geological sense) that is constitutive of the self. For these reasons I have translated *défaillance* as "faultiness" in order to preserve both the semantic and etymological proximity of these two terms. Along these lines, *dé-faillance* is translated as "fault-iness," while the adjectives *défaillant* and *dé-faillant* are translated as "faulty" or "fault-y."

La technique is translated as "technology," broadly construed, whereas *la technologie* is translated as "technics" to refer to technology in its more particular instantiations. *Accomplissement*, which Vioulac uses to capture the German *Vollendung*, has consistently been translated as "consummation." *Le rien* and *le néant* are translated as "the nothing" and "nothingness" (or "Nothingness," when capitalized), respectively. I have retained Vioulac's capitalizations throughout the text. Vioulac uses *abîme* to render the German *Abgrund*, which I have consistently translated as "abyss." He uses *la déité* to capture the German *Gottheit* and Middle High German *gotheit*, which I translate throughout as "deity." Where no prior English translation of a cited source exists, translations are my own.

For all passages from the Bible, I have relied on the New Revised Standard Version (NRSV). However, because Vioulac's analysis depends so heavily on his own close reading of the Greek sources, I follow and prioritize his translations wherever they depart from the NRSV. Throughout the text, Vioulac's own inclusions of foreign terms are marked by square brackets within quotations and parentheses within the main text. Square brackets around French terms outside quotations are my own interpolations to draw attention to any untranslatable wordplay or associations.

I am deeply grateful to Ryan Coyne, who first encouraged me to undertake this project, for his invaluable assistance along the way. I also wish to thank Jean-Luc Marion for several decisive conversations throughout this process. For their willingness to read and comment on various chapters at different stages of completion, my thanks go out to Sam Catlin, Aslan Cohen, Kirsten Collins, Mendel Kranz, and Rebekah Rosenfeld, as well as to William Underwood and the Philosophy of Religions Workshop at the University of Chicago for the opportunity to present a portion of this work. For their translation acumen,

I thank Karin Lopez and Emma Ramadan. Heartfelt thanks to Kyle Wagner, Dylan Montanari, Adrienne Meyers, and Elizabeth Ellingboe at the University of Chicago Press and to Lys Weiss for copyediting the manuscript. My time bringing this work into English has been marked by the companionship of Alex Brewer and the enduring love and support of my family, to whom I am infinitely grateful. Finally, I would like to thank Jean Vioulac for his patience, his encouragement, and his trust.

CHAPTER 1

Clarifications

§1. CLAIRVOYANCE, EVIDENCE, LUCIDITY

"Living without philosophizing is exactly like having one's eyes closed without ever trying to open them,"[1] wrote Descartes to the translator of the *Principles*, and far from "the speculative philosophy taught in the schools,"[2] he compared thinking to "the pleasure of seeing everything which our sight reveals."[3] Philosophy can then be defined by a very simple first demand, that of emerging from obscurity and confusion in order to gain clarity and distinction, to "see clearly":[4] the primordial demand is thus *clairvoyance*. Facing the radiance of the visible, however, there is the constant risk of fascination, and fascination is perhaps more deceptive than obscurity: it is the absorption of sight in the visible, the paradoxical blinding of vision by the very thing that it sees, when "my mental vision is blinded by the images of things perceived by the senses."[5] Fascination is thus the danger proper to knowledge, which gains clairvoyance only to then let itself be engulfed by the visible. Hence the imperative to *take hold of oneself*, in order not to lose oneself in the objectivity of knowledge, and that is the heart of the Cartesian meditation, to isolate vision from what it makes visible. Clear and distinct knowledge, which sees each time what is made visible to the gaze of the mind, actually proceeds entirely from a sight that founds it and makes it possible. Clairvoyance will then be guaranteed by the purity of vision, that is, by exposing the sight without which there is neither clairvoyance nor anything to see. This method consists in rejecting all "my former beliefs," all that is of the order of pre-judice, that is, of the fore-seen. In doing so, it is a matter of getting rid of everything that blocked sight, to free it in its pure essence: by thus methodically eliminating the *seen*, doubt leads *seeing* to appearances, and *evidence* is this "*seem*[*ing*] to see" (*videre videor*).[6] Descartes was then able to pose as a fundamental principle of clairvoyance that "we ought never to let ourselves be convinced except by the evidence of our reason"[7] and that "if there is anything which is evident to my intellect, then it is wholly true,"[8] and in doing so, he was able to base scientific clairvoyance on metaphysical evidence: if clairvoyance is the sight of the visible, evidence is the clarification of sight, where thought takes hold of itself in itself, in its proper element. The fascination for the visible is thus itself found to be naiveté, which allows itself to be absorbed by what is seen without ever stepping back toward the vision that makes it visible.

But evidence is not enough. Through evidence, I gain the sight by which only the visible is made visible to me. For there to be vision and the visible, however, there must first be light. The reduction of the seen to vision therefore cannot constitute a limit; the reduction must be continued toward the light in and by which vision and the visible can be put into relation, or toward the field of brightness in which the visible appears to sight. Since its Greek founding, philosophy has based scientific clairvoyance on metaphysical evidence, but Heidegger's decisive contribution was to take this "step back" (*Schritt zurück*) even outside the realm of metaphysics, and he noted thus: "In order for something to be evident, and that means luminant, there must of course be a light that shines. The shining of this light is a decisive condition for evidence."[9] The evidence in and by which I gain the power of clairvoyance—namely, to see clearly what is—is itself conditioned by a light. The demand for phenomenological radicality then requires bringing to light this conditioning of my thought, and there is thus a naiveté—a transcendental and no longer empirical naiveté; an ontological naiveté—in being based on its evidence without questioning what conditions it. Heidegger's itinerary consisted in radicalizing the transcendental reduction to the extreme, by receding not only from the object to the subjective conditions of possibility of its constitution, but from subjectivity itself to possibility as such, and to the horizon it unfolds and thus assigns to the subject—who most of the time takes hold of himself *from* this horizon. The Heideggerian meditation thus continuously deepened phenomenology, first in order to expand phenomenality from objectivity to beingness, and in so doing opening the subject to the scope of its existance, and then in order to place this existance in the domain of phenomenality into which it must always already be thrown so that phenomena appear to it. It is this domain of phenomenality in and through which beings can appear that Heidegger thought as "Being," specifying however that "'Being' remains only the provisional word,"[10] and then he more precisely named this primordial domain "Open," "Clearing," or "Free Expanse"; he thus emphasized that "originary intuition and its evidence remain dependent upon openness that already holds sway, the clearing."[11] These words state the fundamental site in which, as exi-*stants*, we stand (in Latin *stare*) exposed, and in which alone evidence can arise: because the nature of thought is to situate this place in its limits, it is made the "topology of Beyng" (*Topologie des Seyns*).[12]

If clairvoyance thus proceeds entirely from the evidence of sight, this evidence is itself based on the clearing that alone provides light. This clearing is then the *Urphänomen*, the "primordial phenomenon," which phenomenology must bring to light—that is, the domain of phenomenality in which we are immersed. It is thus a matter of thinking this clearing, which brings all metaphysics, and all science, in its wake. The highest demand of thought is then *lucidity*, understood as the *vision of light*, and no longer only as the "vision of the visible" (in Greek θεαν οραν, which gave θεωρία) or "semblance of seeing" (*videre videor*): in this way "it exceeds all contemplation because it cares for the light in which a seeing, as *theoria*, can first live and move."[13] Lucidity demands calling evidence into question, "not accept[ing] and tak[ing] this 'clear as day' too lightly,"[14] in order to reduce it to the regime of phenomenality of which it is only an epiphenomenon and thus to recede to the condition of possibility of every appearance, to try to specify the nature of its light. And because it is a topology, thought's first requisite is the *elucidation* of this primordial Place in which it stands.

§2. SUFFICIENCY AND FAULTINESS

But evidence does not only concern knowledge, it is the clarity of the act by which I take hold of myself, it is the very taking hold of my being. This was the most radical point reached by Descartes, to show that in evidence, that is to say, thought in all its clarity, the *ego* gains its being and its existance. In this way, evidence is simultaneously the clarification of thought and the discovery that this sphere of clarity circumscribes my very being. Henceforth, the calling into question of evidence required by the exigency of lucidity is quite simply the calling into question of what I am. An uncritical confinement among evidence in fact always runs the risk of circumscribing an identity upon which I would make a base and with which I would be satisfied.[15] With Emmanuel Levinas, we can call this self-satisfaction of thought by which the I is based on itself *sufficiency*: "This conception of the 'I' [*moi*] as self-sufficient is one of the essential marks of the bourgeois spirit and its philosophy. As sufficiency for the petit bourgeois, this conception of the 'I' nonetheless nourishes the audacious dreams of a restless and enterprising capitalism. [. . .] The bourgeois admits no inner division [*déchirement intérieur*] and would be ashamed to lack confidence in himself."[16] Sufficiency is *self-satisfaction*, which defines ipseity (αὐτο) by satisfaction, satiety, in other words by completeness, and a completeness granted by things. This sufficiency finds its expression and systematization in humanism.[17] Humanism believes it has a sufficient definition of the human being, attributes diverse qualities to it, all excellent, and can thus enjoy the satisfaction that there is to be such a being. But lucidity demands recognizing more humbly that we do not know who we are, that no definition of man, however benevolent it may be, is commensurate to his essance. The question "what is man?" is certainly not a settled affair, no answer could constitute an achievement: lucidity demands admitting that "we can only wait for the essance of man."[18] It is thus a matter of overcoming, not only naiveté and fascination, but also sufficiency, of no longer relying on an illusory self-confidence in order to, on the contrary, hollow out the inner fault [*faille*] by which the I receives what it is given to think. If evidence is not sufficient but must be led back to the light from which it proceeds, then the reduction *to* the *ego* must be radicalized by a reduction *from* the *ego*, since the *ego* itself has, at first glance, neither the power nor the freedom to set to work, but must endure—precisely because I cannot renounce my evidence without totally calling myself into question.

Anxiety is a privileged example of such moments of faultiness, when the *ego* falters and discovers the fault that is (in) it. While fear is always fear before a being that threatens us, anxiety is fear before nothing in particular; on the contrary, no being can bring me either bearings or support any longer; thus "in anxiety beings as a whole become superfluous."[19] Anxiety is the collapse of the world, that is, of beings as a whole, and this collapse is the reduction of beings in full, which is thereby the manifestation of what is radically other than all beings: the nothing, which as non-being is Being itself. "Anxiety makes manifest the nothing,"[20] and that is just what I grow anxious in the face of: in the face of nothing; and that is how I take hold of myself after anxiety: it was nothing. But this nothing is what pulls me out of the submersion in the density and indifferentiation of beings to set me at a distance from them and thus to make them visible to me, allowing me to be the existant that I am. Anxiety is thus the trial of the nothing, as what defines both existance and the ipseity of the *ego*: "Holding itself out into the nothing, the existant is in each case already beyond beings as a whole. Such being beyond beings we call *transcendence*. [. . .] Without the original manifestness of the nothing, no selfhood and no freedom."[21] Anxiety is therefore revelation of the *self*, that is, of this transcendence in relation to the *I* itself. "The clear night of the nothing of anxiety"[22] is then always the moment of pure lucidity, it is more essantial than all evidence; in it I grasp the essance of ipseity as the gaping fault where the nothing is hollowed out within myself, and this fault lets the abyss be glimpsed for the first time: anxiety is "the silent voice that attunes us toward the horror of the abyss" (*Schrecken des Abgrundes*).[23] In anxiety, I testify to the nothing (that I am) such that anxiety is the most radical reduction of sufficiency, and in its arche-evidence the very essance of ipseity is revealed to me: *what I am, is that I am nothing.*

Unlike evidence, which is methodically conquered by doubt, anxiety is enforced: by the relation to death. Death is not demise, a simple factual event that would happen at a given moment and would thus be outside of my being, or would simply constitute its limit. Dying is proper to man, if however one understands that to die is neither to perish, nor to demise, but "to be capable of death as death." Heidegger repeated it tirelessly: "Only man dies. The animal perishes. It has death neither ahead of itself nor behind it."[24] Death is a possibility located at the very heart of existance, but this possibility offers nothing to be actualized: "Death, as possibility, gives the existant nothing to be 'actualized,' nothing which it, as actual, could itself *be*. It is the possibility of the impossibility of every way of comporting oneself towards anything, of every way of existing."[25] This means that its only possible actualization is the nothing. Dying, as the assumption of death, is then the conquest of its being: "Only in dying can I to some extent say absolutely, 'I am.'"[26] The tension of existance toward its death is thus the very content of the *ego*: "This certainty, that 'I myself am in that I will die,' is *the basic certainty of the existant itself.* It is a genuine statement of the existant, while *cogito sum* is only the semblance of such a statement." In the clear lucidity of anxiety I am revealed to myself as *sum moribundus*: "but insofar as I am, I am *moribundus. The* moribundus *first gives the* sum *its sense.*"[27] The "courage for anxiety in the face of death"[28] is in this respect a singular mode of lucidity, which allows the essance of existance and that of Being to be elucidated in the nothing at the same time.

The faultiness of the *ego*, which destroys all sufficiency and orders it to stop putting itself on a pedestal, occurs in the event of love as well. We *fall* in love, and this fall immediately reveals the intimate fault that structures me in my essance and which most of the time I evade and deny. This is the fault of my intimate nothingness: "One does not kill oneself for love of *a* woman," wrote Cesare Pavese in *The Business of Living*, "but because love—any love—reveals us in our nakedness, our misery, our vulnerability, our nothingness."[29] In such an event, I am ready to give everything, to give myself away, and at this very moment I discover that I have nothing to give, because I myself am nothing. In that way it is discovered that the gift of self gives nothing; it is the revelation of the nothing constitutive of the self. As such, love is a trembling of beings as a whole as vertiginous as anxiety, since by it all decision and all meaning can be seen to be annulled and reevaluated; especially by the lack that it generates—

when "you miss a single person, and the world is depopulated"[30]—it is proof of an irreducible absence that no presence manages to fill, and which on the contrary sees nothing but absence in the very presence of beings.[31]

Another essantial faultiness occurs in boredom. The ordinary reaction to boredom is entertainment, that is to say, the frantic search for activities, or things, with which I could fill my emptiness. But true boredom, profound boredom, occurs when no being is enough, when nothing is capable of satisfying me anymore: in so doing, it reduces the sufficiency and the self-satisfaction of the *ego* to nothing. In that way it rejects the position of the I on its certain pedestal: boredom [*l'ennui*] (derived from the Latin *est mihi in odio*, "I hate myself") is the revelation that "the self is hateful."[32] But profound boredom is especially the revelation of the abyssal depths of existance: Chateaubriand thus evoked "the abyss of [his] existence," and rightly saw in boredom its irreducible proof: "I was aware of my existence only in a deep sense of boredom."[33] As it "draws back and forth like a silent fog in the abysses of existance" (*in den Abgründen des Daseins*), boredom is this vertiginous revelation of the abyss, such that no being could fill it, a void that no presence could remove. Boredom is thus the simultaneous reduction of the object and the *ego*; it spoils [*abîme*] existance in the nothing and shows that this nothing is the very content of existance; it then lets "the single and unitary universal horizon of time"[34] emerge from the fog: that is, the contours of the Clearing.

§3. HISTORY AND DETERMINATION: DESTINY

The crossing from evidence and access to the sphere of lucidity—that is, the phenomena of elucidation—is thus in truth banal, common to all. The primordial methodological requisite proper to thinking is then the clarification of this luminosity to which we have access because we dwell here: "The guide to thinking strives *for* it to become *brighter* around us, and for us to become more circumspect of the brightness."[35] If this exposure is indispensable, it is because this luminosity *determines* us, and determines our thought: as an existant, I stand in a domain that is going to determine my very evidence. It was one of the major features of the social sciences of the nineteenth and twentieth centuries to recognize—starting from the fields opened philosophically by Marx and Nietzsche—this determination of thought, which led to suspicion about the truth of evidence itself. As sciences, however, they could only ever fold the question of determinations back into the derivative field of systems or empirical and ontic domains by reifying the determination, so to speak. The sciences were only able to be clairvoyant with respect to the determinations that influence us: but the exigency is to be lucid. The determination that it is a question of thinking here is in no way empirical, it is the ontologico-transcendental determination of everything that is by the preliminary opening of the site of the Clearing. Our thought *is determined* by the regime of phenomenality proper to the site in which we stand: I think neither what I want, nor as I want, but I am taken in a flow of light that has always already decided both the mode of appearing of what is and the evidence in which I grasp myself. "Everything coming to presence, and everything coming and going along with it, always appears in a determined and determining light" (*in einem bestimmten und bestimmenden Lichte erscheint*),[36] thus wrote Heidegger, "that which encounters shows itself each and every time in a determined light" (*in einem bestimmten Licht*): if this light is indeed determining, it is determined as well, and an extra step is necessary, which tries to free the very provenance of the Clearing.

To conceive the site in which we stand as a field, a Clearing, is in effect to place it in relation to a darkness surrounding it on all sides: it is thus to think it in its constitutive finitude, as well as to think it as the *result* of a process of clarification, which is a constant struggle against shadow. "Brightness plays in the open and wars there with darkness,"[37] said Heidegger, and the existant always finds itself placed in a site that is already cleared, already arranged, already won against "the totality of beings that remain enveloped within themselves."[38] This clarification is an unfolding of light, which has always already determined the aspect (ἰδεα) or the brightness (ἴδη) of beings, in other words their essence (εἶδος), and it is possible to call this unfolding or this dispensation, recognized in its constitutive mobility, "essance."[39] To recede to the determined modality of the Clearing's arrangement is then to try to think essance's dispensation. It is such a dispensation that opens and furnishes the site in which existance takes place, "for *schicken* ['sending'] originally denotes: 'preparing,' 'ordering,' 'bringing each thing to that place where it belongs'; consequently it also means to 'furnish' and 'admit.'"[40] Being must then be thought as the event of this dispensation that furnishes a site for the existant: Being *is* not—it is the nothing; *there is* Being only as unfolding of light and movement of opening. Being is the event of this unfolding. To think Being is to think its eventality, and this event is that of the diffusion or the dispensation of its essance, which opens the realm of the Clearing: "'Being' means nothing other than the dispensation of the lighting and clearing that furnishes a domain for the appearing of beings."[41] This event, which furnishes the site in which existance takes place, is history. Being is in its essance historical: it does not *have* a history, it occurs *as* history, and it must be said that "the history of Being is Being itself and nothing but this" (*die Seinsgeschichte ist das Sein selbst und nur dieses*).[42] Lucidity is vision of the light that allows us to see, but this light is only the event of its diffusion: Being occurs as "history of the clearing of 'Being'" (*Lichtungsgeschichte*).[43] The thought of Being (of light, of the Clearing, of the free expanse) is in the last instance the thought of the *history* of Being: the "step back" thus consists in thought taking a place within the event of its history.

Humanity is historical in its essance because its essance is existance, that is, the opening and the availability for a dispensation of Being, a dispensation that is the most originary essance of history. In other words, the transcendental arche-reduction that recedes to the Clearing discovers nothing "natural" there, it does not reach a "lifeworld," but a historical world, a situation involved in a history and determined by it, that is to say, enraptured by it: "our being [is] enraptured [*entrückt*] as such, provided that our being is authentic. Inauthentically, it is always—in contrast to such rapture—merely sitting tight on an ever-changing present-day."[44] The situation of existance can therefore only recede to the very movement of this rapture, that is to say, to the dispensation of Being itself, to the essantial occurrence (*Wesung*) of the essance dispensed by a destiny: "The history of Being is never past but stands ever before us; it sustains and defines every *condition et situation humaine* [human condition and situation]."[45] The essance of the human being is itself nothing "natural," it is historical; the question of the essance of the human being is inseparable from that of history: "History is that which is distinctive for the being of the human being, [it] is the distinctive determination in the question concerning the essance of the human being."[46] There is no such thing as "man," timeless entity, to whom would befall all sorts of adventures that could be told in the form of history. Rather, humanity is historical through and through, and we have to recognize that "history constitutes the most proper character of our kind of being."[47] It is the illusion of naiveté to place oneself apart from the history to which we belong, in which we are enclosed, and to thus believe oneself capable of approaching it from the distance of objectivity. But history is not outside of us, it passes right through us; we *are* nothing outside of the realm of Being's dispensation, that is to say, of its destiny: "Always the destining of revealing holds complete sway [*durchwaltet*] over man,"[48] and lucidity demands each time assuming his history.

To be human is to stand in relation to this dispensation in a way that is determined each time. If there is a history of thought, there is also a history of the being of the human being. The Egyptian, Greek, medieval, modern, or contemporary human being are not identical: they do not relate in the same way to things, to animals, to death, to the divine, and to history, nor do they grasp themselves in the same evidence; there is a vibration, a pulsation of ontological luminosity, which offers the humanity that stands within it variations of brightness and hue. The history of Being is a history of the variations of its light: "Initially, as well as later on, Being cleared and lit itself, though in different ways, as having the character of a shining forth, of a shining that lingers, of a presencing, of the over-against and countering."[49] Being's dispensation thus sets itself to work "in a manifold manner."[50] The history of the Clearing is "the history of the formations of Being" (*die Geschichte der Seinsprägungen*).[51] Such a formation of Being, which is each time a "historical formation" (*eine seinsgeschichtliche Prägung*), defines an epoch. The historicality of Being is its epochality, history is made of "particular epochs of the full *Geschick* of Being."[52] These are therefore both the limit of the reduction, which recedes to the epoch in which we stand, and the fundamental methodological requisite: *lucidity demands thinking its epoch*, it needs an epochal situation, which would circumscribe the fundamental site in which we stand, and would thus bring to light the historical formation specific to our time, and in doing so could explain how our thought and our existance are determined.

§4. LANGUAGE AND COMMUNITY

But then it is worth considering what bears and brings essance along, that is, what is the luminous substance that diffuses the primordial phenomenological luminosity. It is language, which is the translucent domain in which this luminosity is at once manifest, broken down, and diffracted. In this sense, language is the realm of primordiality reached by Heidegger at the end of his radicalization of the phenomenological reduction; it is simultaneously the opening and ruling of the world, the primordial spacing that makes beings as a whole visible in a meaningful and structured order: "world announces [*kündet*] itself in the lore [*Kunde*] of historical Being, and this lore is the manifestness of the Being of beings in the mystery. In lore, and through it, world rules. This lore, however, happens in the primal-event of language. [. . .] Language is the ruling of the world-forming and preserving center of the historical existance of the people."[53] Human beings only stand in the light of Being as long as they stand in a language. This is why it must not be said that human beings *have* language, but that they are "within language":[54] "Language is the house of Being. In its home human beings dwell."[55] Language is a house as the mode in which everything dwells, which unfolds the horizon of the familiar by giving meaning to each thing and by assigning it to its limits; it is additionally the collection and guard of meaning: it is especially that *inside of which* we stand. Therefore, there are not first individuals (who would be what they are in themselves and by themselves, which is to say not much), who then would be provided with a tool of expression, to finally be transmitted givens (and which?), but rather there is first the common milieu of language, in which human beings discover a world and dialogue, in order to finally take hold of themselves using this language. Thus the evidence "I am, I exist" by which the *ego* discovers itself is a "proposition" (*pronuntiatum*) which is "necessarily true whenever it is put forward by me" (*quoties a me profertur*):[56] the very evidence by which the *ego* gains its essance is carried by a language—and this is Nietzsche's entire critique of Descartes, to highlight this determination of the *ego* by the grammar of *this* language. In this way, language is "the originary founding of Being. Only when we return to ourselves from out of the essantial power of things experienced in advance do we come to one another and come to *be* with and for one another—of ourselves, and in the strict sense of this phrase 'of ourselves.'"[57] To say that language is the "house of Being" is thus to refuse every temptation to reduce it to one being among others, to recognize that it is the very mode of the unfolding of Being and thought, and that we dwell within it.

In this respect, language is irreducible to simple sound uttering. The element of language is much vaster than simple discourse. Language engages human beings wholly. To be human is to stand in this realm of meaning, and every human attitude and behavior sets meaning to work and is situated in relation to it: all human behavior is speech, to the point that keeping silent, for the human, is an eminent manner of signifying. There are silent words, made of unsaid things or simple glances, and there is also a language of the body, made of gestures. This is why, said Heidegger, the hand is just as much a carrier of language as the mouth: "the hand's gestures run everywhere through language, in their most perfect purity precisely when man speaks by being silent."[58]

To assume one's history is therefore to assume a language: and this is quite simply to assume a community. Indeed, language is first *dialogue*, and in this way the first mode of human beings' reciprocal relation among themselves: it is primordiality as ontological intersubjectivity.[59] Language opens and configures the very site in which we stand as it is dialogue, which is to say, the primordial modality of Being-for-one-another, with-one-another, or against-one-another [*l'un-contre-l'autre*]—in both senses, proximity and hostility, that this last expression has in French. In dialogue it is thus confirmed that "speaking, then, mediates our coming to one another." But dialogue is precisely not only a speaking, it is also a hearing, and in an authentic dialogue—when it is not falling on deaf ears—it is revealed that language is just as much hearing as speaking, that "being able to talk and being able to hear are co-original." In this way, language is communication: if dialogue is authentic communication, then it is availability to what is common, which it manifests: "The unity of a conversation consists in the fact that in the essential word there is always manifest that One and the Same on which we agree, on the basis of which we are united and so are authentically ourselves."[60] As communication, language thus exposes this common essance (*gemeine Wesen*) and attests to everyone's principial belonging to this community (*Gemeinwesen*). There are thus just as many peoples as languages—since "Being speaks everywhere and always, in every language."[61] The Greeks, who never had a common state, homogeneous territory, or unified religion, were this people uniquely defined by their language, this people who dwelled in the λόγος, whose very community was dialogue, and who dismissed all those who were ignorant of it to the rank of "barbarians" (literally: those who only express themselves by rumblings [*borborygmes*], in other words, who do not speak Greek).

To recognize the fundamental character of history and of the epoch, and to recede to the epochality of an essantial unfolding, is then to recognize in the historical community the primordial realm that thought must invest, and in this sense Heidegger wrote in *Being and Time*: "If the destinal existant, as Being-in-the-world, exists essantially in Being-with Others, its historicizing is a co-historicizing and is determinative for it as *destiny* [*Geschick*]. This is how we designate the historicizing of the community, of a people" (*das Geschehen der Gemeinschaft, des Volkes*).[62] To think the epoch is to think a community determined by a history. That is what defines a people, namely, the assumption of such a destiny: "The Being of the people is neither mere occurrence of a population, nor animal-like Being, but determination as temporality and historicity."[63] Just as radicalizing the reduction disqualifies evidence in the direction of lucidity, in the same way it disqualifies the *ego* in the direction of the community, and in this way carries out a "blasting open of the essence of the human existant," and thus recognizes that "the human being is never an individual subject, but he stands always for- or against-one-another, in a with-one-another."[64] The question of the *We* is more fundamental than the question of the *I*: the *I* itself is only possible from the *We* that precedes it. It is the illusion of individualism to try to deduce—by inducing, in this case—a community from separate individuals. A people is not "an assembly of several subjects, who by virtue of agreements first ground a community, but the originally united being bearing exposedness, transportedness, tradition, and mandate can only be what we call 'a people,'"[65] and individual solitude only ever occurs starting from this originary gathering that is the people. This is why, if Cartesian evidence could be satisfied with the question: "Who am I, I who am certain that I am?" Heideggerian lucidity demands asking and ceaselessly repeating the question: "Who are we?"[66] In this respect, "the philosophical question can be posed in the form: *Who are we?*"[67] It is a question not of thereby dissolving the singularity of the existant in an indistinct mass, but of recognizing that each of us belongs, in our own way, to a community, and that to exist in an epoch is always to stand in a determined community: "We as existants submit ourselves [*fügen uns*] in a peculiar manner into the membership of the people, we stand in the Being of the people [*wir stehen im Sein des Volkes*], we are this people itself."[68] The realm of primordiality reached by the reduction is therefore not some sort of state of nature, but a historical community: the site in which we stand is a people. If Being is the history of Being, this history does not float like the spirit over the waters, it is immanent to the destiny of a human community: "Being occurs as the history of man, as the history of a people."[69]

Henceforth, bringing the epochal situation to light cannot happen from the strict point of view of the thinker, it must take on the situation of the community to which he belongs. Yet every thinker is solitary. "The philosopher must remain solitary, because this is what he *is* according to his nature. His solitude is not to be *admired*,"[70] said Heidegger, and thinking indeed demands the most radical solitude. But this solitude is neither selfishness nor sufficiency: it is thought of the community, and the step back of loneliness is precisely what allows the community to be thought as such, insofar as "it is precisely the absence in the lonesome of something in common which persists as the most binding bond *with* it."[71] This is why the thinker, if he is alone, is not independent: he thinks precisely the Being-in-common of a community in its historical determination, and thus must himself assume the tradition constitutive of this destiny. This tradition is gathered together in works of art. Indeed, for a people the work of art is the pole and the pivot in relation to which the historical community can situate itself, and situate the earth, the sky and the divine, in this sense it is a "projection of the Clearing,"[72] which condenses meaning, unfolds it, and transmits it. Heidegger makes this evident using the Greek temple, "the temple work that first structures and simultaneously gathers around itself the unity of those paths and relations in which birth and death, disaster and blessing, victory and disgrace, endurance and decline acquire for the human being the shape of its destiny. The all-governing expanse of these open relations is the world of this historical people."[73]

But as it is the dwelling, language itself is the temple: "Language is the precinct (*templum*), i.e., the house of Being," it is "the temple of Being."[74] Among the works constitutive of historical communities, "the work of language" (*das Sprachwerk*) is what determines the language and thought of the community: it is "the happening of that saying in which its world rises up historically for a people [. . .] In such saying, the concepts of its essance [*die Begriffe seines Wesens*]—its belonging to world-history, in other words—are formed, in advance, for a historical people."[75] The works of language are like the jewels wrought and polished by creators to make the primordial luminosity shine in them, and if the search for lucidity demands assuming the destiny of a language, then it finds in such works the translucent crystals where the light gleams. Among the works of language are literary works, and especially poems: but the poet says his vision in the singularity of an unheard and unrepeatable word, while the thinker says it in a language spun from concepts, which those who come after him can claim for themselves, and speak—and if it is possible for us to think, it is by speaking the languages created by philosophers. All lucid thought, which therefore assumes its historical determination through the destiny of a community, and which attempts to think the epoch of this destiny in which it is situated, then finds in such works "the concepts of its essance" from which it will be able to think what is. The exigency of lucidity demands thinking its epoch and assuming the destiny of the community, and the thinking of such a destiny means confronting its constitutive works: that is, for us Westerners, the works of the philosophical tradition such as it has unfolded since the inaugural *Poem* of Parmenides. Such a confrontation with these works, in order to respond to the primitive essance of language at the same time as to the communal status of these works, can then only take the form of the dialogue. Thinking our epoch therefore demands bringing to light the situation proper to our historical community, and this in a dialogue with the essantial philosophical work of our epoch. This work is precisely that of Heidegger, who took on the destiny of the philosophical tradition all the way through, thought its Greek inauguration, its historical unfolding, and its terminal decomposition, to the point of recognizing in our epoch its "end," and who was above all the only one to think the Clearing of Being as such, and for this reason appears as the most lucid thinker of the West.[76]

The preliminary question to all lucid thought can therefore be formulated simply: *Where are we?* what is our position in this epoch of our history, what are the possibilities that it grants us, and how does it determine us? And if we are allowed to hope to see clearly, it is by searching in Heidegger for "the concepts of its essance." It is therefore a matter of taking up the question asked by Heidegger in 1939: to try "to recognize in what moment of the hidden history of the West we 'stand'; to recognize whether we do *stand* in it, or are falling, or already lie prostrate in it," and to that end, "to stand in *that wherein* every act and every reality of this era in Western history receives its time and space, its ground and its background, its means and ends, its order and its justification, its certainty and its insecurity."[77]

CHAPTER 2

From the Equal to the Same

§5. MACHINATION

An epoch is defined by a determinate modality of essance's dispensation, that is, a regime of phenomenality, a specific ontological luminosity that lucidity must attempt to see. All light first shines starting from the brightness that it gives to things; it is thus starting from the modalities of appearing of what is that we should recede to the Clearing in which we stand. In other words: it is a matter of freeing the essance of our epoch, which can be achieved using a redoubled eidetic reduction, which first reduces the given to its essence, in order to then go back to the realm of phenomenality that fixes its traits to this realm. Precisely because it is a question of exposing the constitutive essance of our epoch, every given whatsoever must be able to lead back to this realm of phenomenality, including "natural" beings: the natural being must even be privileged since it appears in every epoch, and thus makes it possible to observe the metamorphoses of its appearing. The sun is the example of a natural phenomenon that has always given itself to human beings. For an Egyptian of the Middle Kingdom, it is praised each morning as the "good god, well loved, / who offers life to each living thing [. . .] handsome his face when he comes from the God's Land."[1] For Greeks of the classical period, it is a celestial body integrated into the rational harmony of the cosmos, whose movements can be determined, and which can serve, for instance, to find one's bearings at sea.[2] For us, it is a sphere of incandescent gas with a radius of four hundred thirty thousand miles, located ninety-three million miles from the earth, which produces helium by the nuclear fusion of the hydrogen of which it is composed. The same givens (shapes, colors, heat, movements . . .)[3] appear in the first case under the figure of a dispensator god of all beneficence, in the second as a natural body and point of orientation, and finally as a complex system of particles that functions to produce energy: in other words, as a machine.

Thus, at first glance and most of the time, beings are made visible in their "machinational essence" (*machenschaftliche Wesen*). Highlighting the mechanistic essence of beings in our epoch could go on indefinitely, since the constitutive element of reality is now thought, far from the ἄτομος of Democritus, as an extremely complex machine (composed of neutrons, protons, electrons, quarks, bosons, and so forth); the living thing is conceived biologically as a "body machine," that is, as an assemblage of organs; the soul is defined as a "psychic apparatus," ruled by a libidinal economy; and the human being itself is interpreted as a "desiring machine." Contemporary science deploys [*déploie*] the rule of causality unconditionally, and in doing so "brings to light its machinational essence" (*in ihrem machenschaftlichen Wesen*),[4] and scientific interpretation as such today enforces this determined formation of beings, since "the mechanistic *and* the biologistic modes of thinking are always only consequences of the concealed machinational interpretation of beings" (*machenschaftliche Auslegung des Seienden*).[5] Thus, science today has no more than a distant relation with what it was in Greece or in the Middle Ages: it no longer addresses beings with the question: *what is it?* but rather with the sole question: *how does it work?* It addresses everything from the *a priori* of its machinational essence, and now only verifies the mechanics of its models by the efficiency of their functioning. In doing so, contemporary science makes evident that it is *phenomenality itself* that is machinational, and indeed, the great physicists of the twentieth century accepted a redefinition of the phenomenon, based no longer on the conditions assigned to givenness by sensation, but rather on measuring instruments and observation, to the extent that the physical phenomenon is now only "the interaction"[6] between the machine and reality.

This mode of essance's deployment, which enforces the configuration of the machine on all that is, must be called "machination" (*die Machenschaft*), the deployment of phenomenality that constitutes every given in the horizon of machinability, a "machinability in which everything is made out ahead of time to be machinable and altogether at our disposal."[7] The essance of this "machinational epoch"[8] is therefore "machination," which "determines the beingness of beings" (*die Machenschaft die Seiendheit des Seienden bestimmt*).[9] Discovering our epochal situation thus demands recognizing it as the epoch of technology, not, however, because there are a lot of machines, but because its proper regime of phenomenality deploys "its ultimate—which means universal—and planetary form of dominance. In the age of technology, this appears in the form of the machine" (*in der Gestalt der Maschine zur Erscheinung*).[10] Technology is thus primarily nothing thingly or material, it is a determinate mode of phenomenality: "Technology is a way of revealing" (*eine Weise des Entbergens*),[11] it is the artificial luminescence in and through which all beings show through.

The stakes of exposing the essance of our epoch is lucidity regarding what determines us: we are determined by machination. Existance today then consists, not only in seeing beings appear as nothing but machines, but also in having their possibilities circumscribed by machinability. Existance itself is exposure to the power of machination, and that is what is most difficult to grasp: "The essence of technology pervades our existance [*durchwaltet unser Dasein*] in a way which we have barely noticed so far,"[12] its radiation pierces right through us, and without our knowing it; the danger to which thought is exposed remains as long as evidence itself always runs the risk of being reduced to its artificial and spectral luminosity. The evidence by which the human being takes hold of itself from the horizon of machinability is in fact itself machinational: it is "lived experience" (*Erlebnis*), and Heidegger explains that "lived experience" is "the basic form of representation belonging to the machinational and the basic form of abiding therein."[13] There is thus an *ego* specific to the machinational epoch, which is lived experience, and hence the self-satisfaction of this lived experience, which only ever aims to maximize its satisfaction and sufficiency. This *ego* then becomes *ego computo*, which approaches all things in terms of a utility calculus and cost-benefit analysis; this *ego* defines "these all-calculating barbarians"[14] that Hölderlin evoked as early as 1799, and which ever since then has become the norm in societies subject to "the modern 'machine economy,' the machine-based reckoning of all activity and planning [in its absolute form]."[15] Thus subject to this economic machination, human beings are requisitioned by "the unconditioned possibility of the production of everything,"[16] which drives them to "[deliver] the products of production through the market." Machination is absolute productivism, which opens and configures beings as a whole in accordance with its demand for production: in and through it, "what is human about humans and thingly about things is dissolved, within the self-assertion of producing, to the calculation of the market value of a market that is [. . .] a global market spanning the earth."[17] The human, redefined as a calculator and producer, thus stands today in the "global market," and it is henceforth this market that defines the Clearing, the primordial ontological site in which the human being stands and things appear. To exist is to stand in the site of a Clearing and to be exposed to the power of its clarification: man now stands in the market, he is completely dominated by the calculating power of machination. Whether he manufactures machines or whether he is content with putting them to use [*les faire fonctionner*], whether this be in his "work" or in his "free time," man never does anything other than deploy the possibilities assigned to him by machination: "Whether he as an individual knows it or not, wills it or not," he is "a functionary of technology."[18]

§6. CYBERSPACE

In the epoch of technology, the totality of beings is "Machinery,"[19] that is, a machine of machines that has taken on the scale of a global apparatus. The spatiality internal to machinery is the market, which "markets in the essance of Being."[20] But it is important to define the phenomenological luminosity proper to this artificial Clearing. This Clearing is public space *qua* public opinion, which is to say the public realm (*die Öffentlichkeit*), understood as the scene of all that is convened in public and forced to become public: in other words, the ob-scene. As early as 1927, Heidegger recognized in the public realm this neutral and anonymous space whose subject is the They, which "brings tranquilized self-assurance—'Being-at-home,' with all its obviousness—into the average everydayness of existance,"[21] without wondering, however, about the specific historicality of this type of coexistance, and its dependence on the place of mass societies and specific modes of production.[22] Such a loss of self in anonymity certainly belongs to the existant's mode of being, but the fact that "the real dictatorship of the 'they' is unfolded"[23] assumes a determinate exercise of power, which "needs the public, but with the intent of confusing it through and through, and of undermining the possibility of forming an opinion."[24] Power deploys its essance precisely as machination, and in this way Machinery demands "the machinational opening of beings as 'publicness'" (*die machenschaftliche Offentheit des Seienden als "Öffentlichkeit"*).[25] Henceforth, it is "the dictatorship of the public realm" (*Diktatur der Öffentlichkeit*) that expands its empire, in such a way that "so-called 'private existance' [. . .] simply ossifies in a denial of the public realm," and "hence it testifies, against its own will, to its subservience to the public realm."[26] The public realm is the light proper to the market, which thus deploys its absolute demand for transparency in order to subjugate all that is.

Man stands in this realm of spectral luminosity continuously produced by machines, which effectively implement our determination by machination. This determination is called "information," which is simultaneously the transformation, conformation, and uniformalization of existances: "Of course, this sort of 'Information' is also just a sign of the times. The word 'Information'—which is [not a word of German] provenance—speaks more clearly here insofar as it means, on the one hand, the instant news and reporting that, on the other hand and at the same time, have taken over the ceaseless molding (forming) of the reader and listener."[27] In this way, information is the continuous mobilization of the masses by machines: "Radio and film belong to the standing reserve of this requisitioning through which the public sphere [*die Öffentlichkeit*] as such is positioned, challenged forth, and thereby first installed. Their machineries are pieces of inventory in the standing reserve, which bring everything into the public sphere and thus order the public sphere for anyone and everyone without distinction,"[28] and which demands not only the same news, but also the same formatted debates and their childish categories.[29]

Heidegger had understood that the very power of machination would be deployed as public space by "television, which will soon race through and dominate the entire scaffolding and commotion of commerce."[30] And indeed, the tele-vision is a phenomenological machine: its function is to display, and to industrially produce artificial phenomena. The screen, which ever since has been extended to every possible device [*appareil*], is what in fact makes the artificial clearing of public opinion manifest to everyone. The importance of the screen comes from its representational essence: it is not only a reified or objectified representation, as a picture can be, but a machine that produces representation, and in that it is the transcendental structure of the conditions of possibility of the representation that it reifies and mechanizes. Henceforth, representation is no longer (as is the case in Kantian thought) the result of the spontaneity and activity of the finite subject: on the contrary, the subject is passive, and has representations imposed on it of which it is not the author, and of which in reality no one is the author if not machination as such. It especially has imposed on it a massive and continuous flow of data that no one would be able to control: what, from the Greeks to Husserl, philosophy has called hyletic flow, raw material, the indefinite and indeterminate, which it was necessary to differentiate, critique, and inform by the concept. This flow is no longer material, corporeal, or natural, it is digital, virtual, and technological—and this is why, subject to this imperative of managing quantities of data, thought itself tends to become the calculation of all things, to privilege questions of method, and to abide by technical norms.

As early as 1935, Heidegger saw our epoch as a time "when any incident you like, in any place you like, at any time you like, becomes accessible as fast as you like; when you can simultaneously 'experience' an assassination attempt against a king in France and a symphony concert in Tokyo, when time is nothing but speed, instantaneity, and simultaneity":[31] since then this process has only grown to the absolute deployment of its power, with the increase of mobile devices with remote transmission, permanent connection to the internet, live and continuous news channels . . . Each of us is thus continuously confronted with givens that overflow over and breach the finite conditions of our sensation:

"The germination and flourishing of plants that remained concealed through the seasons, film now exhibits publicly in a single minute. Film shows the distant cities of the most ancient cultures as if they stood at this very moment amidst today's street traffic,"[32] said Heidegger in 1950. Thus, not only is each of us passive in the face of representations that are given to us, but these representations are no longer constituted by our finitude: they are produced by Machinery. Henceforth, human beings are no longer "in the world," if by such an expression is meant the region opened and configured by daily work and the project of a finite existance, they are no longer located in a space furnished by their own business, they are "isolated"[33] in this impersonal machination, indeed to the extent that no one *is there* anymore, but always elsewhere, and this elsewhere is not another place, but the virtual space of Machinery, which in reality is nowhere. The unconditional deployment of television has thus constituted its own space, a spectral Clearing bathed in the artificial luminescence of machination, a technological space that has irresistibly absorbed and dissolved the political space of the *res publica*, that has especially replaced what until now could be called the "world," and that absorbs in itself and digests existants themselves: "Hourly and daily they are chained to radio and television. Week after week the movies carry them off into uncommon, but often merely common, realms of the imagination, and give the illusion of a world that is no world."[34] Thus, the site where, as existants, each of us stands is always already relocated in relation to this virtualized universe, which leads to a delocalization of all places, none of which can acquire the primary status of site or center, of There, always already geolocalized because it is in an atopic space: everyone locates their daily environment, concrete and practical, in a global and virtual space that is only known to them via the media system, and everyone is thus enraptured in a spectral universe—while the question "where are we going?" remains "like a specter over all this uproar" (*wie ein Gespenst über all diesen Spuck*).[35]

Lucidity demands the epochal situation, and this involves taking on its historical community and discovering the language that carries and determines its thought. The epoch of technology unfolds the spectral clearing of a virtualized public opinion, itself structured by the mechanistic framework of television broadcasting. Accordingly, human beings no longer stand in a language, understood as the very unfolding of the essence that opens the site of the Clearing, and as the primordial dialogue that relates people to one another in their very essence: they stand in this mechanical space of the production and transmission of information. The epoch of technology is in this respect that of the "technicalization of language by information theory,"[36] and machination requires and imposes the "thoroughgoing technicalization of all languages into the sole operative instrument of interplanetary information."[37] The language of our epoch is the language of the machine, that is, the instrument of coding and information transmission: it is fundamentally informatics. Informatics is in the first instance the regulation internal to Machinery—that is, the software language of "logistics, whose irresistible development has meanwhile brought forth the electronic brain"[38]—but it is also the now dominant model of languages that are actually spoken, purely functional and commercial languages, impoverished and devitalized by the rupture with all literary tradition. This "devastation of language [. . .] under the dictatorship of the public realm" now largely dominates an education cut off from all reference to the history of its works of art. In doing so, language "falls into the service of expediting communication,"[39] it becomes a function internal to the market, finds itself monetized, and it is thus the primordial dialogue constitutive of human communities that is integrated into Machinery. Every language is then reduced to a modality of informatics, an imperfect and confused modality that some, moreover, would like to "purify" in order to give it the efficiency of a symbolic logic.

Informatics is the software of machination, it is the global language toward which all the old languages are moving in order to melt into what today is called *globish*, the global language derived from an English reduced to its simplest expression. Machination thus establishes the "planetary totality"[40] of Machinery, in which "the distinction between 'national' and 'international' has also collapsed."[41] This is why the question of the community to which we belong in reality no longer has an answer, and it is no longer possible, as it was for Heidegger, to think one's relation to one's own people, or even to a European people—in the well-known inability today to recognize in oneself any sort of identity. The epoch of technology is in fact that of "*the burgeoning of the massive*,"[42] where "the increase in the number of masses of human beings is done explicitly by plan."[43] The masses have replaced the people, and the mass is nothing other than the raw material and the stock available for total mobilization in the service of Machinery. Informatics, as the software language of global machination, is in this respect the mode of governing proper to the epoch of technology, the governmentality immanent to machination, which disqualifies all politics in favor of the anonymous imperialism of technocracy. Insofar as informatics is essantially government, steering (in Greek κυβέρνησις), it is cybernetics; the site in which we stand today is none other than cyberspace, the spectral spatiality of the mechanistic universe where people are ordered by every modality of cybernetics: "No prophecy is necessary to recognize that the sciences now establishing themselves will soon be determined and guided by the new fundamental science which is called cybernetics. This science corresponds to the determination of man as an acting social being. For it is the theory of the steering of the possible planning and arrangement of human labor.

Cybernetics transforms language into an exchange of news,"[44] thus wrote Heidegger, and at the end of his itinerary he maintained that "cybernetics"[45] was about to take the very place of philosophy.

§7. EQUALIZATION

The essence of our epoch is machination, which dominates the entire earth and humanity in every aspect of its life. It is thus a matter of specifying the nature of such a domination. If machination deploys an absolute power, this is because it is nothing other than the unleashing of power for the sake of power, and a power that has no other aim than its own growth; Heidegger thus saw in Nietzschean thought the metaphysics proper to the epoch of technology, which actually calls for a new humanity consistent with Machinery's requisites for efficiency: "In the sense of Nietzsche's metaphysics," wrote Heidegger in this regard, "only the Over-man is appropriate to an absolute 'machine economy.'"[46] The un-leashing of power is precisely its rupture with Being, the "unboundedness" (*Ungebundenheit*)[47] of essance with respect to Being and its finitude, and "the empowering" (*Ermächtigung*) of beings: "Being as power unleashes beings into mere effectiveness (force, violence, and the like), and precisely in such unleashing, power is unconditional power."[48] A being is then only ever based on another being with a view to another being, and this is why Heidegger established a connection between causality and machination, to the point of writing: "I understand technology in such an essantial sense that all *causal* experience falls under its jurisdiction."[49] Causal interpretation is this purely ontic thinking, which attributes to beings the effective power to produce beings, it is thinking adapted to the cybernetic regulation of Machinery, which is regulated in itself, by itself, and for itself. In this way machination consummates the very essance of the machine, which, Heidegger specified as early as 1929, is distinguished from the tool by this "autonomous functioning of the structure."[50] Released from Being, beings will unfold nothing but their own beingness: "Beingness is left to its own devices as liberated machination,"[51] and machination *is* "the essential occurrence of beingness" (*Wesung der Seiendheit*).[52] Technology is thus an ontological disappropriation that strips Being of its essance in order to disseminate it into the total system of beings: "Beingness has dissolved into pure machination, in such a way that through this machination, beings attain unlimited power."[53] The advent of Machinery is this toppling of the ontological difference that makes the self-regulated system of beings, and no longer Being, the instance of essance's unfolding. Cyberspace is none other than this artificial space-time opened and configured by the system of beings; and beings as a whole take the figure of the machine precisely because it is the machine itself that assembles them in this way: machination produces the space-time of machinability in which everything is a machine, where "everything we can do confirms all that we have already done, and all that we have done cries out for our doing it; every action and thought has committed itself totally to making out what it is that can be done. Everywhere and always machination, cloaking itself in the semblance of a measured ordering and controlling, confronts us with beings as the sole hierarchy and causes us to forget Being."[54]

How then does machination deploy its power? By fragmentation, the "tearing-to-pieces" of everything, which never admits anything as a being except as a piece of a machine, it thus brings everything to light as a multiplicity of available pieces: "What the machines put out piece-by-piece they put into the standing reserve of the orderable. That which is put out is a piece of the standing reserve [*Bestand-Stück*]." Yet "the piece [*das Stück*] is something other than the part [*der Teil*]": "The pieces of the standing reserve are piece-for-piece equivalent [*die Gleichen*]. Their character as pieces demands this uniformity [*Gleichförmige*]." Thus, through machination, "everything slides into the basic trait of the indifferent [*Gleich-Gültigen*]." This fragmentation of everything puts it at the disposal of Machinery, which can then assemble every piece in its machines. Machination "imposes this equality of the orderable upon everything, that everything constantly position itself again in equivalent form [*gleichen Form*] and indeed in the equality of orderability,"[55] and in doing so it expressly produces "the unconditional uniformity [*die unbedingte Gleichförmigkeit*] of all kinds of humanity of the earth."[56] Human beings themselves are brought back to a condition of equality; as functionaries of technology, they are subjected to a function, and hence they are interchangeable, as long as they fulfill their function: "Men and women must place themselves in a work service. They are ordered. They are met by a positioning that places them, i.e., commandeers them," and in this way machination simultaneously demands the comparison and the parity of everyone with everyone. Completely subjected to Machinery, "recruited" and "ordered" by it, "confined" and "isolated" in it, human beings are more fundamentally equalized [*appareillé*] to it, and thus reduced to being equal [*au pareil*]. "The concernful approach of the indifferent [*der Angang des Gleich-Gültigen*] is a wresting away into monotony,"[57] and thus produces, as Bernanos had seen at the same moment, "a society of beings who do not have equity, but equality."[58]

If machination produces everything as the machine of machines, that is, Machinery, that is how it deploys a power of reduction to the equal, which assembles these entirely equal pieces in order to build devices [*appareils*]. The fragmentation of everything into entirely equal pieces has no other aim than making function the device that reduces everything to being equal, which is why it must be said that its functioning "does not run out to anything; rather it only enters into its circuit,"[59] and it is the rotation of this autotelic circulation that constitutes the essance of automation. Machinery is the global Device of reduction to the equal, and the essance of machination shows itself to be Equalization [*Appareillement*]: "to power there belongs an essantial equalizing [*die wesentliche Gleichmachung*], and this in an unconditional sense."[60]

Reduction to the equal suppresses differences. Equalization is thus the process of indifferentiating of all that is. Such an indifferentiation is manifest through the leveling and standardization of all peoples and all places, in other words, the tangential suppression *of differences*, however it does not come down to just that: the essantial thing is much rather the suppression of difference *as such*, as "lack of differentiation" (*Unterschiedslosigkeit*).[61] This is manifest in the absence of distance: "What is happening when, through the removal of great distances, everything stands equally near and far [*gleich fern und gleich nahe*]? What is this uniformity [*dieses Gleichförmige*] wherein everything is neither far nor near and, as it were, without distance?"[62] Such a suppression of distances is produced by the increasing speed of the means of transit and by the interconnection of all places, it is especially the paradoxical spatiality of cyberspace—coexistence without distance, based on incessant circulation—which presents all that is as equi-distant, and also equi-valent. Thus, for human beings, to be riveted to the global device of this virtual space is to be subjected to the grip of the mechanical power of indifferentiation: "the distanceless has its own standing. Its constancy makes the rounds in the uncanny concernful approach of what is everywhere of equal value [*das Gleich-Gültig*]. The human stands for this in lapsing into it."[63] To say that the human being is equalized is therefore not simply to observe that it is equipped with devices and thus integrated into the device, it is to say that in the intimacy of its Being, it is de-differentiated.

Yet difference is the very essance of the existant. The human being is fundamentally defined by exi-stance, that is, the standing outside oneself in the opening of Being, by the "originary projection of one's possibilities."[64] This transcendence is what keeps beings as a whole at a distance, and thus makes them visible, and in so doing hollows out the place of the self, the place where the human being can receive the essance of Being, and thus be there (*Da-sein*). Existance is therefore pure opening, and the existant is "this being [which] carries in its ownmost Being the character of not being closed off."[65] The difference between Being and beings, and the originary act of differentiation, is thereby constitutive of existance, and transcendence itself "unfolds its essance in the differentiation."[66] To understand that technology is a mode of essantial unfolding, and that this unfolding is equalization, is then to discover that it focuses its power on the very essance of existance, and that as indifferentiation this power is the threat of its annihilation. In this way, the epoch of technology is "the extreme threat to man; that is, the danger that threatens to annihilate his *essance*," it is "danger as the threat of the annihilation of man's essance" (*Gefahr als Bedrohung der Wesensvernichtung des Menschen*).[67]

Machination is the dissemination of Being's essance into beings, it is thereby also the transfer of the human being's essance into the self-regulated ontic system, and that is the very essance of Equalization, to embed the human being within the machine and to reduce it to the rank of an available piece: in the epoch of technology, "mankind has become a 'human resource,' ranked behind natural resources and raw materials."[68] Having become a functionary of technology, the human being can now only make technology function, and this is indeed what it does. In doing so, it no longer projects its own possibilities, it makes the possibilities of Machinery function, it is even compelled to *produce* all these possibilities. Yet the existant's projection of its own possibilities is precisely what opens a world's horizon of positedness, and this is why the existant must be defined as "Being-in-the-world," but why it must also be recognized that "in the essance of its Being it is *world-forming*."[69] Having become a functionary of technology, it therefore no longer configures a world but can only contribute to machination. In this way, the epoch of technology is also the annihilation of the world: thus "the world has become an unworld [. . .] There are effects everywhere, and nowhere is there a worlding of the world."[70] In the horizon of machinability, there is no longer a world, but a universe, in which the earth is nothing but a planet: no longer the inexhaustible base where humanity has its foundation, but a stock of raw materials wandering in the void. Under the artificial lighting of the technological day, the earth is an unworld [*non-monde*], it becomes literally worldless [*im-monde*]: "The earth appears as the unworld of erring," writes Heidegger. "It is the erring star in the manner of the history of Beyng."[71] This annihilation of essance (*Wesensvernichtung*)[72] is then both the provenance and the condition of possibility of the processes of destruction, of man and the earth, which overwhelmingly characterize the industrial era. In this epoch "man as *animal rationale*, here meant in the sense of the working being, must wander through the desert of the earth's desolation [. . .] The laboring animal is left to the giddy whirl of its products so that it may tear itself to pieces and annihilate itself in empty nothingness."[73]

Technology therefore deploys its essance, under all its modalities, as annihilation: essantial annihilation founds "the spreading violence of actual nihilism,"[74] and the epoch of technology is that of the surge of nihilism. Nihilism thought in this way is no relativism, pessimism, or doubt concerning old values: it is the unconditional deployment of the power of non-Being, that is, its essantial occurrence as machination, and this is why, with Günther Anders, technology must be defined as "annihilism" (*Annihilismus*),[75] nihilism in action, the process of annihilation. Because the *nihil* of nihilism is not nothing. The nothing is the essantial void, the emptying through which alone beings can come to appear: the nothing is non-being, the other of being, which is to say Being itself. Equalization connects beings in the density of its equipment, and only bases one being on another being, which is founded in its beingness without Being, and thus enveloped within itself by this unilateral reign of causality. The *nihil* of nihilism is the autonomous system of beings as it carries out its efficacy without Being; it is not non-being, it is *non-Being*: the other of Being, which is to say beings, insofar as they usurp the ontological essance of Being itself and thus dissimulate its forgetting. In this way, the essential void becomes the useless and the superfluous, and also the boring: nihilism is the annihilation of the nothing,[76] and this is why it must be said that "to think the nothing is not nihilism. The essance of nihilism consists in forgetting the nothing in the lostness to the machination of beings."[77]

§8. EQUALIZATION AND APPROPRIATION

The epoch of technology is that of a danger, and "not just any danger, but danger as such":[78] that of annihilation. Annihilation is not incompatible with the persistence of Machinery and its servants, which can actually continue to function indefinitely—but mechanically, without thinking about it—and this is what Heidegger ultimately emphasized: "Everything is functioning. That is precisely what is strange [*unheimlich*]."[79] Technology does not primarily focus its power of annihilation on beings—which, on the contrary, have achieved power and autonomy through it—but on Being itself, and the annihilation is precisely the annihilation *of Being*.

But where does such a threat come from? What is the provenance of the danger? No historiological investigation is in a position to know: technology is a mode of essance's unfolding, and only an "essantial genealogy" (*Wesensgenealogie*) is capable of bringing to light its "essantial provenance" (*Wesensherkunft*),[80] that is, the provenance of this regime of phenomenality that imposes the complexion of the machine upon beings. Machination is this regime of phenomenality that dominates the will with "the mere drive for calculation, for which calculation is above all the first calculative rule," and this is then "the uniformity of calculable reckoning"[81] that produces the uniformity of beings proper to Equalization. Machination occurs first as universal calculation, which identifies phenomenality with calculability and makes objectivity the condition of possibility of the phenomenon: "In this way, all objectification of the real is a reckoning."[82] Technology, in its most immediate applications, implements this calculation of all things. Historiologically, mechanization took off at the end of the eighteenth century in England; the Industrial Revolution, however, was only the response to the Galilean Revolution of the seventeenth century, which led Descartes to establish that within the horizon of phenomenality defined by objectivity, bodies could only be understood *as* machines, then led Leibniz to pose that they *are* machines. Likewise, the fundamental categories of contemporary economism did not appear subsequent to the advent of capitalism in order to describe its functioning, but in the *a priori* determination of the essence of the natural phenomenon by the physical sciences, and Heidegger noted in Newtonian physics "a notable accord with economics, with the 'calculation' of success. All this develops within and according to the fundamental mathematical position."[83] Thus, the advent of Machinery proceeds from a historical metamorphosis of phenomenality: machination proceeds from the "mathematical projection of nature,"[84] which projects onto everything the *a priori* of its calculability by which "nature presents itself for representation as a spatio-temporal coherence of motion calculable in some way or other in advance."[85] The advent of mathematics is in this way the true foundation of the epoch of technology, which only unconceals beings within the horizon of objectivity, representation, and ultimately calculability; machination is first of all the surge of the power of calculation: "*Calculation*—first placed in power through the machinations of technology, which are epistemologically grounded in mathematics."[86]

Machinery thus proceeds from a mechanization of thought, which leads to defining it by the objectivity of a process of deduction that is itself automatic, and this automation of thought finds its consummation in the "thinking-machines" that are computers: "In the age of technology," Heidegger emphasized in 1957, "the computers that are set to work in business and industry, in the research institutes of science, and in the organizational centers of politics, we surely cannot conceive as devices merely employed for more rapid calculation. The thinking-machine in itself is already much more the consequence of a transposition of thinking into a manner of thought that, as mere calculation, provokes a translation into the Machinery of these machines."[87] Mathematization is already machination, and so it is a matter of defining the essance of mathematics. Μάθησις deploys the horizon of calculability that unconceals each being as merely calculable, in other words as μάθημα. Numbers are established straightaway as a typical example of μάθημα: their characteristic is not to be derived from things, but to be added to them by the thought that takes them in view. If I observe that there are three pencils on my desk, it is because I am capable of gathering a given, which in itself is scattered, into the unity of a concept, triplicity, which is a content proper to my thought. A being is therefore taken as μάθημα when thought only retains from it what it already knows about it; mathematics as a fundamental attitude is thus "a taking where he who takes only takes what he actually already has."[88] The "claim" that constitutes the mathematical project lies in this "application of a determination of the thing, which is not experientially created out of the thing."[89] Mathematics is defined by this *a priori* delimitation of phenomenality; the mathematical project is thus characterized by the refusal of every determination of beings that would be imposed on reason by something other than itself, in other words, the will for reason to be constituted as the one and only ontological authority by a refusal on principle of every form of heteronomy and heterogeneity: "This absolutely mathematical principle cannot have anything in front of it and cannot allow what might be given to it beforehand. If anything is given at all, it is only the *proposition* in general *as such*, i.e., the positing, the position, in the sense of a thinking that asserts. The positing, the proposition, only has itself as that which can be posited. Only where thinking thinks itself, is it absolutely mathematical, i.e., a taking cognizance of that which we already have."[90] This fundamental refusal of heteronomy that characterizes the mathematical relation to the given shows in mathematics a project of empowering or absolutizing rationality, in which knowledge is "a self-giving" (*ein Sichselbstgeben*).[91] In this way, reason is based only on itself: it establishes itself as first principle.

The mathematical project is thus defined at its core by the *identification of possibility with rationality*, which recognizes in pure reason the full powers to decide the conditions of possibility of beings: "Pure reason, λόγος so understood, the proposition in this form, becomes the guideline and standard of metaphysics, i.e., the court of appeal for the determination of the Being of what is, the thingness of things."[92] The mathematical project of nature is ultimately based on this basic principle: "every thing counts as existing when and only when it has been securely established as a calculable object for cognition." This principle is the Principle of Reason. Reason is the sole principle of phenomenality, which means that reason alone is recognized as legitimate to decide on what is and what is not: the Principle of Reason "decrees what may count as an object of cognition, or more generally, as a being."[93] Brought back to the foundation of the mathematical project, the epoch of technology is therefore the total domination of the Principle of Reason: "Modern technology pushes toward the greatest possible perfection. Perfection is based on the thoroughgoing calculability of objects. The calculability of objects presupposes the unqualified validity of the *principium rationis*. It is in this way that the authority characteristic of the Principle of Reason determines the essance of the modern, technological age."[94]

The epoch of technology is the consummation of the Principle of Reason understood as the identification of Being and reason, and hence of the being and the concept. Yet the position of a necessary correlation between what is (ὄν) and λόγος constitutes the fundamental and regulatory hypothesis of philosophy such as it was inaugurated in ancient Greece to then determine the destiny of the West. The Principle of Reason therefore names the very essance of metaphysics, namely, the onto-logical hypothesis, and ultimately refers back to the inaugural event of Western history: the Appropriation [*Amêmement*][95] of Being and λόγος. If the Principle of Reason was stated by Leibniz in the seventeenth century, it was as a formulation of a latent principle of metaphysics: Leibniz presents the keystone of its system and its history, namely, the hypothesis of the sameness [*mêmeté*] of Being and λόγος. Henceforth, it is possible to formulate this principle even more clearly, by situating it in the context of the history of metaphysics, and it is Heidegger who gives its complete formulation: "Accordingly, we only hear the Principle of Reason in the second tonality—that is, in a Being-historical manner and hence in an inaugural manner—when we say the theme of the principle in Greek: τὸ αὐτό (ἐστιν) εἶναι τε καὶ λόγος—εἶναι and λόγος (are) the same. In fact one nowhere finds among the Greek thinkers a principle worded in this way. Nevertheless, it names the trait of the *Geschick* of Being of Greek thinking, and this in a manner such that it points forward into the later epochs of the history of Being."[96] The essantial genealogy of technology leads back to the very Beginning of Western history: it "reaches into and shows the essantial provenance of the Western-European and, today, planetary destiny of Being" (*die Wesensherkunft des abendländisch-europäischen und heute planetarischen Seinsgeschickes*),[97] and this is why "the emergence of the machinational essence of beings is historically very difficult to grasp, because that essence has been in effect basically since the first beginning of Western thought."[98] Exposing the provenance of the Danger thus uncovers, not a contingent and accidental event, but the very destiny of the West. Technology, the West, and Philosophy (understood as onto-logy) are the three figures of one and the same event: "'Philosophy,' in its essance, is so primordially Occidental that it bears the ground of the history of the Occident. From out of this ground alone, technology has arisen. There is only an Occidental technology. It is the consequence of 'Philosophy' and nothing else."[99]

Machination is indeed defined by the transfer of Being's essance into beings and the automated deployment of this ontic power released from Being: yet this *transfer of ontological sovereignty* is the most intimate heart of the Greek event, in which "inceptual Beyng [*Seyn*] leaves mastery [*überläßt die Herrschaft*] to the beings which for the first time enter into manifestness as rising in Being [*Sein*]."[100] The Greek institution of metaphysics is the transposition of this event into onto-theo-logy, characterized by the "transferring of Being" (*Verlegung des Seins*)[101] into the highest being [*l'Étant premier*]: "Of course, metaphysics acknowledges that beings are not without Being. But scarcely has it said so when it again transforms [*verlegt*] Being into a being."[102] Machination is then the moment when this transferring is completed, and when the system of beings is effectively the bearer of sovereign power: it is therefore a matter of conceiving "metaphysics, as the ground of this machination, in its consummation."[103] The West is nothing other than this unique event, that of the "decline" (*Abfall, Untergang*)[104] of the essance of Being, which, as soon as it arises, declines into beings: the West (*Abendland*) is *in its essance* twilight. It is then necessary to conclude that the danger of annihilation that today weighs on humanity and the world is nothing other than the consummation of the Greek Beginning, the end of the "*incubation period* of the Principle of Reason,"[105] that is, the completion of the teleology of onto-logy: the Appropriation is the historical provenance of Equalization, Equalization is the destinal consummation of the Appropriation. Machination is the fate of the West, precisely insofar as "metaphysics is in all its forms and historical stages a unique, but perhaps necessary, fate of the West and the presupposition of its planetary dominance."[106] Our epoch is then at its most intimate core the *catastrophe* of the West, understood—in the Greek sense—as the final act of a tragedy, consummation of the logic of the worst, disastrous dénouement that no hero could have prevented. The site in which we stand, the historical situation that lucidity was tasked to circumscribe, is finally nothing other than the Greek event as it has managed to extend the rule of its Western essance to all that is: lucidity requires us to recognize that "in its essantial beginning, which can never be lost, the present planetary-interstellar world condition is thoroughly european-occidental-grecian."[107]

This is why the "end of philosophy" and the "overcoming of metaphysics" are really decisive questions, yet not because philosophy and metaphysics would have become obsolete and outdated forms of thought—in the manner of astrology or alchemy—but rather because they are *actualized* in an effective apparatus that systematically implements all their potentialities. The "step back" that defines the movement proper to thought is henceforth that which leaves the technical apparatus, in order to free its essance:

> What now *is*, is marked by the dominance of the active nature of modern technology. This dominance is already presenting itself in all areas of life, by various identifiable traits such as functionalization, systematic improvement, automation, bureaucratization, communications, [cybernetics]. Just as we call the idea of living things biology, just so the presentation and full articulation of all beings, dominated as they now are everywhere by the nature of the technical, may be called technology. The expression may serve as a term for the metaphysics of the atomic age. Viewed from the present and drawn from our

> insight into the present, the step back out of metaphysics into the essantial nature of metaphysics is the step out of technology and technological description and interpretation of the age, into the *essance* of modern technology which is still to be thought.[108]

Metaphysics exists from now on as technology, today the question of metaphysics *is* the question concerning technology, and the task of thinking is to grasp its essance in order to overcome it.

In doing so, it dives into terror and need: not only does machination extend its domination across the whole planet, devastate the earth, and mobilize all human beings in its service, not only is it the threat of total annihilation, but it is revealed as the necessary consummation of an ancient destiny, decided in Greece at the moment of the very Beginning of Western history. The end of the Principle of Reason's "incubation period" is therefore not a limit, but a start, the start of its implementation, and the technological danger becomes apparent in all its enormity when one considers this fact: it "is only at its start."[109] Unleashing the power of machination actually sets into motion a now autonomous process that is based on the twenty-five centuries of Western history. As the "consummation" (*Vollendung*) is the acting out of the totality of this history, it is not a one-time event, but a long-term process, and it is necessary to insist on the fact that "the 'modern age' is in no way at an end. Rather, it is just entering the beginning of its presumably long-drawn-out consummation,"[110] and that the "process of the consummation of modern times is *just starting*" (*Prozeß der Vollendung der Neuzeit* erst einsetzt).[111] Technology is the death throes of metaphysics, and "the ending lasts longer than the previous history of metaphysics"[112]—in short, it is necessary to envision a technocratic empire of more than twenty-five centuries, and to admit that the devastations and annihilations of the twentieth century were only its prodromes. Because he had thought the fate of its destiny, Heidegger had foreseen the now irreversible and irresistible character of its tendency toward global domination. He had thus understood that despite its enormity and the depth of its history, China would not resist the process of Westernization inherent to technology: "Logistics has developed to such a point that it now plays a frightening role in mathematical research (on machines that think and calculate), which is to say that what began with Descartes has developed in such a way that as things currently stand, several decades from now China will have a European mode of existence, just like Japan," he actually said as early as 1951. "That is Europeanization, this phenomenon in which the essance of modern thought is determined by machines and technology, and in which this fundamental relation to Being determines humanity."[113]

CHAPTER 3

Truth and Its Destiny

§9. ONTOLOGY AND TRUTH

Our epoch consummates the Greek decision (κρίσις), and it is in this sense that it is a crisis: it is then the Greek decision as such that we must attempt to define. The inaugural decision can be formulated as Principle of Reason: this is more essantially the affirmation of the sameness of Being and λόγος, an appropriation that is manifest as the linking of the being and the εἶδος. Yet this relationship defines truth. From one end of its history to the other, with a remarkable consistency, philosophy indeed defines truth by the "link" (ζυγόν),[1] the "likeness" (ὁμοίωσις),[2] the "adequation" (*adaequatio*),[3] the "conformity,"[4] the "relation"[5] between thought and reality, which is ultimately to say by the alignment of λόγος and beings. What in the West is called truth is nothing other than ontology as such, the Appropriation of Being and λόγος—and indeed the Greek ὁμοίωσις, derived from ὅμοις, "the same" [*le même*], would more literally be translated by "appropriation" [*amêmement*]. The Greek decision, which finds its guiding formulation in the *Poem* of Parmenides, is a decision regarding the essance of truth. The West is the event of Appropriation, its destiny is that of the onto-logical configuration of truth, which is to say, the teleology of ontology, the process of *verification* that produces the rationalization of the real and the realization of reason. It fell to Hegel to have thus conceived universal history as a dialectical progression guided by a goal, that of the "reconciliation" (*Versöhnung*) between the rational and the real—in doing so, he highlighted that the very position of truth as adequation was from the outset the demand for the suppression of difference.

But if the terminal consummation of the Greek decision is the danger of annihilating the essance (of humanity, the world, and ultimately Being itself), it is because, far from identifying and circumscribing this essance, the onto-logical configuration of truth missed the essantial thing, which it took for nothing and thus from the outset sent back into nothingness. The Greek moment is the event of a first forgetting, of an inaugural failure, of a foundational refusal: and indeed, the Parmenidean decision to circumscribe the "well-rounded ball" of truth "within the bonds of the limit, which confines it on all sides," to thus define Being as "the Same remaining in the Same which rests in itself," consisted in his denying every origin (ἄναρχον) and in this way "relegating" or "keeping away" (εἶργειν) all alterity, in sending it back from the start to the unthinkable (ἀνόητον), the unnameable (ἀνώνυμον), the untrue (οὐ ἀληθής) and finally nothingness (μηδὲν).[6] The crucial question that imposes itself at the end of Western history is then to think what was forgotten in its Beginning, that is, to place onto-logy within its limits in order to access what exceeds it.

The onto-logical configuration of truth occurs as the linking of λόγος and beings. But if truth is this linking of λόγος and beings as a whole, it presupposes an *environment* where the two can come together, and only the preliminary opening of this dimension makes possible any adequation whatsoever. Hence the fact that adequation is only the derivative phenomenon of fundamental truth, that by which the diaphanous expanse opens up *in which* beings and the forms of λόγος can meet. The opening of this clearing is thereby truth itself: the region of essance, that is, the unfolding of the realm of phenomenality in which alone concept and intuition can agree with each other. The Greek word for truth, ἀλήθεια, is therefore the proper name of the Clearing, the Open, the Free Expanse which lucidity must access, and which Heidegger did not cease to meditate upon. The Greek ἀλήθεια in fact suggests this Clearing: it is literally the negation (privative suffix -α) of λήθη. The word λήθη is a derivative of the verb λανθάνω, synonymous with the passive of κρύπτειν and καγύπτειν,[7] which means "to be hidden," "to happen in secret," with the adverb λανθανόντος, "secretly"; it names all that goes unnoticed: thus in the *Iliad* Glaucus jumped down "from the wall in secret [λαθών], fast, so no Achaean could see him hit and bellow out in triumph."[8] The term evokes that which escapes visibility, and in the *Republic* Plato tries to determine what it is to be just, "whether its possession is unnoticed [λανθάνῃ] by all the gods and human beings or not."[9] The verb λήθω commonly means "to remain unknown," "to stay ignored," and the noun λήθη thus usually designates forgetfulness. The domain of λήθη is thus the domain of all that escapes vigilance, consciousness, and knowledge, of what stands in withdrawal and does not come to appear. The word comes from the same root that gave the English "latent": in this way λήθη is the deep realm of latency out of which alone a phenomenon can become evident [*patent*]. Ἀλήθεια is thus this realm of visibility won against the darkness of what remains hidden; it is not first given, but wrested from λήθη: "'Truth' is never 'in itself,' available by itself, but instead must be gained by struggle. Unconcealedness is wrested from concealment, in a conflict with it."[10] The inaugural establishment of ἀλήθεια is the first ground clearing, which gains a free expanse against what Democritus called the "untrodden" (ἀπάτητον),[11] it is a clearing away of the brush (original meaning of the Greek ὕλη, which for Aristotle will be the material that thought must shape), and this ground clearing is a struggle: there is thus a "conflictual essance of truth [*streithafte Wesen der Wahrheit*] [that] has already been alien to us and to Western thought for a long time."[12] The Greek Beginning places European humanity in "the plain where truth stands" (τὸ ἀλήθειας πεδίον);[13] all of Western history takes place within the limits of this site, it builds on its foundations but does not leave it: "for historical humanity the history of its essantial possibilities is conserved in the disclosure of beings as a whole. The rare and the simple decisions of history arise from the way the originary essance of truth essantially unfolds."[14]

The crucial point here is that ἀλήθεια is *second* in relation to the dimension of λήθη, it is the *result* of a thinning of this Density, of an illumination of this Darkness: "The Greeks understood what *we* call the true, as the un-hidden, as what is no longer hidden, as what is *without* hiddenness, as what has been torn away from hiddenness and, as it were, been robbed of its hiddenness. [. . .] It is curious that 'true' means what something *no longer* has."[15] If ὁμοίωσις is therefore a derivative phenomenon of the truth of which ἀλήθεια is the fundamental phenomenon, λήθη imposes itself here as the primordial environment in which alone there can be a foundation. Truth is established as unconcealment, and thus furnishes the region of the unconcealed, but every *region* [*contrée*] unfolds its horizon *against* [*contre*] an unlimited (ἄπειρον)[16] whose threat it holds back, and within which it makes a home, or a temple. Henceforth, truth is established against a realm where the concealed is maintained in its concealment, which constitutes *that in which* it unfolds its essance. This *other* of truth *in which* truth takes place is "*in*-truth" (*Un-wahrheit*):[17] "Concealment deprives ἀλήθεια of disclosure yet does not render it στέρησις (privation); rather, concealment preserves what is most proper to ἀλήθεια as its own. Considered with respect to truth as disclosedness, concealment is then un-disclosedness and accordingly the in-truth that is most proper to the essance of truth."[18] There is thus an adversarial essance to truth irreducible to falsehood, which is that against which it establishes itself and which extends infinitely beyond the edge of its clearing. In this way, in-truth is "older" (*älter*) than the implementation of truth itself: "The concealment of beings as a whole does not first show up subsequently as a consequence of the fact that knowledge of beings is always fragmentary. The concealment of beings as a whole, in-truth proper [*die eigentliche Un-wahrheit*], is older than every openedness of this or that being. It is older even than letting-be itself, which in disclosing already holds concealed and comports itself toward concealing."[19] The unfolding of the clearing of truth is thus a settlement *within* a primordial in-truth: "The ʾΑ-Λήθεια rests in [*ruht in*] Λήθη, drawing from it and laying before us whatever remains deposited in Λήθη. [. . .] Unconcealment needs concealment, Λήθη, as a reservoir upon which disclosure can, as it were, draw."[20] If truth is won against the depth of concealment, it therefore cannot be established without it; it "needs" the depth of this reserve: "Truth is in-truth in that there belongs to it the originating region of the not-yet- (the un-)disclosed in the sense of concealment."[21] The essence of truth rests in this adversarial environment. Because this adversarial environment is that without which there is no essance, in-truth is the "*in*-essance" (*Un-wesen*) of truth, "what in such a sense would be a pre-essantial essance" (*vor-wesende Wesen*).[22] Truth is therefore in an intimate relationship with in-truth: it is not its pure and simple negation, it only unfolds in a tension, a "primal struggle" (*Urstreit*) with in-truth.

§10. ABYSS AND MYSTERY

But the thought of this "primal struggle" requires complicating the topology of Beyng. The Clearing [*Éclaircie*] of the opening [*clairière*] occurs in and against the density of a primordial undergrowth, and it thus settles in a "surrounding mass"[23] that resists all unconcealment, which Heidegger called Density: "The forest clearing (opening) is experienced in contrast to dense forest, called 'density' (*Dickung*) in older language."[24] The recognition of this Density is inextricably that of the finitude of the Clearing. But the very clarification of the opening within this density proceeds from an event that brought emptiness into this solid fullness, just as in the ancient technique of slash-and-burn, fire is the ground clearing that frees up arable land. Heraclitus saw in "fire" that which "comes upon all things":[25] but the essential thing lies in the original coming of fire, that is, the "thunderbolt" (κεραυνός).[26] And indeed, if the surrounding undergrowth is the *primordial* environment, this remains (pre-)ontic: it is non-unconcealed beings; the crucial ontological question is to determine the *origin* of the Clearing, what allows it to arise and grow (φύσις) within darkness. The thought of the site of truth therefore cannot be content with situating it in relation to the Density that extends beyond its edge, it must furthermore think the arrival of the nothing within beings, that is, the disclosure of Being. Being—that is: the nothing, emptiness, the clearing, truth—is difference, fissure, fault, gaping. It is the spacing established within the primordial density by this fracture that allows beings to appear: the original event is the "fissuring" (*Zerklüftung*) that opens the "clefts of Beyng" (*Klüfte des Seyns*) within "the totality of beings that remain enveloped within themselves."[27] And this fissuring, specifies Heidegger, is subsequent to beings [*l'Étant*]: "Beyng is subsequent (*später*) to beings. Being irrupts within beings, in such a way that this irruption is an *essantial inter-ruption*. This irruption of Being within beings does not change anything about them, but first simply lets them *be* beings, whose being before the interruption was the concealing of Being, even of concealment."[28]

The coming of Being within beings thus proceeds from a gaping: the fissuring is a collapse, it proceeds from an abyssal hollowing out, that is, from an abyss. Heidegger uses the archaic spelling *Seyn* to think the abyss as the origin of Being (*Sein*): the thought of Beyng is thus the most radical point of the Heideggerian phenomenological reduction. If as a first step it leads from beings back to Being, as a second step it leads from Being back to Beyng. This abyss is other than Being, and this is why it is Nothingness: "Beyng as the abyss is Nothingness"[29] (*das Seyn als Abgrund ist das Nichts*), and therefore it is ultimately a matter of thinking this "originary Nothingness" (*das ursprüngliche Nichts*),[30] which the Greeks of the tragic age called chaos (χάος), understood as "that gaping out of which the Open opens itself."[31] If elucidating the essance of truth therefore requires thinking the ontic Density of the undisclosed, it must even more essantially think the ontological undisclosable, that from which the withdrawal, the abyssal collapse, gives rise to the Clearing: it is ultimately a matter of approaching "the essantially Undisclosable" (*die Wesenshafte Unterschließbare*).[32] A radical thinking of truth demands placing its essance (*Wesen*) within its limits, which means specifying its relation to its in-essance (*Un-wesen*): but this in-essance is not only all that extends beyond its opening, it is more authentically the ab-sence (*Ab-wesen*) that alone *gives rise* to this opening; it is not only all that is beyond "the circumference of a circle" (κύκλου περιφερεία),[33] it is more originarily Nothingness as "the proper heavyweight"[34] of the Clearing, which Heraclitus had thought as κρύπτεσθαι, "to escape," "to hide."[35] To think this event, this occlusion of Beyng from which the disclosure of Being comes, is to think an absenting as condition of possibility of presence, an ab-stention that lets be, and it is to think this occlusion as its very essance. The essance of Beyng is thus dissimulation; by such a dissimulation, Beyng withdraws into itself and refuses itself. This mode proper to the essance of Beyng, which consists in refusing itself to all possible unconcealment and thus in covering itself as Nothingness, is veiling: "the ab-stention of Being as such is Being itself. In its ab-stention Being veils itself [*verhüllt sich*] with itself. This veil [*Schleier*] that vanishes for itself, which is the way Being itself essentially occurs in ab-stention, is Nothingness as Being itself."[36]

But by the very movement of this withdrawal, the occlusion in some way manifests itself within the Clearing—just as when a hitherto unnoticed animal suddenly flees into a thicket and thus announces itself: it is precisely its disappearance that makes it appear. The determinate way in which the occlusion of Beyng attests to itself in the very event of disclosure (ἀλήθεια) is a resistance, a refusal, a withdrawal: disappearance is the very mode of its appearance; it is present in the mode of absence, lack, lacuna, or default. "To close," "to shut" in Greek is μῦω, the verb that gave μυστήριον, "mystery." When Luther translates the Bible into German, μυστήριον is rendered by *Geheimnis*, for example, in this verse of 1 Corinthians (2:7): "*Weisheit Gottes, die im Geheimnis verborgen ist*," where the word designates what is concealed. This is how Heidegger thinks the originary essance of truth: "The proper in-essance of truth is the mystery [*das Geheimnis*]."[37] In and through the mystery, the concealed is a *glaring absence*; the mystery is the way in which what is hidden *appears*, the presence proper to absence; *the mystery is the phenomenality proper to disappearance*: "That which shows itself and at the same time withdraws is the essential trait of what we call the mystery."[38] The mystery is the phenomenon of the undisclosable: "That which according to its essance preservingly conceals, and thus remains concealed in its essance and entirely hidden, though nonetheless it somehow appears [*erscheint*], is in itself what we call *the mystery*."[39] The mystery is the mode of manifestation proper to withdrawal, it is the echo or the resonance (*Anklang*) of the closing at the very heart of the opening: "the mystery" is "the intimating-resonating concealment" (*die winkend-anklingende Verborgenheit*).[40] The mystery is this paradoxical mode of phenomenality that indicates a disappearance, an absence, a veiling:

> If the essance of truth is to be sought in the manifestness of beings, then concealment and veiling [*Verhüllung*] prove to be a particular way that is proper to manifestness. The mystery [*Geheimnis*] is not a barrier that lies on the other side of truth, but is itself the highest figure of truth; for in order to let the mystery truly be what it is—concealing safeguard of authentic Beyng [*verbergende Bewahrung des eigentlichen Seyns*]—the mystery must be manifest as such. A mystery that is not known in its power of veiling [*in seiner verhüllenden Macht*] is no mystery. The higher our knowing concerning the veiling [*das Wissen um die Verhüllung*] and the more genuine the saying of it as such, the more untouched its concealing power remains.[41]

The most mysterious aspect of the mystery thus lies in its phenomenality proper, which makes veiling a specific mode of manifestation—just as absence, when we miss someone, is a singular mode of presence: "we shall find in absence—be it what has been or what is to come—a manner of presencing and approaching which by no means coincides with presencing in the sense of the immediate present. Accordingly, we must note: Not every presencing is necessarily the present."[42]

Such a relation to the mystery could seem reserved for a fellowship of initiates: however, it is the most banal phenomenon there is, since it is the common lot of all mortals. Indeed, there is "a concealment appearing in the essance of death [*ein Verbergen, das im Wesen des Todes erscheint*], of the night and everything nocturnal,"[43] this appearance of concealment is the mystery itself, and death thus requires all people, even if by evasion, to take a stand in relation to it. "Insofar as death comes, it vanishes,"[44] it is that phenomenon whose appearance is disappearance, this event of disappearance whose appearance everyone awaits: death is a mystery that it alone can unveil. Death, said Baudelaire, "It is the vibrant light on our black horizon [. . .] It is the portal opening on unknown Skies":[45] it is, at the very heart of the opening of existance, the relation to the closing of its other; it is, at the very heart of ἀλήθεια, the manifestation of λήθη. Death is thus the gateway of Nothingness by which the nothing flows into beings and thus opens the region of Being: "Death, as the shrine of Nothingness, harbors in itself what essances of Being."[46] In the movement of its Being-toward-death, each existant is thus confronted with this advance of Nothingness: but it is also confronted with the appearance of the disappeared in the fundamental phenomenon of mourning. Mourning is this relation to the death *of the other*, and in this relation to the death of another [*d'autrui*] the existant immediately escapes the solipsistic threat of self-closure. Mourning, which intimately combines love and death, is the everyday experience of the presence of absence: "The remembrance of mourning remains near to what has been taken from it and seems to be distant. Mourning is not merely pulled back by a current to something that was lost. It lets what is absent come again and again."[47] It phenomenalizes it and thus works toward the mystery. Mourning thus establishes itself as an eminent case of a phenomenon of faultiness, that is to say, of the emergence of Nothingness at the very heart of existance. Not only does this event hollow out a fault in existance, but the characteristic of mourning is precisely not to flee in horror before this gaping, but rather to make it the crypt of the absent, and to faithfully keep watch over this absence within oneself: existance itself could be defined by the play space of mourning (*Trauerspiel*), that is, tragedy. There is a truth of mourning,[48] which the Greek tragedies, and especially Sophocles in *Antigone*, knew how to endure to the end, and which has become inaccessible in an epoch determined to deny every form of negativity, and which sees in mourning a pathology to be managed with therapeutic techniques.

Truth, as expanse of disoccultation, is therefore in its innermost heart a certain stance in relation to the abyss of concealment, and consequently a certain bearing in relation to the mystery. Yet truth such as it was decided by the Greeks is *defined* by the elimination of this adversarial element: "concealment itself is experienced only as what is to be *cleared away*, what is to be removed (α-)."[49] Through its fascination with the visibility of the visible, through its obsession with clairvoyance and the identification of thought with the sight of what gives itself to be seen (θεωρία), Greek thought focused unilaterally on beings and their beingness. Indeed, the concealed is "eternally non-apparent and therefore Invisible,"[50] its phenomenalization in the mystery no longer goes through seeing, but through listening: "As 'seeing'—θεωρία—was determined by presencing, so Beyng as event now demands *the word and hearing*,"[51] that is, attention to the resonance and the echo. Through its identification with theory, onto-logical truth completely blocked off all access to its essantial origin, and the Greek institution of truth is its loss: "the concealed became, in a typically Greek way, the *absent*; the occurrence of concealment was lost."[52] In-essance is thus for metaphysics the domain of the unexplored: "the 'in-' of the originary in-essance of truth, as in-truth, points to the still unexperienced domain of the truth of Being."[53] This inaugural veiling is the forgetting that defines metaphysics and founds the destiny of nihilism: "The oblivion here to be thought is the veiling [*Verhüllung*] of the difference as such, thought in terms of Λήθη (concealment); this veiling has in turn withdrawn itself from the beginning."[54] The transferring of sovereignty from Beyng into beings, from which proceeds the terminal empowering of machination, is none other than this initial veiling: the Beginning of Western history is "already the veiling of the abyss of Beyng [*die Verhüllung des Ab-grundes des Seyns*] and the relegation to beings themselves."[55]

§11. ORIGIN AND BEGINNING

The Beginning of Western history is a forgetting, and this forgetting is a veiling: "the inceptual forgottenness of Beyng" is the "inceptual veiling" (*die anfängliche Verhüllung*),[56] namely, the "forgottenness of the mystery" (*Vergessenheit des Geheimnisses*).[57] In this way an excess irreducible to the Beginning is revealed: the scope of all that has remained out of the grasp of the Greek λόγος, what Rimbaud called "invisible splendors [. . .] immense unarguable opulence,"[58] which has always been *out of the question* for philosophy. It is the reading of Hölderlin's fluvial poems that leads Heidegger to reflect on "the enigma" of the origin (*Ursprung*), that is, the first springing or flowing forth (*Sprung*). This enigma is that of the unity of "(1) the origin as such (that is, that from which there springs forth that which springs forth), and (2) that which has sprung forth itself, the way it *is* as that which has sprung forth."[59] "What would happen," asked Heidegger, "if the spring, emerging into the light of day, were without the favor of the water flowing to it beneath the ground? It would not be the spring. The spring must belong to the concealed water, a belonging that means that the spring in its essance is secured by means of the concealed water and only from out of it remains the spring."[60] To think the origin is thus to place it in relation to an originary, an abyssal domain *from which* the origin springs forth, that is, the "primordial realms of Beyng" (*Urbereiche des Seyns*).[61] The originary is also not an ancient time, since it unfolds outside all chronology, because it is that from which time emerges and opens up the fissuring of difference within the primordial dark density. Spared from temporal differentiation, the originary can only be defined by uniqueness, from which alone plurality and repetition can emerge: "Beyng itself is uniqueness, is singularity that always lets its time emerge [*entspringen*], that is, lets its truth's 'free-play of the time-space' emerge."[62] The characteristic of the originary is thus to be in withdrawal, the unfolding proper to the originary consists in encrypting itself, in withdrawing into its crypt (κρύπτεσθαι): the originary is in essance the Inaccessible, it is precisely *what does not give itself*. This withdrawal, this abyssal collapse in the chasm of χάος, is the ebbing movement that makes room for the flow of presence, just as the ebb of the sea gives rise to a beach; the withdrawal is thus a giving, and this movement of withdrawal is the essantial occurrence proper to Beyng, whose absenting movement is what gives rise to presence and abandons it to its destiny. Not only does this withdrawal give rise to the manifest expanse of presence, but it is moreover what keeps it intact, it conceals it as "a storing away and safeguarding."[63] If the origin is the source, the originary remains at all times the inexhaustible *resource*: "*The abyss: nothingness*, what is most abyssal—Beyng itself" is "the richest."[64] The originary therefore stands in withdrawal, but it is this withdrawal that guarantees its sovereignty. And because this sovereignty holds itself *in reserve*, because it is a refusal, it is in its truth neither power nor powerlessness, it deprives itself of every form of power and stands "*beyond power and lack of power*—better, what is outside power and lack of power." The originary is withholding, reserve, and this reserve and this withholding found its "dignity," the sign of its "*maiestas*" and "mastery."[65] The originary is sovereign, both inaccessible and untouchable, it is in this sense the "originarily Safe," and because it stays separate, it is the Sacred: "Chaos is the Sacred itself."[66]

The origin (*Ursprung*) is then the springing or flowing forth, or the leap (*Sprung*) out of the originary abyss: the originary "let[s] something flow forth out of itself,"[67] and thus dissimulates itself in withdrawal in relation to this flowing forth. The Beginning is *Anfang*, that is, a capture, an initial taking (*Fang*):

the Beginning is the grasping (*auffangen*) of what flows forth from the originary, it is a reception, a receiving (*empfangen*)[68] of what pours from the source. To begin is to capture the source and thus to circumscribe the origin's effusion basin, which is to delimit the circumference or the periphery (*Umfang*) of a site for existance. A Beginning is thus an inauguration, which traces the limits of a habitable region for Mortals, and this is why it is decisive and destinal: it configures the realm of possibility within which the succession of possibles that will constitute history will occur, it is the "primordial decision for the essantial order [*Wesensgefüge*] of the future history of gods and humanities."[69] This configuration is the initial gathering of the essantial possibilities that will then be deployed and actualized by a history, and in this respect it is destinal: "destiny is the all-gathering Beginning,"[70] and as initial seizure (*An-fang*), the Beginning is defined just as much by what it takes as by what it leaves.

The Beginning is therefore not behind us, it is all around us, in truth it holds us captive (*gefangen*), and the very forgetting of the originary is inseparable from this captivity: "If in forgetting we keep something away from ourselves, then we easily flee into something else that captivates us [*gefangen*],"[71] and as it is finite, the essance of truth is captive to its own limits. The Beginning is not at the start of history: history happens completely within the limits fixed by the Beginning. The inception (*Beginn*) is only the first of the empirical occurrences that happen in this configuration, the first possible carried out in this horizon of possibility. If "the beginning is immediately left behind; it vanishes as an event proceeds,"[72] then the Beginning itself is always regulatory. That is why "concealed within itself, the Beginning contains already the end":[73] from the outset it defines all possible moves, the last move is contained in the Beginning, and insofar as it delimits the circle of possibles, the Beginning has always already projected the horizon of our future. "The Beginning leaps over what has sprung forth, and in leaping ahead outlasts that which remains, embraces the latter coming from its end, and thus, at the same time, becomes the destination for that which remains,"[74] and in this way the Beginning is before us and has always already preceded us. The Beginning must therefore be defined as the *delimitation of the bounds of truth* (ἀλήθεια) in relation to the dark depths of λήθη, and this from what flows forth out of χάος; it is the initial gathering of essance (*Wesen*) in a region of presence (*An-wesen*) introduced from absence (*Ab-wesen*) in an adversarial relation to its in-essance (*Un-wesen*), and it is this inaugural configuration that decides the destiny of a history: "History is only when the essance of truth comes to be decided on primordially."[75] Lucidity is henceforth, in the last instance, the thought of the Beginning of our history, in its finitude and in its limits, which entirely determines our destiny.

§12. DECAY OF TRUTH

The Greek event of the onto-logical Appropriation circumscribes the sphere of essance according to presence alone and refuses absence all positivity. The Other of truth is thus, for it, pure and simple nothingness (μὴ ὄν). Truth is finite, limited in its essance, it is a position in relation to inessance: the trait specific to the Greek inauguration is the *rejection* of the paradoxical phenomenality of the mystery, the refusal or the disavowal (*Absage*)[76] of the originary, the forgetting of its withdrawal. The Greek Beginning is the settlement within the onto-logical region and the assignment of humanity to this ground cut from all ties to the abyss. The one who endures this destiny is thus the existant, who stands in this element. To exist is nothing other than to be *there*; the history of European humanity is this perpetual placement within the site of onto-logy. To exist, for Western humanity, is to *insist* on this place: the existant "not only ek-sists but also at the same time *in-sists*, i.e., holds fast to what is offered by beings, as if they were open of and in themselves." In this way, the human being turns away more and more resolutely from the mystery: "As insistent, the human being is turned toward the most readily available beings. [. . .] However, in taking its standard, humanity is turned away from the mystery. The insistent turning toward what is readily available and the ek-sistent turning away from the mystery belong together. They are one and the same."[77] Onto-logical truth is flight in the face of the mystery to the point of forgetting this flight: and indeed, the opposite of ἀλήθεια was never thought as λήθη—as undisclosable—but as ψεῦδος, what is false, that is, the badly unconcealed. "Western thinking accounts untruth the sole opposite to truth. 'Untruth' is identified with 'falsity,' which, understood as incorrectness, forms the evident and obtrusive counterpart to 'correctness.' The opposition holding sway at the beginning is known to us under the names ἀλήθεια καὶ ψεῦδος, *veritas et falsitas*, truth and falsity."[78]

Philosophy therefore never thinks truth in its founding struggle with in-truth, but only in its derivative relation with the untrue. Western exi-stance is insi-stance in the unique dimension of the Clearing and the resolute denial of the dimension of absence and its paradoxical appearance as mystery. Yet this dimension is not an annex, it belongs to the very essance of truth that only unfolds within it: "the full essance of truth contains the inessance."[79] To turn away from it is to forget the originary essance of truth: "The human being's flight from the mystery toward what is readily available, onward from one current thing to the next, passing the mystery by—this is *erring* [*das Irren*]."[80] In this way the very site of truth, insofar as it closes itself off to the mystery, is errancy (*die Irre*): "The concealing of concealed beings as a whole holds sway in that disclosure of specific beings, which, as forgottenness of concealment, becomes errancy."[81] Errancy is the essance of onto-logical truth, which obsesses over unconcealed beings and wanders [*erre*] from one to the other without ever thinking them in relation to the undisclosable: "Errancy is the free space for that turning in which in-sistent ek-sistence adroitly forgets and mistakes itself constantly anew."[82] Such an errancy belongs essantially to destiny, since the initial gift is a *letting-go* of beings by Being, which abandons them to themselves and lets them go on their way [*erre*]; this way is history itself: "By revealing itself in the being, Being withdraws. In this way, in its illuminating, Being invests the being with errancy. The being happens in errancy [. . .] This is the essantial space of history."[83] History is in its essance errancy, it is the sending of absence back into nothingness, and this is why it is nihilism. The Greek foundation of metaphysics is an inaugural mistake, and as such the kick-off of errancy: "Errancy and the concealing of what is concealed belong to the originary essance of truth." For the existant to stand in the opening of ἀλήθεια is to be condemned to errancy: "The errancy in which any given segment of historical humanity must proceed for its course to be errant is essantially connected with the openness of the existant." The history of the West is now nothing other than this aberrant course. The history of truth suddenly appears as the destiny of Error (*der Irrtum*), "not merely an isolated mistake but the kingdom (the dominion) of the history of those entanglements in which all kinds of erring get interwoven."[84]

The Greek event, which set in motion the process of Western history, is thus, "since the first beginning," the rupture of truth with its proper resource, that is, "the collapse of ἀλήθεια."[85] The contemporary surge of nihilism is the result of this foundational event: "What already happens in Plato is the waning of the fundamental experience, i.e. of a specific fundamental *stance* of man towards beings, and the weakening of the word ἀλήθεια in its basic meaning. This is only the beginning of that history through which Western man lost his ground as an existing being, in order to end up in contemporary groundlessness."[86] In denying its originary in-essance, the onto-logical configuration of truth in effect breaks the link with its proper resource and is condemned to waning: the epoch of technology is defined by the empowerment of the self-regulated system of beings, and as a result it is the epoch of the "impotence of truth."[87] The transferring of Beyng's sovereignty into beings was consummated in machinery, now the holder of an unconditional power. The destiny of the West is none other than the process of transferring and disseminating the essance of Being into beings, and thereby the ineluctable ontological degeneration of essance: the "essantial occurrence" (*Wesung*) that defines historiological becoming is its "essantial decay" (*Ver-wesung*).[88] As systematizing and unleashing ontological verification, machination lets the opening of ἀλήθεια lie fallow and abandons it to darkening, it is the "*burial* of the essance of truth,"[89] and the danger proper to the epoch of technology is this devastation of the Clearing: it constitutes the threat that "every possibility of a truth is destroyed."[90] But this essantial annihilation is only the consummation of the inaugural decision, and it is thus necessary to recognize in the Western destiny the teleology of onto-logical truth: the forgetting of in-truth, the denial of the originary, "is the ground of an innermost need which the existence of man has had to bear ever since. This is what essentially determines the course and direction of the history of the Western spirit and its peoples."[91]

§13. SAFEGUARD OF TRUTH

Lucidity regarding our epoch not only discovers the threat of essantial annihilation, but in this danger it also discovers the "necessary fate of the West,"[92] that is, the consummation (*Vollendung*) of the very decision that inaugurated our history. The danger of annihilation is therefore nothing contingent, and thus easily remediable, but is discovered as destiny and fate. Bringing the essance of our epoch to light then leads thought to terror. But terror is precisely lucidity, which unveils the truth of machination: terror "unveils behind all progress and all domination over beings a dark emptiness of irrelevance and a shrinking back in face of the first and last decisions."[93] By no longer turning back in the face of terror, thought takes on its proper determination (*Bestimmung*) through its affective attunement (*Stimmung*), which alone can give it access to essance. Indeed, thought must always be carried and carried away [*portée et emportée*] by such a fundamental mood: "All essantial thinking demands that its thoughts and utterances be newly extracted each time, like an ore, out of the basic disposition [*Grundstimmung*]. If the basic disposition is lacking, then everything is a forced clatter of concepts and of the mere shells of words."[94] To be determined by this fundamental attunement is thus for thought to escape its determination by machination, and in this sense terror is what frees it from the empire of calculation. And this is exactly what explains the essantial solitude of the thinker, who gains their lucidity through their step back from the phenomenality proper to their epoch, which allows them to see its light precisely because they approach it from another light, that is, from another truth: "Solitude does not come from the fact that usual landmarks slip away from you, it consists, rather, in that another truth arrives."[95]

The disposition of terror thus reveals to thought its own situation of need: "The need compels in the mode of a disposition,"[96] and it is the shock of this situation of need that tears the thinker away from the lethargy imposed by machination, that is, away from the insensitivity and torpor produced by the spectral empire of cyberspace, but also by the demand for the coldness of scientific objectivity characterized by "a certain suppression and blocking of attunement."[97] Determined by the terror of need, thought then discovers for itself a unique task, and also a responsibility: to "save us from lostness in the bustle of mere incidents and machinations."[98] Thought thus ventures beyond philosophy, and there finds itself in charge of the salvation of man's essence, "so that the mystery of man's essance will be *saved* rather than abolished" (*um so dem Menschen das Geheimnis seines Wesen zu* retten).[99] Indeed, it is a matter of preserving, of protecting man's essance from annihilation, and that is what it is to save: "What does 'to save' mean? It says: to let loose, to disengage, to free, to spare, to shelter, to take under protection, to guard."[100] And if the danger originates from Error and proceeds from the decay of truth, then the task of thinking is to safeguard the essance of truth. But the neglect and the denial of this essance are none other than the kick-off of Western history, in and through the onto-logical configuration of truth, which puts the mystery of in-essance out of play in order to guarantee the Appropriation of Being and λόγος. Henceforth, the safeguard of essance is nothing like the conservation of an old asset, it is quite the contrary: the deliverance, for the first time, of what has always been repressed. "'To save' is to fetch something home into its essence, in order to bring the essence for the first time into its genuine appearing."[101]

The task of thinking consists in regrounding truth more originarily than the Greeks. This means to begin history again, and this is how the unique way out of the danger is identified: it is necessary that "the Beginning is begun again *more originarily*."[102] Because the contemporary catastrophe is the teleological consummation of the Greek Beginning, thinking is bound by its need to "the necessity of preparing the other Beginning,"[103] and it is then a matter of breaking with the destiny of Greece as such: the inauguration of "another destiny of Being"[104] can only happen through the unfolding of "the other thinking," which means going "above and beyond the Greek" experience itself and "the surrender of previous thinking."[105] If the danger of annihilation fully defines the site of Western history, then the only possibility for the human being to escape it lies in the "*dis-lodging* of its position amid beings,"[106] the displacement "out of that situation in which we find ourselves,"[107] that is, the region of the clearing. The task of thinking consists in preparing a *dis-location* of truth, understood simultaneously as destruction of onto-logy and change of place: it is a question of preparing the ground for "a wholly other truth" (*eine ganze andere Wahrheit*).[108]

The other Beginning is defined by the regrounding of truth, which dislocates the sphere of onto-logy in order to access what it refuses, and thus gives itself a chance to escape from errancy by no longer turning away from the abyss that constitutes its originary in-essance. The "other truth" is then that which no longer turns away from its originary element but turns *toward* it; it no longer circumscribes its essance within the impassable limits of presence, but quite the contrary maintains it in an essantial relation with absence by authorizing the paradoxical phenomenality of the mystery. Indeed, it is not a question of succumbing to the temptation of immediate immersion in the originary—the lethargy, the inactivity within λήθη—which would condemn the site of the clearing to a darkened wasteland. The "other truth" is *other than* ἀλήθεια, it is especially truth *of the Other*, which opens a clearing site *for* the originary abyss of Beyng—and no longer for beings alone. The Greek decision institutes ἀλήθεια *against* λήθη, in and through a keeping-away (εἶργειν) of self-hiding: the "other truth" institutes a clearing *for* λήθη, in and through an "essantial, 'creative' 'yes'"[109] to the mystery. "Truth as the clearing for concealment is thus an essantially different projection than is ἀλήθεια" (*die Lichtung* für *die Verbergung ist deshalb ein wesentlich anderer Entwurf als die* ἀλήθεια).[110] If first the task of thinking is defined as the inception of another truth, here the configuration proper to this other truth is defined: "*The essance of truth* is the *clearing for self-concealing*" (*das Wesen der Wahrheit ist die Lichtung für das Sichverbergen*).[111] The safeguard of truth is this regrounding of the clearing of Being, which recognizes the paradoxical phenomenality of absence and thus maintains it in its essantial relation to the mystery, a clearing that would be not the denial of the mystery but the conservation of a space dedicated to it. Thought in this radicality, truth is no longer adequation, it is the refuge, the *protection* [*garde*] of essance: "Here, we think the protection in the sense of illuminating-sheltering gathering; what shows itself here is a fundamental trait of presencing—that is, of Being—that has been long veiled. One day we will learn to think our exhausted word 'truth [*Wahrheit*]' from out of the protection [*Wahr*] and learn that truth is the preservation of Being [*Wahrheit die Wahrnis des Seins ist*]"[112]—understanding "preservation" here in its original sense, as it is used in forestry to designate a stretch of woods entrusted to the care of a forest ranger [*garde-forestier*]. The safeguard of truth is its institution as the preservation of the mystery; the mystery is the echo or the trace of the Undisclosed, of the resource, the Unscathed, that is, the Safe, and that is how it grants the salvation of man's essance: to safe-guard truth is then to think truth as protection of the Safe and thus to establish the "temple of Being."[113] *The safe-guard is the very essance* of the "other truth." Within the contemporary catastrophe, the task of thinking consists in preparing the safeguard, and thus in sparing a "glimpse into the mystery out of errancy," in order to make possible the resolute openness toward the mystery within the clearing: "letting beings as such be as a whole occurs in a way befitting its essance only when from time to time it gets taken up in its originary essance. Then resolute openness toward the mystery [*die Ent-schlossenheit zum Geheimnis*] is under way into errancy as such."[114]

§14. TELEOLOGY AND ESCHATOLOGY

It is the possibility of such an openness toward the mystery within errancy that must be thought. Yet the site in which we stand is *defined* by the rejection of originary chaos, and has been since its Greek inauguration; not only does the paradoxical phenomenality of the mystery not have its rightful place within the scope of onto-logical truth, but the spectral luminosity of machination, now all-powerful, withers every trace of absence. Including death, today managed by "the motorized burial industry of the big city,"[115] the anticipation of which is taken over by insurance companies; not only does death itself become the simple putrefaction of the body, but love is reduced to pheromone secretions, boredom and silence are hunted down with wrath, day and night, by an industrial entertainment apparatus that controls the entire earth, and the faultiness that is existance, the fault constitutive of the self, is reduced to all possible forms of psychopathology. In the spectral essance of phenomenological luminosity proper to machination, which totalizes all beings in carrying out its self-foundation and self-determination, there is no originary, but only causes, and as a consequence the mystery is what is false: it is a pseudo-phenomenality that machination has to reduce to its calculations. Moreover, by such calculations, all mystery is subject to the requisite transparency of the artificial clearing of public space, and in this way destroyed as mystery, which is why it is necessary to insist on the fact that "we never know a mystery by unmasking it or analyzing it to death, but only in such a way that we preserve the mystery *as* mystery" (*das Geheimnis* als *Geheimnis hüten*).[116] Yet no one can believe that they are sheltered from such a power, which determines even our evidence: lucidity demands taking on man's dependence with respect to his epoch, and no more can he decide to implement calculation than he can decide to accept the mystery. "It would surely be simplistic and not thoughtful at all if we were saying that the little ego of some individual man were capable of elevating calculability to the rank of the measure of the reality of the real. Instead, the modern age corresponds to the metaphysical depth of the course of its history, when, in accordance with its will toward the unconditional 'residuelessness' of all procedure and all organizing, it builds broad avenues through all continents and so no longer has a place free for that residue in which the mystery would still glimmer in the form of mere inexplicability."[117] The relation to the mystery therefore falls under the jurisdiction not of the *ego* of any individual person whatsoever, but of the epoch as such, and of the abyssal withholding (the epochality) of Beyng in it.

"The resolute openness toward the mystery [. . .] under way into errancy as such" therefore does not come under the jurisdiction of us humans. The dislocation of truth, capable of opening the totality to what it expressly veils, can thus only happen as an event. Such an event is by definition impossible: these are the conditions of the phenomenon's manifestation, which means the very configuration of possibility by onto-logy, which denies the paradoxical phenomenality of the mystery. Thus, the mystery can never *manifest* itself, since manifestation *is* its veiling. It can only appear *against* manifestation's conditions of possibility, in an annulment—however provisional—of the very configuration of phenomenality. The mystery can never be unconcealed—only beings are unconcealed, and the unconcealment is a step into presence—it can only be unveiled, that is, recognized as the sign of an abyssal ab-stention. The event of an appearance of what the conditions of manifestation expressly dissimulate must be called *revelation*.

The revelation of the mystery within ἀλήθεια is the condition of possibility of its overcoming, and this revelation is itself only possible by the annulment of ἀλήθεια: such a dislocation of the very structure of phenomenality is not within the reach of human beings, who remain dependent on the possibilities assigned by the epochal configuration of essance. *But it is precisely such an event that defines the epoch of technology*, which is "the collapse of truth,"[118] and this is how "the essance of technology is in a lofty sense ambiguous," it threatens humanity and the world with annihilation—and, at the same time, grants the perspective on the mystery capable of opening truth to its other: "When we look into the ambiguous essance of technology, we behold the constellation, the stellar course of the mystery."[119] If the catastrophe of truth is not unilateral, this is because, for the first time, it allows the mystery of the originary to be glimpsed. The thought that reflects on the technological danger is seized by the terror of need, and this need is never purely negative: it is the shock by absence, the experience of lack, the pain of abandonment, and in this way a first discovery of absence as a singular and haunting mode of presence, and a premonition of the mystery. As collapse of ἀλήθεια, the technological catastrophe allows what ἀλήθεια expressly dissimulated to be glimpsed; it is *in itself* revelation:

> Everywhere and always machination, cloaking itself in the semblance of a measured ordering and controlling, confronts us with beings as the sole hierarchy and causes us to forget Being. What actually happens is that Being abandons beings: Being lets beings be on their own *and thereby refuses itself.*

> Insofar as this *refusal* is experienced, a clearing of Being *has already occurred.* For such refusal is not nothing, is not even negative; it is not some lack, is not something truncated. It is the primordial and initial revelation of Being [*Offenbarung des Seins*].[120]

Such a terminal revelation was in reserve from the very Beginning. The abyssal withdrawal of Beyng is its withholding by which it gives rise to ἀλήθεια's zone of presence, and it is this withdrawal that, in the clearing of ἀλήθεια, appears as mystery. The mystery is precisely the mode of manifestation proper to withdrawal, it is the echo or the resonance of the closing within the opening, it is thus the voice (*Stimme*) that makes itself heard in affective attunement (*Stimmung*). As this withdrawal manifests itself in this way, it does not keep quiet, but declares itself (*sich zusprechen*) for human beings. Thus, the withdrawal into absence announces itself to humanity, and what announces itself is that Beyng is not nothing, "but the richest."[121] As its absence announces itself (*sich vorsprechen*) as such a richness, Being promises itself (*sich versprechen*). In this way, the mystery is the promise of Being: "But insofar as Being is the unconcealment of beings as such, Being has nonetheless already addressed itself to the essance of man. Being has already spoken out for and insinuated itself in the essance of man insofar as it has withheld and saved itself in the unconcealment of its essance. Addressing in this way, while withholding itself in abstention, *Being is the promise of itself*" (das Versprechen seiner selbst).[122] This withdrawal that is simply a promise constitutes the most intimate essance of history, and that is why the destiny of the West must be defined as "*the history of the mystery of the promise of Being itself*" (die Geschichte des Geheimnisses des Versprechens des Seins selbst).[123] It is thus absence qua announcement as mystery, withholding as promise, that founds the constitutive epochality of history: "As the promise of its truth [*als das Versprechen seiner Wahrheit*], Being keeps to itself with its own essance. The admission of the omission of the ab-stention takes place on the basis of its keeping to itself. From the respective distance of the withdrawal, which conceals itself in any given phase of metaphysics, such keeping to itself determines each epoch of the history of Being as the *epochē* of Being itself."[124] Ab-stention as promise is therefore the originary temporalization of history. Ab-stention is the temporality of absence, the temporalization proper to the movement of withdrawal, the différance[125] that defers the consummation of the promise. Such a consummation, however, could not consist of a full presence of Being: by no means could it be a question of gaining access to "the essantially Undisclosable,"[126] of reaching the bottom of the abyss, or of bringing Being out of its retreat, but rather a question of becoming able "to experience the *ab-stention* of Being's unconcealment as such for the first time *as an advent* of Being itself, and to ponder what is thus experienced."[127] Such an experience, which recognizes in absence a determinate mode of phenomenality, is precisely what defines the openness toward the mystery.

Yet our epoch is that of "the most extreme release of beings as such," which only opens the clearing as "publicity" and "information," understood as "the metaphysical securing and establishment of the everydayness of our dawning age": it is the epoch of machination in which "man himself and every aspect of human culture is transformed into a stockpile which, psychologically reckoned, is incorporated into the working process."[128] The sovereignty of technology is the consummation of metaphysics as the forgetfulness of Being, it institutes "the age of the darkening of beings, our age of confusion, of violence and despair in human culture," which is precisely the "threat of the annihilation of man's essance": this epoch is the one in which humanity is capable of "experienc[ing] with trepidation the ab-stention of Being itself."[129] If history is the promise of the unconcealment of Being itself as essantial absence, our epoch, and precisely because it is the full availability of beings offered to consumption, is the one where this absence of the essantial is experienced, where Beyng itself is grasped as what has always withdrawn itself, and at the same time it can be apprehended that "withdrawing is not nothing. Withdrawal is an event [*Entzug ist Ereignis*]."[130]

Lucidity requires thinking our epoch in the radicality of its essance, which is revealed in its structural complexity. Our epoch is the technological catastrophe, which is the threat of total annihilation as the consummation of the destiny of the West. In this respect, our epoch is that of the end, and it must be said that "the history of Being is at an end" (*zu Ende*).[131] It is really a matter of the end *of Being*, and not of beings, which is why this end remains unnoticed to every thought obsessed with beings: the end is the darkening of the clearing, the closing of the Open, the closure of difference, and hence the return, in the ontic density of global Equalization, to "the totality of beings that remain enveloped within themselves."[132] This is why the end is not a limit, but the moment of the total and unreserved unfolding, the unleashing, of all the possibilities of the Beginning. This consummation is then simultaneously the moment when history can be grasped in its constitutive totality, and when thought can, for the first time, *leave* this totality: the "step back," explains Heidegger, "leads us away from what has been thought so far in philosophy. Thinking recedes before its matter, Being, and thus brings what is thought into a confrontation in which we behold the whole of this history."[133] Because, for the first time, it exceeds the onto-logical totality, thought gains lucidity regarding this destiny. It is in a position to think the Greek Beginning: "In essantial history the Beginning comes last. [. . .] To be sure, at first, at the outset, the Beginning appears veiled in a peculiar way [*erscheint der Anfang in einer eigentümlichen Verhüllung*]."[134] The terminal consummation of the destiny of Greece is in this way, first, the revelation of its hidden essance. This hidden essance is nihilism, that is, the reduction of the mystery of originary absence to nothingness. It is therefore this forgetting that is revealed. The terminal decomposition of truth is then the moment when the forgetting it is based on becomes manifest, and when what is *not* part of its history is revealed, and what is not part of history because history *is* its denial [*dénégation*]. And this revelation can only happen *as* catastrophe: "Before Being can occur in its primal truth, Being as the will must be broken, the world must be forced to collapse and the earth must be driven to desolation, and man to mere labor."[135] The revelation of what unfolds beyond the historiological totality, as this revelation happens in and through the completion of its teleology, defines the eschatological event. In this respect the most intimate law of this destiny is "the eschatology of Being" (*die Eschatologie des Seins*), which is what the catastrophe reveals: "As destining, Being itself is inherently eschatological [*in sich eschatologisch*]."[136] The contemporary event is that of the eschatological advent of what Beyng is in its own right—that is, ab-stention, absence, withdrawal, abyss, originary Nothingness—and through this return that is an adieu to the first Beginning it founds the possibility of the other Beginning.

Our epoch is that of the danger, which makes the threat of the annihilation of the essance of humanity and the world weigh upon us. Reflection on this danger discovers, not an accident of history, but the consummation of its very logic, founded in the Greek inauguration of truth. In this way, our epoch is the catastrophe of onto-logical truth. This catastrophe is not unilateral, however; as the collapse of truth, it dislocates the conditions of manifestation, which allows, for the first time, what these conditions expressly dissimulate to be glimpsed: the teleological destruction of truth founds the possibility of an eschatological revelation of the mystery. This revelation abruptly convicts truth itself of error and shows an errancy in its destiny. The revelation of the mystery is a crisis, which judges and condemns destiny as such and in full by confronting it with the originary in-essance of truth, which it denies, and which thereby offers resource and salvation. Such an event must be circumscribed by the concept of apocalypse.[137]

CHAPTER 4

Apocalypse and Truth

§15. THE CONCEPT OF APOCALYPSE

Ἀποκάλυψις is the first word of the last book, to which it will give its title, of the New Testament. Written on the island of Patmos in the Icarian Sea in the 90s of our era, the Apocalypse of John describes "the hour of trial that is coming on the whole world to test the inhabitants of the earth" (Apoc. 3:10 NRSV) at the time of "the consummation of the age" (ἐν τῇ συντελείᾳ τοῦ αἰῶνος: Mt 13:40), that is, "the hour of crisis" (κρίσις: Apoc. 14:7) when true Life defined as ἔσχατον (Apoc. 2:8) will confront the empire of the "Beast" (τὸ Θηρίον)[1] that "in amazement the whole earth followed" (Apoc. 13:3). Since then, the term "apocalypse" has served as a generic term to designate a literary genre proper to late Judaism and then early Christianity, characterized by grandiose descriptions of cosmic cataclysm coming to sound the death knell of history. The apocalypse is thus the very event of judgment by which history as such is confronted with truth, when those who "erred from the truth" (πλανηθη ἀπο τῆς ἀληθείας: Jas 5:19) are condemned.[2] The term has passed in everyday language to the modern epoch to evoke the end of the world, understood as total and definitive devastation: this meaning is not illegitimate, but it omits the essential dimension of the apocalyptic event, which is the coming of salvation. The apocalypse thus circumscribes an event defined simultaneously as the terminal epoch and consummation of history, as the implementation of a monstrous power of destruction jeopardizing humanity and the earth, and as the coming of what saves, a coming that thereby convicts the totality of history of errancy and error, and thus judges it. In this respect, the concept of apocalypse allows for all the epochal determinations previously brought to light to be gathered: it defines the very essence of our epoch, as the catastrophic completion of the metaphysical teleology that is, quite simply, the eschatological coming of that which this teleology denies.

If the concept of apocalypse is necessary here, it is more essantially so in that it allows the dazzling confrontation of onto-logical truth with the mystery from which it turns away to be thought. As the obsession with the being-unconcealed of beings, ἀλήθεια is in its essance, however unknowingly, the veiling of its in-essance, without which it is nevertheless errancy, and error. Ἀλήθεια only collects and gathers beings within the scope of its translucence as long as it throws a veil over the abyssal absence of λήθη. In this sense λήθη is what remains veiled. The apocalypse is the lifting of this veil and confrontation with the mystery: it is what alone makes possible the "resolute openness toward the mystery [. . .] under way into errancy as such." The Greek word ἀποκάλυψις is in fact a derivative of the verb κάλυψεν which designates all activity that covers, envelops, and dissimulates: thus, in the *Iliad* the god Hephaestus "shroud[s] [κάλυψας] in night" the son of the priest Dares to camouflage him at the moment of the enemy assault; in the *Odyssey*, a "black wave covered [κάλυψεν]"[3] the goddess in order to conceal her from the eyes of Odysseus. The verb κάλυπτειν[4] thus designates the activity of veiling that allows light to be isolated: it is itself actually derived from κάλυμμα, "the veil," that with which one covers one's head to hide one's face. Ἀποκάλυψις, built with the prefix ἀπο-, "away," "apart," therefore literally means "un-veiling," it designates the exposure of what was previously invisible. The word exists in the classical language, but it is its usage in the Septuagint that is decisive for its later meaning. The Book of Daniel (2:27–30), the oldest example of what will later be called "apocalypse," is for this reason crucial:

> Daniel answered the king, "No wise men [σοφοι], enchanters, magicians, or diviners can show to the king the mystery [τὸ μυστήρια] that the king is asking, but there is a God in Heaven who unveils mysteries [ἀνακαλύπτων μυστήρια], and he has disclosed to King Nebuchadnezzar what will happen at the end of days. Your dream and the visions of your head as you lay in bed were these: To you, O king, as you lay in bed, came thoughts of what would be hereafter, and the unveiler of mysteries [ὁ ἀνακαλύπτων μυστήρια] disclosed to you what is to be. But as for me, this mystery [τὸ μυστήριον] has not been unveiled to me because of any wisdom [σοφία] that I have more than any other living being, but in order that the interpretation may be known to the king and that you may understand the thoughts of your mind."

The apocalypse is the unveiling of what is at first glance concealed: but this unveiling is not within the reach of "wise men," it is inaccessible to "wisdom," even that of Daniel. And necessarily so, in that it discovers not nature, but the "mystery." Ἀποκάλυψις is a mode of manifestation incommensurable with ἀλήθεια. The mode of manifestation that defines the wisdom of wise men is strictly limited to ἀλήθεια, that is, to natural phenomenality. But the field of this clearing is finite and unfolds from an originary in-essance that it dissimulates and that only signals itself as mystery. Thus, if the wisdom of wise men *cannot* show the depth from which ἀλήθεια arises, it is not for contingent reasons—for example, its primitive and insufficiently developed character—but by its very essance that *is* blindness to the mystery. Unconcealment only unconceals by veiling the Undisclosable. This denial of the Undisclosable's positivity (its reduction to nothingness) founds the onto-logical claim to the totalization of essance, that is, the unreserved identification of truth with the clearing of ἀλήθεια. Ἀποκάλυψις is then the lifting of the veil that lets the mystery appear as such, manifests the abyss of an infinite absence, and thus abruptly reveals the originary vastness of truth's in-essance. The appearance of the mystery, the paradoxical appearance of what phenomenality as such dissimulates, is revelation, that is, the lifting of the very horizon of phenomenality: it is ἀποκάλυψις, which will be translated into Latin as *revelatio* and then into English as "revelation." Every revelation is eschatological, in that it reveals to the totality of manifestation the excess or surfeit of essance that it dissimulates; it opens a tear in the envelope of presence to expose it to the pure essential offering from which it proceeds and in which it takes hold. And every revelation is catastrophic in that it convicts what until then was called "truth" of error and shatters the world that had been built upon it.

§16. PAULINE THOUGHT OF THE APOCALYPSE

But if the concept of apocalypse is definitively established in the problematic of access to an "other thinking" by going "above and beyond the Greek"[5] experience itself, defined as a "leap" into the "wholly other,"[6] this is because it was thought exactly in this way in the first texts that tried to subordinate Greek philosophy to an inaccessible mystery, those of Saint Paul,[7] the Apostle. Jewish spirituality unquestionably offers the example of a thought fully heterogeneous to Greek thought and irreducible to it: if the few texts of Saint Paul that have come down to us have a crucial importance—at least comparable to that of the verses of Parmenides and the aphorisms of Heraclitus—it is because they are the very site of a confrontation of the Hebraic tradition with the Hellenic tradition. Paul, "of the people of Israel, of the tribe of Benjamin, a Hebrew born of Hebrews" (Phil 3:5), who writes in the Greek language for the Nations, is precisely the one who brings the mystery to wisdom, and thus finds himself obliged to consider the relationship between the Jews and the Greeks. For if the sharing of tasks made Peter "an apostle to the circumcised" and Paul an apostle "to the Gentiles" (Gal 2:8), Paul always thought this distinction as the opposition of the Jews and the Greeks. Within the empire ushered in by Octavian Augustus, it is to Hellenism that Judaism is opposed; to evangelize the Nations is therefore to try to convert Greece. Yet "Greeks desire wisdom" (Ἕλληνες σοφίαν ζητοῦσιν: 1 Cor 1:22): Paul identifies Greek culture with "philosophy" (φιλοσοφία: Col 2:8). One thus finds in the epistles of Saint Paul a thematic thinking of the coming of the mystery within onto-logical truth.

By "philosophy," Saint Paul means Greek thinking such as it constitutes the vulgate of the Hellenistic epoch, and more precisely the doctrine of the "Epicurean and Stoic philosophers" (Acts 17:18–19). The Greeks have wisdom, but a wisdom "according to the elemental spirits of the world" (κατὰ τὰ στοιχεῖα τοῦ κοσμοῦ: Col 2:8), which is always defined as "wisdom of the world" (σοφία τοῦ κοσμοῦ: 1 Cor 1:20). Greek thinking is thus brought back to what it is at its core: a physics, which is to say, a logical unconcealment of beings as a whole; it only unfolds "in the wisdom of the Logos" (ἐν σοφία λόγου: 1 Cor 1:17). To this "wisdom of the world," Saint Paul opposes "the wisdom of God" (σοφία τοῦ θεοῦ: 1 Cor 1:21). Yet this wisdom is incommensurable with the wisdom of the world, it even constitutes its "antithesis" (1 Tm 6:20), it remains inaccessible to the wise who specifically enclose themselves within the onto-logical sphere, and Jesus himself thus praised God: "you have hidden these things from the wise [σοφῶν] and the intelligent and have unveiled [ἀπεκάλυψας] them to infants" (Mt 11:25). Such a wisdom therefore cannot be transmitted in the element of the Logos, and that is why the Apostle "did not come proclaiming the mystery of God to you in the Logos or in wisdom" (1 Cor 2:1). It is only given in, and as, "the Logos of Christ" (Col 3:16). The Logos of the Greeks only gives the world, which is why "the world did not know God through wisdom" (1 Cor 1:21); the Logos (of) Christ gives what the world "veils" and "hides," even refuses, that is, the wisdom of God, which from the point of view of the world is thus the "mystery." The Logos incarnated in the person of Jesus of Nazareth makes the mystery visible in a flesh: "the mystery," writes Saint Paul, "was manifested in flesh" (τὸ μυστέριον ἐφανερώθη ἐν σαρκί: 1 Tm 3:16). Such is the unique task of the Apostle: to teach "God's wisdom, hidden in the mystery" (θεοῦ σοφίαν ἐν μυστερίῳ τὴν ἀποκεκρυμμένην: 1 Cor 2:7), that is, to introduce it within the realm of clarity that defines natural phenomenality, and thus "to make everyone see what is the plan of the mystery hidden for ages in God" (Eph 3:9).

As a whole, Saint Paul's preaching is the unfolding of the unique event by which the mystery was given: "the mystery that has been hidden throughout the ages and generations but has now been manifested" (Col 1:26). The dissimulation proper to the mystery is the veil: "Indeed, to this very day, when they hear the reading of the old covenant, that same veil [κάλυμμα] is still there [μή ἀνακαλυπτόμενον]" (2 Cor 3:14), and the lifting of this veil is the event by which the mystery was given to Paul: "but when one turns to the Lord, the veil [κάλυμμα] is removed" (2 Cor 3:16). The event of revelation is the event of *unveiling*, that is, the apocalypse, the moment when "the mystery of God will be consummated" (Apoc. 10:7). The Apostle thus speaks "according to the unveiling of the mystery [κατὰ ἀποκάλυψιν μυστερίου] that was kept secret for long ages but is now disclosed" (Rom 16:25–26); he repeats it ceaselessly: "the mystery was made known to me by unveiling [κατὰ ἀποκάλυψιν]" (Eph 3:3). And not only does the unveiling of the mystery constitute the founding event of Pauline preaching, it constitutes also, and especially, its very content. To convert, for a Greek as for a Jew, is to turn away from what veils the mystery in order to acquiesce to it; it is to no longer veil one's face. This is how Saint Paul defines the condition of the Christian: "we act with great boldness, not like Moses, who put a veil [κάλυμμα] over his face [. . .] And all of us, with unveiled faces, see the glory of the Lord as though reflected in a mirror" (2 Cor 3:12–18).

Yet the unveiled cannot simply slip into the world and occupy a place there among others: indeed, it is the very truth of the world that it comes to refute by making evident its veiled nature,[8] and therefore by diminishing its claim to unconceal the fullness of essance. The Epistle to the Romans is without a doubt Saint Paul's most important text, where he addresses the capital of the Western world, and where for this reason the tension between Jews and Greeks, mystery and wisdom, that is, the conflict between two antithetical regimes of truth, reaches its peak: it unequivocally makes explicit revelation as judgment of ἀλήθεια by ἀποκάλυψις. Indeed Saint Paul writes: "For the wrath of God is unveiled [ἀποκαλύπτεται] from heaven against [. . .] those who by their wickedness hold the truth [ἀλήθεια] captive" (Rom 1:18). Revelation is primarily about the status of truth; it shows that until then truth was "held captive": the verb κατέχειν used here commonly means "to retain," "to contain," "to detain"; Homer used it in the sense of "to cover," "to envelop," "to wrap," as a synonym of καλύπτειν. Revelation does not import some content into a context that would remain unchanged, it focuses first and foremost on the nature of this context, whose finitude, narrowness, and finally opacity to the essential it reveals. The unveiling of the mystery is the uncovering of the excess irreducible to the limits of knowledge; it lays bare these limits and annuls its claims: "as for knowledge, it will come to an end. For we know only in part, and we prophesy only in part; but when the complete comes, the partial will come to an end" (1 Cor 13:8–10). This is precisely why a revelation is never ontic, in which case it would only be manifestation: it is essantial, which means that it concerns the configuration of possibility that circumscribes a world in its essance. By abruptly revealing its boundaries and its shutting out of the mystery, revelation shows in the truth of the world a pure and simple error: those who held to this truth "became futile in their thinking, and their senseless minds were darkened. Claiming to be wise [σοφοὶ], they became fools; [. . .] they exchanged the truth about God for an error [ψεύδει]" (Rom 1:21–25). Unveiling the excess that truth dissimulates by its very claim to totalization demands recognizing that it is, in its essance, error; likewise, it demands recognizing that its knowledge is in reality ignorance, and indeed Saint Paul clearly distinguishes wisdom and ignorance from the mystery: "So that you may not claim to be wiser than you are, brothers and sisters, I want you to understand this mystery" (Rom 11:25). From then on, the search for wisdom that defines the Greeks is confinement persisting in error, it is, in the words of James, "errancy" (Jas 5:19), or, in the words of Paul, "foolishness:" Revelation has "made foolish [ἐμώρανεν] the wisdom of the world" (1 Cor 1:20). The word μωρός used here by Saint Paul is most often translated as "madness," yet it is not a question of μανία, madness conceived as delirium or dementia—the word that Acts uses when Festus reproaches Paul, "Too much learning is driving you mad!" (Acts 26:24)—but of stupor, stupidity, folly. The verb μωραίνω means "to lose its flavor," "to make bland," "to become insipid," used in this way in the Gospels: "You are the salt of the earth; but if salt has lost its taste [μωρανθῇ], how can its saltiness be restored?" (Mt 5:13). When it designates somebody, the verb certainly means "to go mad," but in the sense of "to become stupid," "to sink into a stupor," "to be stunned," "idiotic," "narrow-minded." To write as Saint Paul did that God ἐμώρανεν the wisdom of the world is to say that He struck it dumb and in that way made it foolish: "Do not deceive yourselves. If you think that you are wise [σοφὸς] in this age, you should become fools [μωρός] so that you may become wise. For the wisdom [σοφία] of this world is foolishness [μωρία] with God" (1 Cor 3:18–19). It should be translated: God struck *dumb* the wisdom of the world.

Saint Paul's conclusion is abrupt: "See to it that no one takes you captive through philosophy and empty deceit" (Col 2:8). It is a question not of renouncing thinking as such—the Epistle to the Romans concludes with the appeal: "be transformed by the renewing of your minds [νοῦς]" (Rom 12:2)—but of "avoiding the profane chatter and contradictions of what is falsely called knowledge [ἀντιθεσις τῆς ψευδωνύμον γνώσεως]" (1 Tm 6:20), that is, of not enclosing oneself within the limits of a truth defined exclusively by an unconcealment of the world. The challenge to phenomenality's autonomy is explicit in the Epistle to the Hebrews: faith is defined there as "the conviction of things not seen. [. . .] By faith we understand that [. . .] what is seen is not made from phenomena" (μὴ ἐκ φαινομένων τὸ βλεπόμενον γεγονέναι) (Heb 11:1–3). We understand that there is another possible mode of essential unfolding, beyond onto-logical luminosity, in an "unapproachable light" (1 Tm 6:16). The philosophy that Saint Paul assimilates to a "captivity" and a "deceit" is therefore the "wisdom of the world" that encloses Being within the limits of phenomenality, that is, the philosophy that persists and becomes rigid within onto-logical wisdom, and makes logic the very essance of truth. This wisdom is "a powerful errancy, leading them to believe what is false" (ἐνέργεια πλάνης εἰς τὸ πιστεῦσαι αὐτοὺς τῷ ψεύδει: 2 The 2:11); the truth that it unfolds is established as a "search for error" or even a "method of errancy" (μεθοδεία τῆς πλάνης: Eph 4:14). The Apostle's task then consists in "destroy[ing] arguments" (2 Cor 10:4): Saint Paul's warning concerns liars [*le pseudo-logos*] (ψευδολόγων: 1 Tm 4:2). To refute philosophy is thus fundamentally to refute the Greek thesis of the identity of ἀλήθεια and λόγος, which is ultimately to refute the identity of Being and λόγος by affirming the positivity of what unfolds beyond logos, and this is what it means to overcome onto-logy. The apocalyptic event is the "earthquake" (σεισμὸς: Mt 27:54 and 28:2) that dislocates the onto-logical totality, and this is indeed the most radical Pauline formulation to think the coming of the mystery within the world: "God chose what is low and despised in the world, things that are not [τά μὴ ὄντα], to reduce to nothing things that are [τά ὄντα]" (1 Cor 1:28).

§17. THE APOCALYPTIC REGROUNDING OF TRUTH

Saint Paul's preaching inaugurates another history through the event of an apocalypse of truth. The influx of the mystery into wisdom is in fact inseparable from a trembling of temporality itself, since from the outset it challenges the very thing by which nature closes in on itself, namely, the eternal return of the same [*du pareil*]:[9] a temporality proper to the mystery, but one that ontology, as it is developed first and foremost as λόγος of φύσις, took up and conceptualized in ancient Pythagoreanism,[10] and then in stoicism.[11] The thought of the circle as a figure of perfection in fact led to thinking the time of the world as recurrence, to thus rejecting in advance all coming of the new, but also to making the κόσμος a perfect and complete totality, which consequently could be neither perfected nor completed:[12] thus eternity remained immanent to the κόσμος, *perpetuum mobile* of its rotation, and the eternal return of the same thus again became the temporality proper to the technological totality. It is this onto-logical totalization that is dislocated by the entry into presence (παρουσία) of "things that are not," that is, by ontology's other. This other is not nothing; quite the contrary, it brings salvation and lays bare the narrowness, the bias, and finally the errancy of onto-logical truth, as well as its *insufficiency*, its inability to satisfy finitude and to fill the gap of its constitutive fault: the apocalypse of truth consists in revealing the finitude of a "captive truth" (Rom

1:18) by suddenly opening it to "all the truth" (Jn 16:13) through recognizing the phenomenality proper to the mystery.

In this way the New Testament thematically develops the thought of an "other truth," irreducible to the onto-logical truth of the Appropriation, and it is even its essantial content to bring the news of this "other truth." The various texts that make up the New Testament indeed all proceed from a unique and radical thesis about the essance of truth,[13] one based on a redefinition of λόγος that identifies it with the person of Jesus of Nazareth. A thesis absolutely implausible for metaphysical thought and its scientific developments, but a thesis that precisely is radically opposed to metaphysical logic and its onto-logical truth: against the metaphysical refusal of originary Nothingness, the λόγος of Christ is defined by an unreserved acquiescence (2 Cor 1:19) to the Wholly Other; as opposed to the rejection of the mystery, it is defined by its welcome and reception (Col 2:9); instead of the closed totality of a perfectly defined universal concept, it occurs as pathetic and singular flesh. Thus, to affirm as Saint Paul does that "in him the whole fullness of the deity dwells bodily" (Col 2:9) is to recognize in this body the *safeguard* of the mystery, and to establish "the temple of his body" (ὁ ναός τοῦ σώματος αὐτοῦ: Jn 2:21) as the center opening a site *in which* humanity could now "stand" and "abide" (Jn 15:9). By establishing a new temple, inseparable from the "destruction" (Jn 2:19) of the old one, another truth could be established, and thus ἀλήθεια could be regrounded. This is confirmed by a Greek biblicism (an expression absent from classical language) that is found simultaneously in the Septuagint and the New Testament: "to make" or "to produce" (ποιεῖν) truth. As early as Genesis (32:10), Jacob thanks YHWH in these terms: "I am not worthy of the least of all the steadfast love and all the truth that you have made" (ἀληθείας ἡς ἐποίησας). Likewise, it is said in the New Testament that if we "are walking in darkness," then we "do not make truth" (οὐ ποιοῦμεν τήν ἀλήθειαν: 1 Jn 1:6). But the most significant occurrence of the expression is in the Gospel of John (3:21): "Those who make truth [ὁ ποιῶν τὴν ἀλήθειαν] come to the light [πρὸς τὸ φῶς], so that it may be clearly seen [φανερωθῇ] that their deeds have been done in God." Truth is established as the work of a ποίησις, of a creation and a production, which unfolds a luminosity in which human works are manifest *otherwise*. "To make truth" is then to contribute to the furnishing of this realm of phenomenality, it is to implement the translucent expanse of the clearing, which is no longer truth of the Same, developing in the tautological logic of identity, but truth of the Other, which develops in the altruistic logic of love.

"Why is it," asked Nietzsche, "that from Plato onwards every philosophical architect in Europe has built in vain? That everything they themselves in all sober seriousness regarded as *aere perennius* is threatening to collapse or already lies in ruins?"[14] He then responds: it is the "cornerstone [*Grundstein*] of those sublime and unconditional philosophical edifices [. . .] Plato's invention of pure spirit and the Good in itself."[15] Henceforth, it is apparent that Christianity occurs from the outset as a rival project, which was conceived by the Church Fathers as "true philosophy,"[16] and was thus placed on the terrain of philosophy, whose truth it contested in the name of another λόγος. Its coming destroys the onto-logical edifice in order to rebuild everything on the basis of another keystone, another cornerstone: the pathetic and singular flesh of the most humble. It is a constant assertion in Saint Paul: "like a wise architect [ὡς σοφὸς ἀρχιτέκτων] I laid a foundation, and someone else is building on it. Each builder must choose with care how to build on it. For no one can lay any foundation other than the one that has been laid; that foundation is Jesus Christ" (1 Cor 3:10–11); "you are citizens with the saints and also members of the household of God, built upon the foundation of the apostles and prophets, with Christ Jesus himself as the cornerstone. In him the whole structure is joined together and grows into a holy temple in the Lord" (Eph 2:19–21). But it is a verse from the Psalms (118:22), cited four times in the New Testament (Mt 21:42, Mk 12:10, Acts 4:11, 1 Pt 2:7), that is the most significant here: "The stone that the builders rejected has become the cornerstone." In this way, it is no longer the highest being, the being par excellence that constitutes the principle, it is no longer "a stronger and more immortal Atlas to hold everything together more,"[17] but quite the contrary, it is the weakest, with "no form or majesty that we should look at him, nothing in his appearance that we should desire him" (Is 53:2) who becomes the cornerstone: a "living stone" (1 Pt 2:4). By moving the principle (ἀρχή) from the Idea to the flesh, the Incarnation of the λόγος abandons the metaphysical "yoke" (ζυγόν)[18] of onto-logy, and promises rest to "all you that are weary and are carrying heavy burdens": "Take my yoke (ζυγόν) upon you, and learn from me; for I am gentle and humble in heart, and you will find rest for your souls. For my yoke (ζυγόν) is easy, and my burden is light" (Mt 11:28–30). In this respect, the Incarnation of the Logos is the event by which the originary instance of truth's unfolding leaves the "beyond"[19] to come "among us" (Jn 1:14): the principle of phenomenological luminosity is therefore no longer the sun, which in Plato's thought constantly figures the Idea of the Good, but the singular flesh. Through the apocalyptic event of such a regrounding of truth, "the sun became black as sackcloth" (Apoc. 6:12), and it is thus "the icon of the invisible God" (εἰκὼν τοῦ θεοῦ τοῦ ἀοράτου: Col 11:15) that takes its place: "his face was like the sun shining with full force" (Apoc. 1:16).

It is henceforth possible, on the basis of its elaboration in the New Testament, to delineate a historical concept of apocalypse. The apocalyptic event is the *crisis of truth*, which reveals what it is, what it was, what it can become.

Indeed, the terminal crisis of Western history happens as the revelation of the decision by which it was begun. This decision, namely, the Greek establishment of metaphysics, was the de-finition of truth, that is, the delimitation of a site—the one where Western existance stands—within an undisclosable originary. Thus, the *finitude of truth* is revealed, which is only ever the furnishing of a region cleared from an undisclosable abyss, which only ever appears as mystery. A Beginning occurs through such a delimitation of a clearing: *a Beginning is a configuration of truth*, a "clearing projection."[20] The most intimate essance of a Beginning is then its *position in relation to the mystery*: every delimitation of a clearing is located in relation to an unlimited opacity, every foundation is confronted with the abyss, every definition of presence is surrounded by absence. Yet the Greek Beginning was nothing other than a *rejection* of this adversarial element: the Greek Appropriation of Being and λόγος was an introversion of truth that condemned the West to tautology, even to autism, by "keeping away" (εἶργειν) the original alterity. The Greek inauguration was an apocalypse *manqué*, or refused, and this is what Parmenides's *Poem* testifies to. Indeed, the tenth verse of the exordium says of the maidens who guide the thinker that they had "pushed back the veils from their heads with their hands" (ἄπο κερσὶ καλύπτρας);[21] καλύπτρα is an old form of κάλυμμα, "veil," used metaphorically by Aeschylus to describe being "veiled in darkness":[22] the exordium of the *Poem* therefore describes, literally, an apo-calyptic event. This unveiling is the one by which the maidens "had left behind the palace of Night towards the light," and it confronts the thinker with the alternative of the "paths of Night and Day";[23] Parmenides then responds with the destinal decision on the essance of truth: "Well, it has been decided, as is necessary, to abandon the one as unthinkable, unnameable (for it is not the true road)."[24] Confronted with the "road" (ὁδός) of nothingness, Parmenides immediately prohibits it by setting down: "nothingness is not" (μηδὲν δ´οὐκ ἔστιν).[25] To the Greek apocalypse, the revelation of Beyng's abyssal crypt (κρύπτεσθαι),[26] Parmenides responds with a rejection, its an-*nihil*-ation [*a*-néant-*issement*], which bars it from entering the sphere of thought and language, and in doing so imposes anonymity (ἀνώνυμον) on it. It is upon this inaugural *no* that all the weight of nihilism ultimately rests. The apocalypse is then the terminal catastrophe of this tautological teleology, which conceals the promise of a revelation of the mystery of the originary from which all truth proceeds and in which it settles. To sense this event is to discover the need for a regrounding of truth, that is, for another Beginning, defined by an *acquiescence to the mystery* capable of opening up the site of its *safeguard*.

CHAPTER 5

On the Edge of the Abyss

§18. APOCALYPSE OF THE WEST

Our epoch is the epoch of technology. All that is and exists now stands within a Machinery that constitutes the very framework of reality and whose machination conditions both the way things have of appearing and humanity's mode of being. Machinery's functioning aims at nothing other than the growth of its power, and there is nothing that is not now mobilized to contribute to it: all the earth's resources, to the point of fracturing the very ground on which we stand in order to extract from it a little more fuel; all the peoples of the planet, to the point of proletarianizing the last so-called primitive peoples and thus reducing Zulu warriors and Chukchi hunters to the dismaying position of television viewers. In this respect, our epoch is the epoch of *risk*, of a risk concerning humanity as such, one that its great thinkers were lucid enough to see. There is the risk that people may remain assigned to the function of producer-consumer, and that Equalization may freeze humanity into a payroll [*masse salariale*] for the capitalist production apparatus and into mass tourism for the entertainment industry, masses determined "in real time" by the mechanical drives of cyberspace. There is the even greater risk that such a degeneration of humanity[1] is imperceptible, which is why Heidegger stressed that devastation is so unearthly: "The devastation of the earth can easily go hand in hand with a guaranteed supreme living standard for man, and just as easily with the organized establishment of a uniform state of happiness for all men. Devastation can be the same as both, and can haunt us everywhere in the most unearthly way—by keeping itself hidden."[2] There is also the risk that man's integration within Machinery may reduce him to a *high-tech* product: Heidegger asserted in the 1940s that "since man is the most important raw material, one can reckon with the fact that some day factories will be built for the artificial breeding of human material, based on present-day chemical research"; the unstoppable advances in genetic engineering, the current research in cloning and artificial wombs, connected to new demands for assisted reproduction, have only hastened the approach of this day, which is also the day of what its proponents call "augmented humanity," embedded with equipment such as artificial organs or microprocessor implants in the brain to treat such or such disease. The installation of humanity within the cybernetic space of Machinery, its subjugation to machinational possibilities, as well as technology's inherent requirement to realize all its possibilities without delay, the technical efficiency standards that it imposes on everyone, and the possibilities that it offers for adaptation, themselves technical, thus open the perspective—in a process we must recall is only at its start—of an effective reduction of the human being to a cerebral machine. There is the concomitant risk that thinking itself may disappear through its analytic dilution in the mechanical computation of all things. But there is also the risk that the desertification of the earth may definitively condemn humanity to "wander through the desert of the earth's desolation,"[3] since the early decades of the twenty-first century extend to the entire planet the sober and lucid observation that Nietzsche made in 1884: "*The desert grows*,"[4] and to such an extent that the total desertification of the planet is now possible.[5] Finally, there is the risk of an effective and total annihilation, since the twentieth century gained that possibility in the form of nuclear machinery, which now condemns humanity to live in the drop shadow of "the hydrogen bomb, whose detonation, thought in its broadest possibility, could be enough to wipe out all life on earth."[6]

In the face of what Heidegger himself called the "technological revolution" (*Revolution der Technik*),[7] only another revolution would be capable of annulling the threat that is inherent to it. Marx is its thinker: the first to have seen in the advent of capitalist Machinery a "total revolution" and a direct threat to humanity and the earth, and the first to have grasped the urgency of a revolution to overcome it. But such a revolution, in order to be authentically revolutionary, could not consist in a simple change of personnel in the device, which would only be the new assignment and transfer of functionaries, and would in no way succeed in influencing its functioning: Marx expressly stated that the revolution could in no way be brought about by the "conspiracy" of "professional conspirators."[8] Technology is danger precisely because it has become autonomous in relation to humans, and now only moves in the circle of its auto-matism. "An attack with technological means is being prepared upon the life and nature of man," Heidegger observed in 1955. "No single man, no group of men, no commission of prominent statesmen, scientists, and technicians, no conference of leaders of commerce and industry, can brake or direct the progress of history in the atomic age. No merely human organization is capable of gaining dominion over it."[9] Machinery functions in a purely immanent way, it governs itself through cybernetics, it is therefore ungovernable in principle—and all the more so when the (pseudo-)elites who claim to govern it are meticulously formatted by it, methodically formed to its management requirements and preserved in the sufficiency of the "specialist." Once Machinery has become a planetary totality, "no 'revolution' is 'revolutionary' enough."[10] The divestiture of the existant and the alienation of its essance, the universal transfer of sovereignty that establishes the dominant power of Capital and that Marx was the first to think, is in fact nothing other than the technological consummation of metaphysics. It proceeds historically from the transfer of Beyng's sovereignty into beings, which leads—through an essantial modality of fetishism, which gives rise to the metaphysical idolatry of the highest being, then is disseminated into commodity fetishism—to assigning beings the originary essance of Beyng, and as a result to transferring it into them: "inceptual Beyng leaves mastery to the beings,"[11] and the Greek Event (*Ereignis*) is none other than this disappropriation (*Enteignung*) and this transfer (*Übereignung*), now accomplished in and through the empowerment of the self-regulated system of machinery. The only revolution commensurate with the epoch is humanity's recovery of its essance disseminated into the autonomized mechanistic apparatus, that is, a reversal (*Umkehrung*) or a Turn (*Kehre*) into Being; the revolution capable of warding off the threat can thus only occur as a historical event (*Ereignis*), that of the terminal reappropriation (*Aneignung*) of the initial expropriation (*Enteignung*), which could thus lead humanity back to its proper (*eigen*) essance.[12]

This event has not occurred: perhaps it will occur, in a form that is inconceivable today, and perhaps it will not. In any event, it can be neither decided nor planned—which would still be a technical calculation—and this is why thinking must remain in withdrawal. If thought is distinguished from every science by its relation to the ab-stention of Beyng, and if it is this ab-stention that makes it thinkable, then on principle thought must abstain from all political involvement—and that is the motto that must be remembered from Epicurus: λάθε βιώσας καί μὴ πολιτεὺεισθαι, "live hidden and don't play politics," which means: stand as close as possible to λήθη, withdrawn in relation to the ob-scene of public space, abstain. The thinker must not have the naiveté—which Heidegger himself had—to believe himself capable of in any way influencing the sovereign power of machination. His only responsibility is to think, and the thinker's solitude is the abstention that gives him the distance and the freedom to think: that is, to think the event that defines our epoch, to try to unconceal what in it is capable of warding off the threat, and to wait for it. This is ultimately the attitude that Heidegger advocated: "We should *do* nothing at all, but rather wait."[13]

It is a matter of circumscribing the essence of the contemporary event, and this event is defined as apocalypse. To speak of apocalypse is, then, not to predict, but to name an event that has already taken place and continues to occur, which is the very unfolding of our epoch at its core, which is to say its essance. This essance is crystallized in its crucial event, which is why it must be said that "in the Auschwitz apocalypse, it was nothing less than the West, in its essance, that revealed itself—and that continues, ever since to reveal itself."[14] Thought in the radicality of its essance as well as in its provenance, such an event is the "necessary fate of the West,"[15] in other words, the end of the "baleful destiny of Being" (*das böse Geschick des Seins*).[16] This fate and this destiny are ultimately led back to the essantial configuration of truth proper to the Greek Beginning. This is why our epoch must be defined as καταστροφή, "catastrophe," that is, dénouement of Greek tragedy, consummation of the destiny of onto-logy. This consummation unconditionally requires the sovereignty of science, technics, capitalism, and democracy, these apparatuses of a specifically Western provenance, and equalizes all that is within the "planetary totality"[17] of Machinery, which implements metaphysical nihilism and therefore unfolds as annihilation. To recognize and take on the apocalypse allows us first and foremost to admit the enormity of the danger—to no longer veil one's face—and thus to shed light on what is. If the concept of apocalypse allows us to embrace the scale of the catastrophe, it especially allows us at the same time to recognize that in this event something is said that until now had remained unheard: it is in fact the very meaning of the concept of apocalypse to circumscribe a revealing catastrophe—a revelation that can only occur in the total destruction of a world.

The catastrophe is that of the West. But this catastrophe is apocalypse: this means that it is revelation. It is the revelation of the nihilistic essance of the West, but also and above all the first glimmer of the mystery of Beyng that nihilism took for nothing. That is why this terminal revelation of the nihilistic essance of the destiny of the West in no way constitutes a pure and simple condemnation of this history, which would lead, for example, to abandoning this "civilization" in order to go search for a way elsewhere[18]—and not only because there is no longer any elsewhere. Western history is that of the opening *of* Being and the opening *to* Beyng, and in this way it is opposed to the immobility of all closed societies and to the lethargy of the Asian element against which the Greeks of the tragic age rebelled and which they managed to interrupt; but by this opening it reveals the essance common to all humanity. The West is *effectively* the revelation of Being in λόγος: the extension of its logic to all peoples of the planet does not refer simply to a political or economic imperialism, but to a real universality of which this λόγος is the bearer. What happened in ancient Greece is the common heritage of humanity, the Greek λόγος makes explicit an essance that is implicit in the human community, and which allows people to be defined in this way: those who share λόγος, those to whom λόγος is common. What characterizes the West is the making explicit, within the determinate configuration of metaphysics, of this λόγος immanent to the human community, which succeeds in manifesting its universality. The end of the destiny of the West reveals, however, that, from the outset, this manifestation has been deceptive: the Greeks were certainly exposed to the light coming from the abyss of Beyng, but they never saw it elsewhere than in the brightness (ἴδη) of beings, and thus from the outset the luminous specter of the Clearing deteriorated in this initial "collapse of ἀλήθεια,"[19] and λόγος was at once stranded and stuck within beings.

Yet it could be that not only does λόγος define the human being as such, but that this deterioration and this degeneration define it just as much. As existant, the human being is, in the midst of beings, the very place of difference, it is the one who introduces, within "the totality of beings that remain enveloped within themselves,"[20] the fissuring through which Beyng can occur. In this way, it is the "breach" (*Bresche*) or the "draft" (*Riß*) through which surges the excessive violence of the originary: "Historical humanity's Being-here means: Being-posited as the breach into which the excessive violence of Being breaks in its appearing, so that this breach itself shatters against Being."[21] The human being is this irruption; it is, in the natural continuity, a breakage, "an irruption and an essantial *inter-ruption*";[22] its coming is an earthquake that opens the fault from which the originary springs. Humanity *is* faultiness: "As the breach for the opening up of Being in beings—a Being that has been set into work—the existance of historical humanity is a *fault-iness* [*Zwischen-fall*], the faultiness in which the violent forces of the released excessive violence of Being suddenly emerge."[23] As fault-iness [*dé-faillance*] the human being is this finite Being whose ipseity is the fault that vertiginously opens it to the abyss, and thus hollows out beneath its feet an originary that is limited by no bottom, no ground, and in this way imposes itself as infinite. The definition of existance by finitude therefore is not sufficient, since a rock, a tree, or a bird are unquestionably finite beings: finitude, understood as de-finition and thus self-enclosure, is precisely sufficiency, and immediately the claim to infallibility [*infaillibilité*]. But the human being's finitude is inseparable from this opening to the infinite, which could be called in-finitude, if one thereby understood a finitude that *is* opening to the infinite, which is only ever the finitude of a breach that gapes toward an infinite abyss. This is why taking on man's essantial fallibility [*faillibilité*] is not his debasement, but the recognition of what opens him to the space of his elevation: the recognition that "man's greatness comes from knowing he is wretched."[24]

The breach within beings, existance, is thus the surge of an infinite power. That is why man can never control it, and why, as Sophocles had said in the tragic age, man is τὸ δεινότατον, the most uncanny. Man is the most uncanny, first, because he finds himself the custodian of a power that most of the time he cannot tame, because he "is thrown this way and that between fittingness and un-fittingness, between the wretched and the noble"; he is thus defined by the possibility of "plunging into what has no way out and has no site: perdition." This, however, does not come from the fact that someone "does not succeed in a particular act of violence and mishandles it; instead, this perdition holds sway and lies in wait fundamentally."[25] It is in his essance that man is exposed to the possibility of perdition, and as such the "ontological privilege" of existance is paid for at the price of inquietude. This inquietude defines him in his essance. Such an inquietude, however, comes from the excessive violence of the originary that arises from the abyss, therefore it could not be reduced to one simple state of mind of a living thing among others: in-quietude is none other than the abyssal quality of Beyng, which provides no stable ground and thus imposes on humanity essential instability and exposes it to vertigo, and it must be said that "uncanniness [*die Unheimlichkeit*] does not first arise as a consequence of humankind; rather, humankind emerges from uncanniness and remains within it." If humankind is the most uncanny because it is the holder of an excessive violence that it cannot control, it is even more so because it stands unstable above the abyss. The most uncanny is this exposure to the enormity of the originary excessive violence, which "looms forth in the essance of human beings."[26] It therefore belongs to the essance of human beings to flee from the originary's unbearable proximity: "the mortals flee, turn away [. . .] Mortals flee before the origin, want to forget it, avoid its frightfulness."[27] As a springing-forth, the origin is a projection toward us, humanity, and Being is this pro-ject. By fleeing from this pro-ject, we are "disavowing the proper work of Being: *we cast Being away from us*."[28] This turning away from the essential is made evident in language as a prism of essance: precisely because it is such a prism, it unfolds in a spectrum, from meaning (of Beyng) to simple designation (of beings), that is, from speech to discourse, which itself gets bogged down in idle talk. Language includes within itself its own decline in the expression and transmission of information: in this sense it is "dangerous," because "by its very essence it bears decline within it, whether into a mere reciting or reporting of what has been said, or the decline that falls into idle talk."[29] The essance of language is inseparable from its own decay, and this decline that belongs to the essance of language is one with the decline of Being into beings, since "in saying something about Being we make it into a 'being' and thus cast it away."[30]

The human being is, therefore, in its essance, the fault-iness that institutes the fault of Being within beings, but at the same time it defaults [*fait défaut*] on its project. It is the breach that initiates the ontological fissuring through which surges the originary excessive violence, an excessive violence that not only is it unable to tame, but before which it turns away in order to turn back unilaterally toward the stability of beings, thus breaking with its proper essence. In this way, it *is* catastrophe: "The uncanniness of the unhomely here consists in the fact that human beings themselves in their essance are καταστροφή—a reversal [*eine Umkehrung*] that turns them away [*abkehrt*] from their own essance. Among beings, the human being is the sole catastrophe [*der Mensch ist innerhalb des Seienden die einzige Katastrophe*]."[31]

Henceforth, it is necessary to conclude that the West does not initiate the catastrophe, a catastrophe from which other peoples would be exempt: it manifests it, and manifests it as the essance common to the human community, and brings it to its completion. The Western catastrophe is the revelation of man's catastrophic essance, which has always missed itself. In this sense man is his own decline, he is the twilight of his own essance toward beings, which always leads him to give himself the mode of Being of a worldly thing, and that is why the West, the Occident (*Abendland*), is the crepuscular light fit to reveal him as what he is. At the very moment when he risks ending up in the hideous figure of the cerebral machine, "the mystery of man's essance"[32] can be sensed, and the most intimate heart of the risk inherent to our epoch is to miss this eschatological encounter. Heidegger thus asked in 1951: "What becomes of the man—not of the brain but of the man, who may die under our hands tomorrow and be lost to us, and who at one time came to our encounter?"[33]

Man's essance can be discovered as availability to the originary, as listening to the voice (*Stimme*) that murmurs in affective attunement (*Stimmung*) and thus determines him (*bestimmt*): that is, as "the thinking being" (*das denkende Wesen*).[34] That is why it is up to thinking to take on the responsibility of ensuring that "the mystery of man's essance will be *saved* rather than abolished,"[35] which is what Heidegger, citing a word of Meister Eckhart, calls "the great essance [*das große Wesen*] of the human [that] lies in its belonging to the essance of Being. It is needed by the essance of Being so as to guard it in its truth."[36] Thinking, in its simplicity and poverty, certainly seems paltry, fragile, and powerless in the face of the annihilating device's planetary hold, and without a doubt it is: it alone, however, is capable of receiving what is revealed in such an event, at the same time as it brings back to its intrinsic vanity the activism that claims to be pragmatism and deems idle the meditations of thinking, without seeing that in reality it does nothing other than implement the fundamental forms and structures of metaphysics, and thus collaborates daily in annihilation. That is why Heidegger's thought is in the proper sense of the word crucial. Heidegger is in effect the most radical thinker of our history: by continually deepening the eidetic reduction, he actually stripped thought of all that was not it, and thus led it to the purity of its essance. In doing so, he freed its constitutive eventality, which proceeds from Beyng's ab-stention, which opens the leeway of a history defined precisely by its epochality, that is, its withdrawal, and he was able to define the very essance of thinking by putting it back within its limits, which are those of ἀλήθεια such as the Greeks configured it. But if, by his step back, he was able to free thought from the metaphysical structure that since the Greek Beginning has constituted its framework, its structure, its backbone, this is precisely because he is situated at its end—that is, after Nietzsche, who exhausted all its possibilities—at the moment when metaphysics is completely past (*gewesen*), and therefore when its essance has been completely gathered together (*Ge-Wesen*). The end of Western destiny is the end of philosophy, and this end is the moment of its gathering, the moment when time becomes space, when all the philosophical minds, from Anaximander to Nietzsche, coexist in the same place. The end of philosophy is this place: "The end of philosophy is the place, that place in which the whole of philosophy's history is gathered in its most extreme possibility. End as completion means this gathering."[37] Heidegger's thought is this place, it is the terminal recapitulation of the destiny of the West insofar as it is, in its essance, philosophy. Heidegger's work, made from "the apparently random bestrewal of blocks quarried from the bedrock,"[38] is, in its very perdition, the final work of our destiny—and that is because it is destinal, through its intimacy with the "baleful destiny of Being,"[39] because it belongs to its errancy, has its share of fatality, and thus brushed against the abyss of the German catastrophe. Heidegger's thought is the apocalypse of the German soul,[40] and of the German soul such as it is, since the high period of idealism, the coming of age of the Greek spirit. It is then a matter of asking oneself how Heidegger thought the eschatological revelation proper to our time.

§19. POETICS OF TRUTH

To recognize that the danger of annihilation is the collapse of a truth whose essance has always been decay demands as its task the "ground[ing]" of "a wholly other truth." This other truth is immediately defined by openness toward the mystery and the safeguard of the abyss of the originary Nothingness within the Clearing itself: grounding a wholly other truth establishes a site *for* the "wholly other."[41] Such a possibility is in reserve within the "condition of our world [as] a needful one"[42] that characterizes our epoch. This need, as the experience of the absence of the essantial, gives a sense of ab-stention as givenness proper to Beyng and of absence as its essance. The question remains, however, to know *how* to respond to this situation of need and to this shock by absence, and how, from there, to reground a truth.

The regrounding of truth is the pro-position of a "clearing projection."[43] In this sense it is creation. Indeed, there is only creation through the *refusal to play the game* of existing truth. Creation is irreducible to "invention," which is merely the simple "application of faculties that the human being has":[44] the inventor is content to make use of his faculties, and thus assembles in a new way what is given to him in the site in which he stands; in contrast, the creator is defined by the will to exceed this site, and to gain unheard-of powers from the originary excessive violence. That is why creation is not an innocuous or peaceful activity, it is fundamentally violence. It is first of all the will to destruction, that is, "strife with the ordinary" that "thrusts up the extra-ordinary." This destruction of the ordinary is an opening to "the undisclosed fullness of the extraordinary" (*die unerschlossene Fülle des Ungeheuren*).[45] If, therefore, the human being is the fault-iness that opens within beings the fault through which springs the originary excessive violence, most people flee from this fault and seek sufficiency; the creator is the one who endures his own faultiness, seeks it out, stands resolutely in the region of the interval, at the limit, right on the edge of the abyss. Creation is first the "capture" (*Einfang*) of the originary, and then the attempt at "disciplining and disposing of [its] violent forces."[46] Violence is exercised first to bring about breaches within the limits of the Clearing, and it is exercised in return as the irruption, within this Clearing, of the excessive violence unleashed from the originary. Creation is thereby the most dangerous activity there is, it is the senseless risk taken by the one who stands "on footbridges spanning the abyss," on the edge of "gulfs of azure, wells of fire,"[47] and is thus nakedly exposed to vertigo and chaos. It is risk pure and simple: "The one who is *violence-doing*, the creative one, who sets out into the un-said, who breaks into the un-thought, who compels what has never happened and makes appear what is unseen, this violence-doing one stands at all times in risk."[48]

Thus, the creator (*Schöpfer*) is the one who draws (*schöpfen*) from the abyssal reserve of the originary in order to bring forth the "extra-ordinary" into the clearing of the unconcealed: "everything with which man is endowed must, in the projection, be drawn forth from out of the closed ground and explicitly set upon this ground. In this way, the ground is first founded as a ground that bears. Because it is such a drawing-forth, all creation is a drawing, as in drawing water from a spring."[49] The creator draws from the unheard-of, the unthought, the invisible, and from absence, he draws from the unscathed reserve of what has been spared by its own ab-stention. But to truly be a creator, he must give this influx the form of creation: that is, of the work. The characteristic of the work is to maintain—with a firm hand—among beings the originary power drawn from the abyss, which "happens only in so far as it is brought about by the work: the work of the word as poetry, the work of stone in temple and statue, the work of the word as thinking, the work of the *polis* as the site of history that grounds and preserves all this."[50] The work is then the proclamation of the unheard-of, the disclosure of the unthought, the manifestation of the invisible, the presentation of absence—and that is why every work is mysterious. The work is in itself a repository of the originary, it gathers and focuses its power: it makes the luminosity of Being shine from and around it, and so we must recognize its eminently paradoxical status as "Being that *is*" (*das seiende Sein*).[51] The work is the foundation that the creator installs out of the abyss, it is always a "platform in the center of chasms,"[52] and this work "guards [*bewahrt*] what is originally gathered [*das ursprüngliche Gesammelte*], and thus the word stewards *phusis*, which holds sway."[53]

To this exact extent the work is truth, and this is what defines art. But it is important here to think art in its originary power, as "the setting-into-work of truth" (*das Ins-Werk-Setzen der Wahrheit*),[54] and therefore not to confuse it with what most of the time gets taken for it, namely, the simple invention of amenities. This is the point of view of aesthetics, which evaluates the work according to a level of satisfaction, which is to say, according to its role as a guarantor of sufficiency, and this approach to art is predominant in our terminal epoch: "for us today, the beautiful is the relaxing, what is restful and thus intended for enjoyment. Art then belongs in the domain of the pastry chef. Essentially it makes no difference whether the enjoyment of art serves to satisfy the refined taste of connoisseurs and aesthetes, or serves for the moral elevation of the mind."[55] But the beautiful is none other than the stability of the originary power disciplined within creation and thus maintained within the enclosure of the Clearing: "What the Greeks meant by 'beauty' is discipline."[56] Art is therefore a rare thing, very rare: art is the violence of the initial act through which the originary power is captured and disciplined in order to grant it the position of the work that will unfold its essance in and as a site for existance. Art is rare because it only occurs at the origin, and as origin: it allows the originary to arise and unfolds it as truth: "Art allows truth to arise [*entspringen*]."[57]

In this sense truth is the product of a creator, that is, of a τεχνίτης. The τεχνίτης is the one who sets τέχνη to work. The word is most often translated either as "art," or else as "technology," two terms that are opposed today: but such an opposition is a late one, linked to the autonomization of technics within Machinery, and determined by the destiny that it is a question of thinking; it lacks the originary essance of τέχνη. To think τέχνη demands rejecting both the devaluation of art in aesthetic consumption and the devaluation of technology in mechanistic production. The τεχνίτης cannot be reduced to the technician, if the technician is content with handling logistics and inventing instruments, but nor can he be reduced to the artist, if art is conceived of as the invention of amenities, refuge in a world of beautiful forms, or flight before the harshness of reality. The τεχνίτης is defined, in contrast, by the effective setting to work of truth, which imposes it through violence. That is why the authentic creator does not seek to produce pieces of work conceived of as "contributions to the furthering of culture and progress," since "only insignificant times—eras when our entire existance declines into something contrived—foster the true, the good, and the beautiful and then have corresponding ministries in their state."[58] He never seeks to be defined as an author, which would be an affectation of sufficiency—"so many *egoists* call themselves authors"[59]—he is only ardor and fury, and the will to destruction: "Therefore the violence-doer knows no kindness and conciliation (in the ordinary sense), no appeasement and mollification by success or prestige and by their confirmation. In all this, the violence-doer as creator sees only a seeming fulfillment, which is to be despised. In willing the unprecedented, the violence-doer casts aside all help. For such a one, disaster is the deepest and broadest yes to the overwhelming."[60]

Τέχνη is art understood as the establishment of truth—and that is why the emancipation of τέχνη within machination is the annihilation of truth. The establishment of truth is the clarification of the site of ἀλήθεια, which is to say ἀληθεύειν as such. Τέχνη is the ground of ἀλήθεια, it is fundamentally clarification, and the illumination of the expanse thus cleared. What brings the light that opens a clearing and simultaneously consumes the old site is fire. Heraclitus had already stated the destinal power of the "thunderbolt" (κεραυνός), and in so doing had recognized the identity between fire and "judgment" (κρίσις):[61] creation is in its essance inaugural pyro-technics, understood as the thinning out [*éclaircissage*] of the Open by setting to work the fiery essance of τέχνη. It is thus with the most extreme rigor that Rimbaud was able to conceive of himself as a "thief of fire": if the creator is always uncanny, if he "becomes among all men the great patient, the great criminal, the one accursed,"[62] it is indeed because there is always something Luciferic about him, because he is the one who brings the light.[63] Heidegger rethinks the myth of Prometheus in precisely this way: "If Beyng inceptually came to word as φύσις and if φύσις and φάος [= *light*] say the same in the manifoldness of the same, that is, the rising clearing within the interlocution of opening and en-glowing, then the inceptual metaphysical experience of the living being who has λόγος entails at the same time the experience of man as a being that 'has' the glow, the fire—the experience of the one and only being that can make 'fire.' In that case 'fire' is not only, as conflagration and brightness, a 'means' of τέχνη, but is also as the clearing—ἀλήθεια—the essantial ground of τέχνη."[64]

A regrounding of truth is therefore possible through the creation of a work by τέχνη. Yet truth is said essantially as discourse [*langage*]. Not that all truth should be in the form of a proposition—which is only ever one derivative and degraded form of this essantial relation between speech and truth—but truth unfolds as language [*langue*], language is the very unfolding of the Clearing. To stand in the site of truth as ἀλήθεια is to stand in a language: "language is the house of Being in which the human being ek-sists by dwelling, in that he belongs to the truth of Being, guarding it."[65] Language is thus a primordial world, which not only leads all beings to appearances through its words, but moreover constitutes, as dialogue, the originary modality of coexistance. In this way language is what makes the world at the same time as it makes the community, and it opens the essantial space of the history of this community. Henceforth, to reground truth is to reground language: "the event of language is the Beginning" (*das Sprachgeschehnis ist der Anfang*),[66] and consequently the question is to know what establishes it, that is, what is the "primal-event of language" (*Urgeschehnis der Sprache*)[67] that primitively unfolds such a ruling. To that, Heidegger responds: it is poetry. But poetry conceived in this way could not be reduced to harmless versification meant to put refined aesthetes at ease: "the poet is not he who writes verses about the respective present. Poetry is no soothing for enthused little girls, no charm for the aesthetes, who believe that art is for savoring and licking. [. . .] Poetry, and with it, proper language happens only where the ruling of Being is brought into the superior untouchability of the original word."[68] Poetry is the merciless combat against worldlessness [*l'immonde*], and it is through the bitterness of this combat that it can open a world. The poet is defined therefore by the violence of this combat, he is "the one who is *violence-doing*, the creative one, who sets out into the un-said, who breaks into the un-thought, who compels what has never happened and makes appear what is unseen."[69]

The creator is thus the one who endures the excessive violence of the originary, who does not flee into beings but has the courage to turn back toward his essantial origin. Because he en-dures this flow from the abyss, the creator submits to the duration of originary time. Every creator spends a long time (*lange Weile*) enduring this duration, and that is why he exposes himself to boredom (*Langeweile*). The authentic creator says: "I am still bored a great deal. I have never known anyone who is bored as much as I am"[70] because boredom is the proper time of creators, it is the long time in which originary time unfolds; in this time "there is no passing or even killing of time there, but a struggle for the duration and fullness of time that is preserved in awaiting. [. . .] This long time, however, 'once' lets the true—the revelation of Beyng—come to pass."[71] But this boredom is only creative because it is availability to the originary. Boredom is in an intimate relation with nostalgia, and is thus deepened in melancholy. Melancholy is the attunement proper to creation: "All creative action resides in a mood of melancholy [*Schwermut*], whether we are clearly aware of the fact or not, whether we speak at length about it or not. [. . .] As a creative and essantial activity of human existance, philosophy stands in the *fundamental attunement of melancholy*."[72]

Through this self-exposure to the originary, the creator is then available and sensitive to its signs: he does not take refuge in the common designation of beings, but exposes himself to the meaning of Beyng. He is in this sense first and foremost "the witness of Beyng" (*der Zeuge des Seyns*).[73] This means that he collects signs from the originary, then in his work offers them to a people: "The poet's saying is the collecting of these signs [*das Auffangen dieser Winke*], in order to pass them on to his people. The collecting [*Auffangen*] of signs is a receiving [*ein Empfangen*]."[74] The quality of the poet is to be receptive in relation to the originary powers, to discipline them and collect them in a work of speech, and thus to hold them captive in the language opened by this work. By offering this work to his people, he thus gives them the basis upon which they will be able to found themselves, and that is what defines the Beginning: "Bestowal and grounding have in themselves the abruptness of what we call a Beginning [*Anfang*]."[75] Poetry, as the inauguration of language, is the inception of truth, it is the Beginning: "The essance of poetry is the foundation of truth [*Stiftung der Wahrheit*]. 'Founding' is understood, here, in a threefold sense: as bestowing, as grounding, and as Beginning."[76]

Creation is therefore never the simple production of a work: it is the offering of this work to a people. Without the acceptance of this offering by the people, the work remains powerless and is *not* creative. This means that the veritative power of the work remains null and void if it is not received by people, accepted and taken up by them, who will situate themselves in relation to it and will dwell in its sphere of power. The history of Being is inseparable from the history of human beings: the dispensation of Being, the breath of emptiness into the density of fullness, the thrust of the nothing within beings does not come about "on its own," it only happens through existances who coexist, undergo a determination of common essance, and thus gather together in community. The Beginning that occurs in the creation of a work is therefore quite simply the institution of a historical community of those who go to work at the same "clearing projection."[77] There is history only "insofar as historical humanity is engaged in constructively inhabiting the lighting and clearing of Being."[78] The creator is thus, in truth, not simply a technician, he is more essantially an architect: he is the ἀρχιτέκτων who establishes the ἀρχή, the foundation upon which his people are going to labor, and the community is then one of co-builders. The historical community is therefore fundamentally a community at labor, but this labor, with respect to the essance that it sets to work—that is, when it unfolds in the time freed from immediate needs, the production of time that defines economy—is the labor of the builder who sets the architect's plan to work. Because the clearing projection is inseparable from this setting to work (ἐνέργεια) through labor (ἔργον), and because labor actualizes the possibilities opened by this clearing projection, there is an essantial connection between labor and truth, and Heidegger expressly stated that "a new fundamental experience of Beyng [. . .] entails, first, a transformation in the essance of truth; and second, a transformation in the essance of labor."[79] Indeed, as existants, people not only stand within the possibilities granted by the initial event of their history, but contribute daily to arranging beings as a whole, whether they do it fully consciously (in a state of wakefulness) or else without knowing it (fully asleep): that is why Heraclitus said, "those who sleep are constructors and collaborators [ἐργάτας καὶ συνεργοὺς] in what happens in the world."[80]

To the question of knowing how to ground another truth, how to inaugurate another Beginning, it is now possible to respond: through the inaugural event of poetry. The poet is the one who institutes language, and language is the very realm in which a humanity stands. Because it is a Beginning, a Poem is destinal, and configures the site of truth in which a historical humanity stands. It is then possible to characterize the poet conceived in the following way. The poet is first the one who knows how to unconceal signs from the originary, and thus makes himself an augur by observing "birds from mystery plays";[81] in doing so, he exceeds the region of the clearing that lucidity circumscribes, and in this way the authentic poet is always visionary; he is, as Rimbaud saw well, a "Seer," that is, someone who "reaches the unknown" and thus sees "unheard of and unnamable things."[82] Thought and poetry may be distinguished in this way: the thinker is lucid [*lucide*], the poet is visionary [*extralucide*]. But if he is a Seer, it is also because he pre-dicts, not because he knows in advance what is going to happen, but because his saying configures the play-space where he makes what he drew from the abyss flow in. He "define[s] the amount of the unknown awakening in his time in the universal soul,"[83] and in so doing configures the site of Possibility and opens the space of the future to come [*l'à-venir*], he establishes the Beginning that contains already, in reserve, the end. That is why it is more rigorous to call him a "prophet," and to recognize the prophetic violence in creation. Poets prophesy, "their word is the foretelling word in the strict sense of προφητεύειν. The poets are, if they stand in their essance, *prophetic*."[84]

CHAPTER 6

Abyss of the Deity

§20. THE NAME OF THE PROPHET

The inaugural saying of the destiny of the West is Parmenides's *Poem*, which gains its status as a historical work in Plato's *Dialogues*: Parmenides is the prophet of the West, and we always stand in "the Same remaining in the Same which rests in itself,"[1] in the tautological sphere of onto-logy consummated today in the planetary totality of technics. The saying of this *Poem* is a disavowal (*Ab-sage*), which refuses to think Nothingness and decides to leave it "unnameable" (ἀνώνυμον).[2] The Greek event is the advent of λόγος; the characteristic of the Greek λόγος, what gives it its historical and destinal character, is its translucence to Being, which unfolds it as the realm of phenomenality (in which onto-logy is phenomeno-logy), but at the same time this λόγος is burdened by a lack and a failure, which is its opacity to the mystery. Parmenides's decision (κρίσις) to leave the other of Being in anonymity therefore has nothing contingent about it, it is the most necessary and rigorous way of making explicit the very essance of the Greek λόγος, which *is* the impossibility of naming the originary Nothingness: "This *not*-naming [Nicht-*Nennen*] of the covering-over that fundamentally unfolds in all revealing is an omission and failure of enunciation [*Ausbleiben und Fehlen des Aussprechen*], one in which the innermost secret of the fundamental essance of Greek thinking perhaps lies concealed."[3] Henceforth, the ultimate task that comes down to thinking today is the reception [*accueil*] and collection [*recueil*] of Nothingness in thought by naming it.

Philosophy is then confronted with its own limits. First, because the radicality of the continually deepened meditation drove it into its ultimate entrenchments. The task to which it is devoted is the regrounding of truth, which can only happen starting from a lucid assumption of the site of the Clearing and from an availability to what wells up from the abyss. Yet this position is gained for the creator through the destruction of a world and the refusal to play its game: none of the criteria, none of the verification procedures usually implemented can therefore be of any use to him. He is situated on this side of truth and falsehood, he is situated on this side of belief and knowledge as well, which are only ever judgments whose verification procedures are opposed according to these canceled criteria. It is thus a matter of establishing a truth even though all the objectivo-logical criteria of clairvoyance, but also the criterion of evidence, have been abandoned. In its essantial relation with truth, thinking itself is dislocated, and thus redefined. The creator is fault-y exi-stance, that is, resolute holding within the site of truth inasmuch as it proceeds from an abyssal fault, and is thus recognized as the safeguard of the mystery: this resolute position, understood as the "*abiding in the essance of truth*" (*das Sichhalten im Wesen der Wahrheit*), is what Heidegger calls "originary faith" (*ursprüngliche Glauben*). Thus, reflected upon in its essance, faith is no longer the "deeming true" (*das Für-wahr-halten*), which is only ever a superficial judgment of belief, but an abiding-in-truth, which is an existential determination and an ontological position. In this sense faith is "essantial knowledge," which allows "the originary and proper believers" to be defined as "those who in a radical way take seriously *truth* itself, not only what is true."[4] The most radical determination of the poet as prophet is therefore deepened by exposing his relation to truth as faith.

But if the philosopher finds himself pushed into his ultimate entrenchments, it is equally because he must "learn to exist in the nameless" (*im Namenlosen zu existieren*).[5] Indeed, from one end of its destiny to the other, philosophy was the thought of Being, and *the forgetfulness of Being* that characterizes it as metaphysics finally appears as the adequate response to the *ab-stention of Being*: it is "Being itself" that "determines the fact that its omission takes place in and through human thought."[6] Being is the property of thinking, the property of thinking is Being, and the Western event is this reciprocal appropriation. Yet our epoch is the one where "the history of Being is at an end,"[7] and so the ultimate—which is to say eschatological—challenge of our time is to *exit from Being*. Our thinking is thereby forced to recognize its incompetence—in the juridical sense of the term, when a court removes itself from the function of judging—and to admit that, taken as it is in a λόγος whose "innermost secret of the fundamental essance" is "an omission and failure of enunciation" that imposes on it "*not*-naming,"[8] it cannot complete this task. It is a question of saying the "wholly other" (*das ganz Andere*),[9] but thinking remains permanently installed within the Western event of the Appropriation. From this point of view, it can only think its other as the negative side of the Appropriation, that is, as an essantial Alteration. Considered from the site of ἀλήθεια, this alterity is λήθη; thought from truth, it is in-truth; from the clearing of the unconcealed, it is the darkness of the Undisclosable; from the domain of evidence it is absurdity; from Being interpreted as Ground [*Fond*] (*Grund*), it is the depths [*tréfonds*] or abyss (*Abgrund*); from the onto-logical sphere, it is Nothingness; considered from the region of presence, it is absence. All these names are locks serving to enclose the sphere of the Same. The word "Being" itself is only an expedient, a word that suggests, but does not say anything: "'Being' remains only the provisional word,"[10] thus writes Heidegger, a word that calls thinking to the demand for remembering, but vanishes when what it prepares is achieved. The task of the "other thinking" requires naming the anonymous otherwise in order to seek out a more original name: "Nevertheless, the name *Being* at the same time loses its naming power in the step back [from metaphysical representing] [. . .] Being no longer allows itself to be defined as—'Being.'"[11] And if at the end of its meditation thinking abandons the name of Being, that is because what it tends toward is other than Being: "It is no longer 'Being' at all," and therefore it is necessary "to relinquish the isolating and separating word 'Being.'"[12] A paradox then arises, according to which the essance of Being is *other* than Being: "the discussion of Being as just that—Being—still speaks an inadequate language, insofar as, in our perpetual references to Being itself, it is addressed with a name that continues to talk past Being as such. In making this remark, we are voicing the assumption that Being—thought as such—can no longer be called 'Being.' Being as such is thus other than itself, so decisively other that it even 'is' not."[13]

This is precisely why philosophy finds itself obliged to delegate its task, or at least to make itself the servant of a more originary word: that of poetry. "There must first be thinkers so that the poet's word may be perceptible":[14] *philosophia* is thus made into *ancilla poesis*, and the task of the thinker is to pave the way for the poet's word. Indeed, it is poetry's proper and essantial mission to reveal the mystery:

> Unveiling the mystery [*die Enthüllung des Geheimnisses*] of what has purely sprung forth is the singular and authentic mandate for poetizing as such in general. [. . .] Poetizing is essantially a scarcely being allowed to unveil the Mystery. This unveiling is not a special mandate for particular poets, in the sense that these poets would select a particular object for themselves. Rather, this mandate of scarcely being allowed to unveil the mystery of that which has purely sprung forth is *the* poetic mandate pure and simple—the only one.[15]

Because its proper mission is *unveiling the mystery*, the poetry in which Heidegger recognizes the possibility of responding to the eschatological situation of our time is in its essance apocalyptic.[16] And because the poet is, even more essantially, a prophet, the ultimate task of thinking is to identify an apocalyptic prophet, that is, a poet who measures up to the moment, "the moment of the sweat lodge, of seas snatched away, of underground conflagrations, of the angry planet, and the resulting exterminations."[17] The challenge is therefore to know the prophet's name: not only to learn the name of the poet for our time of apocalypse, but also, and above all, the name that he gives to the originary Nothingness that, since the Beginning, has remained anonymous.

§21. THE DEATH OF GOD

A prophet who stands in the essance of truth by faith and brings his people a name for the mystery—such is the creator capable of "regrounding a wholly other truth." "Prophet," "salvation," and "faith," at first glance and most of the time, are the prerogative of religion. It would then seem that religion provides, immediately, the long-awaited possibility of warding off the danger. Yet the scale and imminence of the threat, the destructive power of real nihilism, the need and urgency of the crisis prohibit being satisfied with ancient forms of fallback solutions,[18] themselves withered by devastation. The essantial demand of thinking is lucidity, that is, the resolute taking-on of our epoch, and that is why it is necessary to insist on the scale of the global production apparatus and on the naiveté of those who believe themselves to be spared: "What threatens man in his essance is the opinion that this assertion of production would be risked without danger if only other interests in addition to it, perhaps those of a faith, remain valid"[19]—but one could not imagine a more radical profanation than reducing the divine to the keystone of a system of "values" or the basis of a political ideology, that is, by holding onto sufficiency and infallibility. The sovereign and absolute force [*puissance*] today is that of technology, which confiscates and monopolizes all power [*pouvoir*], and, in fact, no counter-force exists today. In a course on Heraclitus, Heidegger thus evoked "the historical bankruptcy of Christianity and its church" and asked: "Is a third world war needed in order to prove this?"[20] Indeed, the least one could say is that the twentieth century showed the superficiality[21] of the conversion of the peoples of Europe to the love commandment, and highlighted that, before the force of a Machinery become precisely autonomous, religion was unable to oppose the surge of nihilism and its power of mobilization and totalization.[22] And to assume that one defines, as Kant still does, the project of Christianity by the establishment of a "*kingdom* of virtue"[23] on earth, it must be observed that we are not taking its path—unless it is under the obscene pharisaical caricature of "the empire of the Good"[24] described by Philippe Muray.

Such disarray, however, is nothing contingent: our epoch is indeed that of "the loss of the gods" (*die Entgötterung*).[25] According to the word of Léon Bloy in the volume of his diaries precisely entitled *On the Threshold of the Apocalypse*: "God withdraws."[26] This "default of God," it should be specified immediately, "does not contradict the fact that a Christian relationship to God continues among individuals and in the churches, and it certainly does not disparage this relationship to God. The default of God means that a God no longer gathers men and things to himself visibly and unmistakably and from this gathering ordains world-history and man's stay within it."[27] In our epoch, this gathering of men and things is no more than the total mobilization of all that is by machination, and the human stay order in the midst of beings is imposed by the available apparatus that defines its functioning: this means that beings as a whole, even the dimensions of earth and sky, human and divine, are under the yoke of an ontic, and mechanical, entity.

In this technological totality, "not only have the gods and God fled, but the radiance of the deity [*der Glanz der Gottheit*] is extinguished in world-history," and "not only does the sacred remain hidden as the track to the deity [*Gottheit*], but even what is whole, the track to the sacred, appears to be extinguished."[28] As the epoch of the absence of God, ours is the epoch of atheism: but this atheism is nothing superficial, it is inherent to its essance, which is the teleological consummation of the destiny of metaphysics. Metaphysics is in fact atheist in its essance, which only ever approaches the question of the divine in the idolatry of a Groundwork, a Cause, an Idea, or a Substance, and moreover makes the eminent being [*Étant*] privileged in this way the yoke that envelops the sphere of onto-logy. The contemporary consummation of the destiny of metaphysics within the autistic and enclosed sphere of the technocratic empire is inseparable from the process of the loss of the divine, and atheism is the truth of this cosmos:[29] its essance, the very mode of its unfolding, the specter of its light. This is why today *atheism is evidence* for everyone, because it is the evidence illuminated by the spectral light of cyberspace, it is the fundamental position that technology assigns to its functionaries: "Thus where everything that presences exhibits itself in the light of a cause-effect coherence," wrote Heidegger in "The Question concerning Technology," "even God can, for representational thinking, lose all that is exalted and holy, the mysteriousness of his distance."[30] Lucidity then requires reducing this evidence to the luminosity that determines it, that is, to the artificial luminescence of machination that does not allow anything of the mystery to show through and dissimulates the glimmers of the sacred, in order to situate this essantial configuration of phenomenological luminosity within the destiny of the West—and likewise, the question of the relation to the enormity of the divine cannot be posed in terms of evidence, nor of subjective certitude, but demands thinking a destiny of truth, which is the history of a community.[31] Here as elsewhere, the problems must not be approached from an *I*, but rather from a *We*, that is, from a historical community: in any case, the statements "I believe" or "I do not believe" do not refer to a theology, but only to an egology. It must also be recognized that atheism, far from being an achievement of free spirits, is their mere determination by the destiny of the West: "'A-theism,' correctly understood as the absence of the gods, has been, since the decline of the Greek world, the oblivion of Being that has overpowered the history of the West as the basic feature of this history itself. 'A-theism,' understood in the sense of essantial history, is by no means, as people like to think, a product of freethinkers gone berserk. 'A-theism' is not the 'standpoint' of 'philosophers' in their proud posturing. Furthermore, 'a-theism' is not the lamentable product of the machinations of 'freemasons.' 'Atheists' of such a kind are themselves already the last dregs of the absence of the gods."[32]

The prophet whose word must be received by thought must endure to the end the absence of the gods as such, and think this event: "a godless time is not nothing," thus said Heidegger, "but an uprising of the Earth that can neither be alleviated, nor even recognized, whether by the mere continued existence of various denominations, or by an organizational change in the governance of the church on the part of the state. The gods of a people cannot be acquired so readily. The flight of the gods must first become an experience."[33] Nietzsche is the historical thinker of the "death of God,"[34] understood as the consummation of the destiny of the West: and because he was simultaneously a philosopher, poet, and prophet, he remains one of the rare ones up to the task of our time. But his thinking of the loss of the divine is in the wake of Hölderlin, whom he presented from his school years as his "favorite poet," acknowledging having been "deeply shaken by the reading of this work."[35] Indeed, Hölderlin is fundamentally the thinker of the *Entgötterung*, understood as the absence and withdrawal of the divine, and his thought, which is situated at the height of speculative idealism all while renouncing from the outset its logic and metaphysical conceptuality, is the essantial testimony of this experience of the flight of the gods.

§22. FRIEDRICH HÖLDERLIN

In 1802, Hölderlin wrote a hymn entitled "Patmos," named after the island in the Icarian Sea where the Book of Apocalypse was composed. In it the poet follows eagles—the symbol of Saint John—"over the abyss" (*über den Abgrund*) to head toward "Asia's gates." Thus "carried" toward this "radiance fresh, / Mysteriously"

(*Geheimnisvoll*) the poet "greatly desired [. . .] To approach the dark grotto [. . .] where the field's / Flat surface cracks," that is, the grotto of the "God-beloved / The Seer" who "saw the face of God exactly." It is in this meditation on the Apocalypse of John that Hölderlin writes: "But where Danger threatens / That which saves from it also grows,"[36] and it is the very meaning of the concept of apocalypse that the most extreme need and the greatest risk are in themselves the bearers of a revelation capable of bringing salvation. Hölderlin's entire poetic enterprise thus consists in trying to collect what is revealed in this way, and to say it, in his poetry, to his people. The apocalyptic climate proper to modern Germany is described in the first lines of "Germania": "On us a heaven today [. . .] casts prophetic shade. / With promises it is fraught, and to me / Seems threatening too," and it is this very hymn that formulates with the most extreme density the necessary task for this age of the world, that of naming the veiled mystery:

Und nenne, was vor Augen dir ist
Nicht länger darf Geheimnis mehr
Das Ungesprochene bleiben
Nachdem es lange verhüllt ist.

And name what you see before you;
No longer now the unspoken
May remain a mystery
Though long it has been veiled.[37]

It is thus Hölderlin whom Heidegger identifies as the essantial prophet of our time: Hölderlin's work is the site of the "*revelation of Beyng*" (*Offenbarung des Seyns*),[38] and it is therein that Heidegger sought the salvation promised by the apocalypse of the West.

Hölderlin is first the thinker of destiny, and of its power against which mortals can do nothing, because "in the face of destiny / Imprudent it is to wish."[39] The cycle of his fluvial poems is the ceaselessly deepened meditation on the relation between the course of a river and its source, between a destiny and the "enigma" of its Beginning: that is, its intimate relation with the originary element from which it originates. This is precisely what is suggested by the course of rivers that, like the Rhine, the Danube, or the Rhône, have their source within the same mountain range, the "sacred womb" of the "holy Alps." The Alpine mountain range constitutes the unique originary domain from which the great rivers emerge: but what gives each its course and decides its direction [*sens*]—whether it will head toward Asia like the Danube, or toward Europe like the

Rhône—is the reception of the water, that is, the configuration of the valley and the arrangement of the rocks in which it springs forth; after having specified that "the source must follow the river's course," "The Blind Singer" thus distinguishes between the "holy chalice, pure golden source" and the "verdant earth, our cradle of peace."[40] If the originary is therefore that from which the source springs, the Beginning is the capture that provides it with its first configuration. It is this configuration that is decisive. Whether the underground source emerges on such or such hillside determines whether the river is destined to the North Sea, the Black Sea, or the Mediterranean. In this way the Beginning is "the master craftsman" (*der Bildner*) who "drafted the paths of the rivers," and a "well-allotted destiny" is circumscribed by "the bounds / Which God at birth assigned / To him for his term and site." The Beginning is what decides destiny: "For as you began, so you will remain,"[41] because the Beginning establishes the Law that orders and regulates everything that happens starting from it. But this "fixed Law" is itself "begotten, as in the past, from holy Chaos" (*aus heiligem Chaos gezeugt*).[42] This "lawless" (*gesezlos*) and "orderless" (*ordnungslos*)[43] chaos is the originary itself, and because it is essantially outside destiny, it is "older than the ages":[44] it is "the best thing of all, the find [*der Fund*] that's been saved up beneath the / Holy rainbow of peace, [that] waits for the young and the old,"[45] and hence "inexhaustible" (*unerschöpfliche*). The originary is thus the invisible and chaotic depth of a mountain range that saves up water in its rocks, even saves up "time's quick torrents" (*die Fluthen der Zeit*)[46] that break within the river of destiny. To think destiny is therefore to think the house arrest on a ground that emerged from the abyss:

Vom Abgrund nemlich haben
Wir angefangen und gegangen
(. . .) *das wille aber heißen*
Das Schicksaal.

From the abyss indeed we have
Begun and gone
(. . .) but that is what is called
Destiny.[47]

To think the river is to think destiny, and the poetic meditation on its source and its course is in this way an entrance to the essance of history: to the springing-forth of the source that is Greece, to the river that is the history of the West, to its delta that Rimbaud will call "the western swamps."[48] Yet the Hölderlinian thought of the source is precisely that of a *tension* between these two divergent movements, which are, on the one hand, the closure of an originary mountain range within its own opacity, and on the other, the effusion of torrents toward the delta; between the abyss that remains a constant reserve and resource of the waters, and the well-drawn limit of the banks. To think Greece is therefore, for Hölderlin, to think the tension and the difference between two antagonistic elements. This antagonism occurs in Greece as the opposition between the Asian element and the European element: Greece *is* the region of the interval, it is the archipelago where the prism unfolds from East to West. Hyperion elaborates this distinction, and opposes "the Egyptian," who has "an urge to do homage, to idolatrize," and has always been cast "to the ground" by the splendor and radiance of the Eastern climate and is thus "devoted" to the Whole, to "the son of the North" for whom "knowledge has corrupted everything," who "learned so thoroughly to distinguish [him-]self from what surrounds [him]" and finds himself "solitary in the beautiful world, an outcast from the garden of Nature, in which [he] grew and flowered, and [is] drying up under the noonday sun": it is the Greek who stands "in the golden mean."[49] This tension between Eastern and Western is the one that exists between chaos and measure, between enormity and moderation, between πάθος and λόγος, between drunkenness and sobriety, between darkness and light, between night and day. The Greek dawn is therefore not the pure element of clarity isolated from the dark from which it comes: the dawn is this glimmer that both reveals the unfathomable depth of darkness and promises the brightness of day, and this is why Hölderlin specifies: "Dearer even than Night reasoning Day is to you. / Nonetheless there are times when clear eyes too love the shadows."[50] It is thus "more bacchantically" that "morning approaches": it never comes down to the sobriety, measure, and cold clarity of the concept but, through the pallor and isolated location of its rays, reveals the embracing vastness of the darkness. The Greek dawn is not reducible to Enlightenment [*Lumières*], it is the interval of night and day: the Greek genius is having known how to dwell in it.

The Greek moment is thus the discovery of the leeway between the "bounds that are timeless" and the dwelling of this spacing. This is why Hölderlin calls it "loving discord":[51] to speak of "love" to evoke "discord," a "dispute," an "opposition" (*Streit*) is precisely to think a difference that does not await its own resorption, but on the contrary enjoys its difference. Hölderlin's meditation thus leads him to recognize in the Greek moment the occurrence of a difference *and its maintenance*. In this sense, Greece is pure harmony, if it is remembered that this word first designated the crossed layout of planks of wood in the construction of a ship, whose opposing tension ensured the solidity and cohesion of the hull: the exact sense in which Heraclitus used it when he thought how "diverging, it accords with itself: a backward-turning harmony [παλίντροπος ἁρμονίη], as of a bow and a lyre."[52] The decisive achievement of Hölderlin's meditation, breaking totally with the work of Johan Winckelmann[53] who still dominated the thought of Goethe, Schiller, and Hegel, is thus to have highlighted that *the characteristic of Greece is not the Western element*, but the balance reached between, on the one hand, Eastern excess [*démesure*] and its obscurities, and, on the other, Western moderation [*mesure*] and the clarity of the concept. The Western element is of course the rational, the clearing within the Dark, the lull within the furies of the Unlimited: but its meaning and its function consist in allowing for dwelling within these immensities, in supporting, enduring their power and not fleeing from them. The function of the poetic word is precisely to accompany human beings in their "wandering below the Unthinkable,"[54] it occurs so that "deep in the dark there shall be something at least that endures."[55] This is precisely what the Greek tragedies did. "Greek art is foreign to us," thus wrote Hölderlin in 1803, "and I hope to present it to the public in a more lively manner than usual by bringing out further the oriental element it has denied."[56] The Greek moment is the one when the aorgic immensity of the Eastern sacred is collected within the organic measure of Western clarity, when each "is entirely what it can be, and one combines with the other, compensates for the shortcomings of the other."[57] The genius of Hellas is condensed in the Homeric poem, which found and crystallized the equilibrium point between these two elements: "Hence the Greeks are less master of the sacred pathos, because to them it was inborn, whereas they excel in their talent for presentation, beginning with Homer, because this exceptional man was sufficiently sensitive to conquer the Western *Junonian sobriety* for his Apollonian empire and thus to veritably appropriate what is foreign."[58]

Yet in this relationship of the Greek moment to the East, the very meaning of Modernity is at stake. For to define the essance of the Greek moment by the right balance between East and West is then to refuse to see in the total realization of the concept the legitimate achievement of Greece's destiny. It is in this sense that Hölderlin's poetry is directly opposed to Hegel's system: Greek measure only had meaning in relation to the sacral splendor that radiated from the East. To those who would like to define Greece by its works, Hyperion thus responds: "Athenian art and religions, and philosophy and form of government, [. . .] are flowers and fruits of the tree, not soil and root. You take the effects for the cause."[59] Greek philosophy itself does not constitute a separate absolute, but the reaction to the wonder constituted by the excess of χάος, and it owes its meaning to the wealth of its origin. Torn from its Eastern soil, rationality is sterile: "Mere intellect produces no philosophy, for philosophy is more than the limited perception of what is. Mere reason produces no philosophy, for philosophy is more than the blind demand for ever greater progress in the combination and differentiation of some particular material."[60] The Greeks certainly provided a model, but by the harmony of their existence, and not by their works. Greece remains a paradigm for us, but for the balance it was able to find between Eastern and Western, between frenzy and measure; Greek greatness is to have established that "the most beautiful harmony [καλλίστην ἁρμονίαν] comes out of what diverges."[61]

The task of the thinker, then consists in determining our situation, how these two contrary elements appear today. This is the heart of Hölderlin's meditation starting from the Homburg period, in particular in the 1799 essay *The Perspective from Which We Have to Look at Antiquity*. It is about knowing the innate drive [*tendance*] proper to the Moderns, and thus determining their strengths and weaknesses: "for this is man's only mistake, that his formative drive goes astray, takes an unworthy, altogether mistaken direction or, at least, misses its proper place or, if it has found it, comes to a halt in the middle of the way with the means that are supposed to lead him to his goal. That this happens considerably less frequently is assured by our knowing from where and with what goal this formative drive emerges."[62] Yet the Greeks only had to "drive" toward the Western because they came from the East, they only had to gain the calm and measure of the concept because they endured and suffered from the enormity of χάος, and it is this "sacred pathos" that constituted their proper drive [*pulsion*]. Their task thus consisted above all in *comprehending themselves*: "the Greek representations change insofar as it is their chief tendency to comprehend themselves, which was their weakness; on the other hand, it is the main tendency in the mode of representation of our time to designate something, to possess a skill, since the lack of destiny, *the dysmoron*, is our deficiency."[63]

Yet our epoch is characterized, not by an overabundance that must be contained, but quite the contrary by scarcity: it is a time of "lean years."[64] The Western is weakened, secluded within the empty interiority of the concept; what the Greeks had to achieve has become the native element of the Hesperians: "the clarity of the presentation that is so natural to us as is for the Greeks the fire from heaven."[65] We are effectively the heirs of the Greeks, and if our native element is the "clarity of the presentation," "presence of mind," the "talent for presentation," and the "Western *Junonian sobriety*,"[66] it is because the Greeks were able to win this kingdom and settle there: as Hegel masterfully shows, Modernity is the empire conquered by this kingdom. But precisely because he defined the Greek essence by the balance between this kingdom of moderation and the wild vastness that surrounded it on all sides, Hölderlin grasped in the autonomy conquered by this kingdom not a fulfillment, but a catastrophe. Indeed, bringing to light Greek perfection as balance allows its debacle to be explained by the rupture of this balance. A draft of a hymn thus says:

> Indeed they wanted to establish
> A kingdom of art. But thereby
> The patriotic among them
> Were neglected and pitifully went
> Greece, the most beautiful, to ruin.[67]

If, therefore, Greece is this moment of equilibrium, its destiny is one of disequilibrium that destines the West to the coldness of the rational. The Greeks themselves were unable to maintain harmony lastingly: the fascination for rational clarity, the singular quest of the Western element led them to a catastrophic rupture with their own nourishing soil. The seventh stanza of "The Rhine" offers the same diagnosis; there Hölderlin asks the question: "Who was the first to coarsen, / Corrupt the bonds of love / And turn them into ropes?" and he answers it by designating those who "[. . .] of the heavenly fire / Defiant rebels mocked, not till then / Despising mortal ways, / Chose foolhardy arrogance."[68]

But this risk is inherent to destiny. Indeed every Beginning, insofar as it springs from the originary, and thus extracts itself from it, is tempted to flee from it, and thus to abstract itself from it. It is in principle that rivers "rush on" and "roar seaward,"[69] and the direction of a river consists in moving it ever farther away from its source to go flow into the sea. Those who are carried away by its flow are thus commonly captivated by the display of the delta; thereby they turn away from the originary: "Many a man / Is shy of going to the source; / For wealth begins in / The sea."[70] The poet can thus reproach the "fettered river": "in yourself wrapped up, / And by the cold bank linger, too patient youth, / And do not heed your origin."[71] This forgetfulness is the threat of an essantial decline: "For sooner the dwelling shall be destroyed, / And all the laws, and the day of men / Become iniquitous, that such as he / Forget his origin,"[72] and this is why "A great Beginning can come / Even to humble things."[73]

This humble thing is Germany. Because it consummates this bad destiny, Germanic modernity is "the shipwreck of the world" (*der Schiffbruch der Welt*).[74] The fundamental drive that defines our epoch is a deadly drive; its acceleration and systematization by the project of imitating the Ancients therefore constitutes a danger: "Hence it is also so dangerous [*so gefährlich*] to deduce the rules of art for oneself exclusively from Greek excellence. I have labored long over this and know by now that, with the exception of what must be the highest for the Greeks and for us—namely, the living relationship and destiny—we must not share anything identical with them."[75] Far from completing Greek perfection and consummating its promises, the actualization by the Moderns of "reason, the cold reason abandoned by the heart"[76] is the setting to work of a new barbarism. The penultimate letter from Hyperion to Bellarmin is thus the occasion of a violent "diatribe" against the Germans: "Barbarians from the remote past, whom industry and science and even religion have made yet more barbarous, profoundly incapable of any divine emotion [. . .] there is nothing sacred that is not desecrated, is not debased to a miserable expedient among this people; and what even among savages is usually preserved in sacred purity, these all-calculating barbarians pursue as one pursues any trade, and cannot do otherwise."[77] The source of this German barbarism, which Rimbaud will call more generally "modern barbarity,"[78] is contempt for the origin; the diagnosis formulated in "The Rhine" already provides *Hyperion* with its conclusion: "everything is so imperfect among them only because they leave nothing pure uncorrupted, nothing sacred untouched by their coarse hands, [. . .] nothing thrives among them because they do not respect the root of all thriving, divine Nature." Hyperion must therefore make the observation: "The incurable corruption [*die Unheilbarkeit*] of my century became so apparent to me from so many things that I tell you and do not tell you."[79]

But it is the poet's task to try to remedy this incurable century. Because he understood that our situation is opposed to that of the Greeks, that it is even exactly the "reverse" (*umgekehrt*),[80] his search for harmony and perfection can in no way consist in imitating Greek works, but must on the contrary take the opposite view: not to reproduce the cold rationality idealized by Winckelmannian classicism, but to revitalize [*ressourcer*] rationality in its wild origin. Greek culture as a whole is strained in a rationalizing, organizing, and formalizing effort because it comes from chaos, the aorgic, and the unformed; yet the native element of Hesperia is precisely form and the organic: "antiquity seems to be entirely opposed to our own original drive, which aims to fashion the unformed, to perfect the original and the natural."[81] Our spiritual effort must therefore be *umgekehrt*, inverted, reversed. Against the whole tendency stemming from the Renaissance and renewed in an "Enlightenment that is clear as mud,"[82] Hölderlin rejects the imitation of the Greeks, but on the contrary thinks the task of the poet as "patriotic reversal" (*vaterländische Umkehr*). It is important to reject from the outset every reductive interpretation in terms of nationalism or chauvinism: for Hölderlin, it is not a matter of suddenly discovering the virtues of what Rimbaud called "patrolling [*patrouillotisme*]"[83] and Nietzsche "patriots,"[84] but of poetizing in accordance with our situation, the "reverse" (*umgekehrt*) of that of the Greeks. The *Umkehr* is a reversal, an inversion, a conversion, even an about-face; indeed, it is about counteracting the "formative drive" of the Moderns, which destines them to ever more rationality in order to revitalize them in the fullness of the Sacred, that is, to make "the entire form of things" "convert to wilderness" (*Wildniß*): "For patriotic reversal is the reversal of all modes and forms of representation. However, an absolute reversal of these, as indeed an absolute reversal altogether without any point of rest is forbidden for man as a knowing being. And in patriotic reversal the entire form of things changes, nature and necessity, which always remain, incline toward another form—be it that they go over into wilderness [*Wildniß*] or into a new form."[85] The destiny of the West is that of the decline of Greece, which is its flight from the origin: the task of modernity is the return, if not *to*, at least *toward* the origin. "The Fettered River" thus says: "[You] do not heed your origin, you / Son of great Ocean, the friend of Titans! / Those messengers of love whom your Father sends, / Do you not know those winds breathing life at you?"[86] The return is patriotic in that it tries to reconnect with the originary element understood as the "Father's land" (*Vater-Land*), and perhaps *vaterländische Umkehr* could be rendered as "repatriation."

The task of the poet is then to go back to the source, in order to access the moment outside time where destiny is decided, where "Destiny for a while [*eine Weile*] / Is levelled out, suspended"[87]—and that is precisely why boredom (*Langeweile*) is its proper time. This moment is pure hesitation, it is the "hesitant moment" or "wavering moment" (*zaudernde Weile*),[88] when nothing is "yet" decided. The poet is thus essantially the *mediator* between the originary immensity and the land of mortals, he stands in the very place of the emergence of truth, which he then collects in his word: "But where more superabundant than purest well-springs / The gold has become and the anger in Heaven earnest, / For once between Day and Night must / A truth be made manifest."[89] In this way the poet is charged with inaugurating a new Beginning, in that he is the one who goes forth, alone and without protection, into this interval to collect signs from the Father:

> Yet, fellow poets, us it behoves to stand
> Bareheaded beneath God's thunder-storms,
> To grasp the Father's ray, no less, with our own two hands
> And, wrapping in song the heavenly gift,
> To offer it to the people.[90]

The poet is then the one who interprets what wells up from the abyss, he is always first an augur, and that is why he inaugurates. The originary is announced by signs. A fragment of Heraclitus says: "The Prince whose oracle is the one in Delphi neither speaks nor hides, but gives signs" (οὔτε λέγει οὔτε κρύπτει ἀλλὰ σημαίνει). The Prince (ὁ ἄναζ) is the only one who rules, and this only one only speaks through the mouth of an oracle: he is the "One" who "does not want and does want to be called only by the name of God [Ζηνὸς ὄνομα]."[91] Therefore, between the self-withdrawal, the abyssal concealment of κρύπτεσθαι, and the illumination by the fire of λόγος is this gap, this fissure out of which emerge signs from the abyss. The poet is the one who bears the burden, and the enormous risk, of going to collect these signs.

Hölderlin is thus the thinker of the dis-aster [*dés-astre*]: of the Beginning as the turning-away of the gaze before the blinding light of the originary star [*astre*], of history as the flight before this star and the consequent march toward twilight, of modern barbarism as the result of this flight and also the desire to rediscover this star. But for "master and novice alike," the "divine fire" of this star is "too bright, dazzling" for man's weak receptivity: "For not always a frail, a delicate vessel can hold them, / Only at times can our kind bear divine fullness."[92] "When the Holy Cloud is hovering round a man, / We are amazed and do not know the meaning,"[93] observes Hölderlin, and he specifies furthermore that "not even wise men can tell what is her purpose."[94] If Hölderlin therefore is the one who accomplished the about-face and headed right toward the star, if he took on the mission of going forth "bare-headed beneath God's thunderstorms" to "grasp the father's ray, no less, with [his] own two hands," this was at the cost of being struck by lightning himself, and he will thus confess in the second letter to Böhlendorff: "The tremendous element, the fire of the sky and the silence of the people [. . .] has continually affected me, and as it is said of the heroes, so I may say that Apollo has struck me."[95] Hölderlin's poetry remains this "wavering moment" when the poet falters [*défaille*] before the excessive violence of the originary. He certainly formulates his task with the most extreme rigor: "And what I saw, the Sacred, my word shall convey,"[96] and that, in effect, is his highest mission, to name this originary that since the Beginning has been renounced and remained anonymous. As a resource that is unscathed and has always been held in reserve, this originary is capable of making that which saves grow: this dimension of the Unscathed (*das Heile*) is the opening of the Sacred (*das Heilige*), and this dimension conceals "the best thing of all, the find that's been saved up beneath the / Holy rainbow of peace, [that] waits for the young and the old."[97] The task of the poet—and this is how he is essantially a prophet—is therefore to give his people a divine name.

But the time of need that Hölderlin lives in is precisely that of the "gods who are fled," when it is no longer possible to invoke the "images of gods [*Götterbilder*] in the ancient land,"[98] that is, the names given by ancient prophets. It is therefore on *this* question—namely, that of the relation between language and the divine, a relation for which there could be no question of being content with approximations or expedients—that Hölderlin's itinerary ultimately focuses. Indeed, God is in *essance concealed behind a veil*: "God has put on a garment. / And his Face is concealed from the knowing" (*Gott an hat ein Gewand / Und Erkentnissen verberget sich sein Angesicht*).[99] It is the question of divine names that haunts Hölderlin's poetry, and this theonymic stammering leads him to evoke God, the god, the divine, the most High, the Father, Heracles, Dionysus and Christ, the Celestials, but also holy Chaos, sacred Earth, and divine Nature. His probity and rigor, and also "shy[ness] of going to the source,"[100] then lead him to see in silence the name most loyal to its absence:

> Much in the meantime I've heard of him, the great Father, and long now
> I have kept silent about him [. . .]
> Him, the most High, should I name then? A god does not love what's
> unseemly,
> Him to embrace and to hold our joy is too small.
> Silence often behooves us: sacred names are lacking.[101]

If in this age of the world the divine name is silence, piety becomes "sacred mourning."[102] Mourning is faith, insofar as faith is an abiding in the essance of truth: mourning is then simultaneously the recognition that the space-time of truth (ἀλήθεια) is granted by an initial death, which is an absenting (of the originary) into the mystery of Nothingness, and the faithful safeguard of this absence within the clearing. Mourning is this essantial modality of existance that consists in standing in what the hymn "Patmos" calls "the loved one's shadow," and thus allows us "to dwell in loving Night and in fixed, / Ingenuous eyes to guard [*bewahren*] / Abysses of wisdom":[103] mourning is the guard of the abyss that opens a truth where the gate of death lets Nothingness arise as love. This is what makes Hölderlin, before Nietzsche, the thinker of the death of God, who tried to take on this time of mourning, but in order to ensure that his place is held until his return. This is how Heidegger defines Hölderlin's historical situation: "It is the time of the gods who have fled *and* of the god who is coming. It is the *time of need* because it stands in a double lack and a double not: in the no-longer of the gods who have fled and in the not-yet of the god who is coming."[104]

§23. THE LAST GOD

"Only a god can still save us"

The task of "grounding a wholly other truth" finds its possibility in a poetics of truth, which itself assumes finding the name of the prophet: Heidegger identifies Hölderlin as the essantial prophet of our time, and Hölderlin himself grants the divine name to the wholly Other that has remained unnamed and is capable of granting salvation. At the terminal moment of the completion of the eschatology of Being, Heidegger thus stands at the heart of Hölderlin's poetry, that is, precisely in the abyssal need of this gap between the gods who have fled and the gods to come: the eschatology of Being is in an essantial relation with the divine. In the face of Machinery's monstrosity and the omnipotence of its machination, in the face of the danger inherent to it of the annihilation of thinking and consequently of man's essance, confronted with the real risk of "the complete annihilation of humanity and the destruction of the earth"[105] and the "more and more hopeless attempts to master technology,"[106] Heidegger concluded his itinerary with a word that he himself wanted as a testament: "Only a god can still save us."[107] In it there is the recognition that it is too late for us, human beings, to still be able to do something, that a threshold has been crossed that only leaves us with the possibility of waiting for the occurrence of an event. But there is also, faithfully to Hölderlin, the expectation of a new coming of the divine: the posthumous treatises, drafted in the solitude of the 1930s and in constant proximity to the thought of the poet, are occupied with the expectation of the "passing by of the last god" (*Vorbeigang des letzten Gottes*).[108] Evoking Nietzsche's atheism in his first course on Hölderlin, Heidegger stressed that "the necessity of renouncing the gods of old, the enduring of this renunciation, is the *safeguarding* of their divinity":[109] Nietzsche's absolute and honest a-theism then appears as a process of dismantling and liquidating onto-theo-logy, of destroying metaphysical idolatry, which opens the possibility of an opening to the truly divine god: "The god-less thinking which must abandon the god of philosophy, god as *causa sui*, is thus perhaps closer to the divine god."[110] The god capable of saving us, specifies Heidegger, "is neither a 'being' nor a 'nonbeing' and is also not to be identified with *Beyng*," and, if it is indeed "the Only One" or "the Singular," it is situated beyond all "-theism": "The last god has his own most unique uniqueness [*seine einzigste Einzigkeit*] and stands outside of the calculative determination expressed in the labels 'mono-theism,' 'pan-theism,' and 'a-theism.'" Like Hölderlin, Heidegger in the *Contributions to Philosophy* often speaks "of gods," in the plural, however he specifies that there is no "polytheism" there, but simply the necessity of holding open the very question of the relation between Being and the divine: "To speak of the 'gods' does of course not mean that a decision has been made here affirming the existence of many gods instead of One; rather, it is meant to indicate the undecidability of the Being of gods [*die Unentschiedenheit des Seins der Götter*], whether One or Many. This undecidability carries within it the question of whether something like Being can be attributed to gods at all without destroying everything divine."[111]

The god's mode of being is in effect its ab-stention: "The god comes to presence only by concealing himself,"[112] and in doing so it refers to neither Being nor Nothingness, but to the passing of the one into the other. The god only comes into presence through its withdrawal into the originary Nothingness, and this is why Heidegger sees in Dionysus the "distinctive" demigod. Commenting on Hölderlin's evocations of the god of wine in "Bread and Wine" and "As on a Holiday . . . ," Heidegger specifies: "in being, he at the same time is not and in not being, he is. Being, however, for the Greeks means 'presence'—παρουσία. In presencing, this demigod is absent, and in absencing he is present. The symbol of the one who is absent in presencing and present in absencing is the mask. The mask is the distinctive symbol of [. . .] the originary relatedness to one another of Being and Nothingness (presence and absence)."[113] But this essantial evanescence of the god, its occurrence under a mask and as mask, makes its naming all the more difficult, and requires the "modesty" that Hölderlin already had. This modesty, which is also shyness, demands being wary of discourse as such, and especially of all rhetoric that, concerning the divine Name, can only turn to the obscene, and, strictly speaking, to profanation: "This nearness of the gods is of a unique sort," thus said Heidegger in a course on Heraclitus. "Hence, we would do well not to speak too much, too loudly, or too often about the gods."[114] The nearness of the gods is evanescence, which is to say, their absence, but this absence is not a pure and simple blank, an empty nullity; it is, on the contrary, the haunting experience of lack: "The default of God and the divine is absence," wrote Heidegger, "but absence is not nothing; rather it is precisely the presence, which must first be appropriated, of the hidden fullness and wealth of what has been and what, thus gathered, is presencing."[115] In "The Poet's Vocation," Hölderlin deploringly observed the reduction of the divine to the use that people make of it, that is, to a (metaphysical) function or a (moral) value, when not to a (political) pretext: "Too long now things divine have been cheaply used / And all the powers of heaven, the kindly, spent / In trifling waste by cold and cunning / Men without thanks." However, he concluded the poem by affirming: "God's being missed in the end will help,"[116] thus suggesting that it is indeed this lack that today constitutes the most authentic relation to the divine. God's *lack*, comments Heidegger, is always *God's* lack, and the lack must be understood in both senses: people are lacking God, but only because the divine remains-lacking, that is, ab-stains and defaults, and the mystery proper to the divine is this withdrawal (this veiling) by which it is announced and manifest. Such a lack is thus essantially divine, its content is the divine, which is manifest in it. Therefore, lack is "not absence of the God, but presence—the fact that the vocation imposed by the God is not suspended. Such vocation is, in its being taken up, always lack and faultiness [*Fehl und Verfehlung*]—not out of weakness, but out of having to bear the overpowering. Yet precisely 'until'—that is, insofar as—the lack is one coming from the God, the fidelity to this calling persists":[117] lack, Heidegger expressly states, is human faultiness before the divine overpowering, but this faultiness, insofar as it assumes the fault that gives it the divine, is fidelity. Lack is not nothing, *lack is fidelity*, and thereby a way of receiving and maintaining what lacks: of safeguarding it.

Absence is the mode under which the divine goes forth toward humanity, and silence is then the word capable of welcoming such an absence and making oneself available for it. Though silence seems to be only a deficient and secondary mode of speech, it is in truth its abyssal ground. The primordial unfolding of λόγος is "a (silent) deliberation,"[118] and this deliberation proceeds from an originary Silence that is the voice of the abyss: "language itself has its origin in silence (*im Schweigen*). It is first in silence that something such as 'Beyng' must have gathered itself, so as then to be spoken out as 'world.' That silence preceding the world is more powerful than all human powers."[119] Therefore, such a silence is not the simple interruption of a worldly speech, it "precedes the world" and unfolds in the domain of originarity from which the world emerges, and in the abyss from which all language is built, because it is first pure listening. "*As silence, Being would also be the origin of language*," said Heidegger in a course from 1941. "The animal does not speak because silence is impossible for it, and an animal cannot be silent because it has no relation to what can be kept silent about, i.e., to keeping silent, i.e., to concealment, i.e., to Being."[120] Because silence is essantial, because it is the pure and sovereign calm that rules in the abyss, silence about God is itself essantial, and originary: "Someone who has experienced theology in his own roots, both the theology of the Christian faith and that of philosophy, would today rather remain silent about God when he is speaking in the realm of thinking."[121]

If Heidegger therefore tends to privilege silence, it is because this silence is the voice of the abyss. This abyss is that of the Sacred. In the poetic theiology that Heidegger develops in his posthumous manuscripts and in his commentaries on Hölderlin, Beyng (*Seyn*) as abyss of the Sacred is in effect this *whence* the gods emerge: "the godhood of gods arises out of the essance of Beyng" (*aus der Wesung des Seyns entspringt*),[122] and Beyng as abyss of the Sacred "prevails (saves) and unfolds its essance *before* gods and men" (vor *den Göttern und den Menschen waltet (heilt) und west*).[123] The abyssal opening of the Sacred is therefore the precondition for the coming of the god, and it is only from the originary space-time opened by this abyss that god and man can come up against one another: "In this Openness alone do gods and men find one another [. . .] This opening in advance is the Sacred."[124] The Sacred thus remains "that which is 'above' [the god]"; gods and men find one another in the same relation of dependence with respect to the originary dimension of the Sacred, and in the same inability to endure "an immediate relation to the Sacred." The gods are necessary to men, who need "someone higher, who is nearer to the Sacred and yet still remains beneath it, a god, to throw the kindling lightning-flash into the poet's soul."[125] But, conversely, the gods need men, who, as essantially fault-y, have a more immediate relation to the abyss; here Heidegger relies on a passage from Hölderlin's "Mnemosyne":

> *Nicht vermögen*
> *Die Himmlischen alles*
> *Nemlich es reichen*
> *Die Sterblichen eh'an den Abgrund.*
>
> Not everything
> Is in the power of the gods.
> Mortals would sooner
> Reach toward the abyss.[126]

Because men and gods are in this relation of reciprocal dependence, "there is love between them."[127] But both "belong not only to each other, but to the Sacred." The abyss of Beyng thus remains for Heidegger the ultimate dimension where god and men can come to appropriate one another and thus each achieve its proper essance. If, therefore, "the passing by of the last god" is capable of "saving" us, it is as an event in Beyng. To speak of passing by is in effect to oppose the expectation of a full and definitive presence, in order to consider humanity's being brushed by an advance of the divine, a fleeting but sufficient brush to make them tremble *in their Being*: "passing by is precisely the kind of presence belonging to the gods: the fleeting character of a scarcely graspable beckoning that, in the flash of its passing over, can indicate all bliss and all terror."[128] In this sense, the last god is waited for to provoke a trembling in the history of Beyng, an earthquake capable of reconfiguring the constellation of men and gods, of the earth and the world, that is, to originarily unfold the Crossing of these four cardinal points of the topology of Beyng.

The god arises from the abyss of the Sacred, which constitutes the originary rule where the essantial space-time of the history of Beyng unfolds; as mediator between the originary Nothingness and the clearing of truth, it occurs, just like Dionysus, under the figure of a mask. But this mask masks the abyss: more radical than the question of naming the god is then the question of identifying the abyss, an authentically abyssal and properly vertiginous question. Yet Heidegger tends to think the abyss of the Sacred as Earth [*Terre*],[129] by thus privileging, in Hölderlin's theonymic hesitation, what had led him to plead:

"Once only, daughter of sacred Earth, / Pronounce your Mother's name."[130] "The Sacred is the essance of nature" (*das Heilige ist das Wesen der Natur*), writes Heidegger to comment on "As on a holiday . . . ," and "'abyss' means the all-enclosing which is borne by 'Mother Earth,'"[131] and it is the Earth that constitutes "the essantially Undisclosable."[132] In the thought of the "patriotic reversal," that is, of turning toward the Father's Land (*Vaterland*), Heidegger thus emphasizes the Land [*La Terre*], where Hölderlin, hesitating, emphasized the Father equally.[133] The mystery that constitutes the in-essance of truth, which is the originary in-truth, is then understood as the "mystery of the Earth,"[134] and the resolute openness toward the mystery within truth is identified with a patriotic reversal understood as "rootedness in a landscape" (*landschaftliche Verwurzelung*), "being enjoined back into the Earth of his homeland" (*Rückfügung in die heimatliche Erde*), and "turning back and turning in toward the homeland" (*Rückkehr und Einkehr in die Heimat*).[135] The German word *Heimat* designates the homeland, understood as familiar environment (*heimisch*), original home, the place where one grew up, where one feels at home; it is the proper place where each of us derives our authenticity and where we ultimately have our essance: Heidegger thus makes the mystery (*Ge-Heim-nis*) the gathering in itself and the concealment in the Depths of the Earth of what grants to each of us such a native home (*Heimat*). It is this native home, rooted in the depths of the Earth, that then constitutes the origin: "The homeland is the origin and the original ground of the spirit" (*die Heimat ist der Ursprung und der Ursprungsgrund des Geistes*).[136] The abyss of the Earth is therefore what conceals the fatherland [*patrie*]: "the fatherland is sealed in a mystery, and indeed essantially and forever. [. . .] *The 'fatherland' is Beyng itself.*" If, therefore, the poet is a prophet, it is because he says originary Nature, he is the prophet of Nature, who gives voice to its silence: "the saying of the poets as the self-saying of Nature is of the same essence as the latter." Poetry can grant salvation through its promise of rootedness: "the poetic work as a projection (taking root and saving) of Beyng grounds the existance of human beings upon the Earth in the face of the gods."[137]

If he kept the last god in a strict anonymity, Heidegger nevertheless always took care to specify that it was "wholly other than past ones and especially other than the Christian one":[138] he thus expressly opposed the mystery's rootedness[139] to its incarnation. His entire thinking is in fact inseparable from an "argument" with Christianity, an argument that in truth is a distancing, an attempt to break with it, and thus a systematic critique. His path thus led him to cross philosophy from one end to the other in order to find what preceded its arrival: a primordial poetry equal to a new Hesiodic theogony based on a neo-Hellenic mythology. His thought comes down to waiting for a chthonic divinity and a neopaganism devoted to the cult of a new figure of Demeter (Γῆ Μήτηρ in Greek, "Mother Earth"). Thus, following the slope of a Germanic pantheism characteristic of romanticism and German idealism, Heidegger undoubtedly indulged in what Emmanuel Levinas called "the fascination of nature [. . .] the eternal seductiveness of paganism," where nature is "impersonal fecundity, faceless generous mother, matrix of particular beings, inexhaustible matter for things."[140] The Earth constitutes the immemorial base of history, no world is possible without its primordial holding, and its contemporary devastation in the unfolding of worldlessness is a direct threat to the very survival of humanity; it is furthermore the native dimension from which people can welcome the divine and turn toward it, and Judaism shows that sacred history is inseparable from the relation to a promised land: nevertheless, it remains problematic to make it into the abyss from which spirit, meaning, Being, truth, and salvation arise.

Against this tendency inherent to a certain German romanticism,[141] however, another poet had given a warning, and in doing so did the work of a prophet in the most common sense of one who sees what is going to happen, and thus predicts it. In *On the History of Religion and Philosophy in Germany*, which he published in 1835 for the French public, Heinrich Heine showed the gifts of a visionary seer by announcing even more precisely than Hölderlin in *Hyperion* what "German barbarism" could be. His lucidity regarding a German philosophy that he defines as "naturalism" in effect allows him an authentic prophecy of what he himself described as a "catastrophe":

> so the *Naturphilosoph* will enter into terrible association with the original powers of nature. He will be able to conjure up the demonic forces of Old Germanic pantheism, and that lust for battle which we find among the Old Germans will awaken in him, which does not battle to destroy, or to conquer, but solely for the sake of the battle itself. Christianity—and this is its greatest merit—has to some extent tamed that brutal Germanic lust for battle, but could not destroy it; and if ever that restraining talisman, the Cross, breaks, the savagery of the old fighters will rattle forth again, the absurd frenzy of the berserker, of which the Nordic poets sing and tell so much. That talisman is brittle, and the day will come when it breaks apart miserably. The old stone gods will then emerge from their forgotten ruins and rub the dust of millennia from their eyes. Thor, with the giant hammer, will spring up at last, and destroy Gothic domes. [. . .] Do not take lightly the visionary, who expects in the realm of appearance the same revolution which has happened in the province of the spirit. Thought goes before deed as lightning before thunder. German thunder is certainly German; it is not very agile and begins

> to rumble very slowly. But it will come and when you hear crashing, as it has never crashed before in all of world history, you will know, German thunder has finally reached its goal. With this sound, eagles will fall dead from the sky, and lions in the most distant desert in Africa will put their tails between their legs and crawl into their royal caves. A play will be enacted in Germany which will make the French Revolution look like a harmless idyll.[142]

By opposing paganism to Christianity, by seeing in the disappearance of the Cross the risk of an unleashing of barbarism, Heine truly made himself an apocalyptic prophet—and surely, no one could "take lightly the visionary" today. But here Heine also shows himself to be an essantial poet through the formulation that he gives of the original essance of this event—namely, the death of God: "A unique horror, a mysterious piety does not allow us to write any further today. Our heart is full of a terrible compassion—it is old Jehovah himself who is readying himself for death. [. . .] Do you hear the bell ringing? Kneel down—Sacraments are being brought to a dying God."[143]

Meister Eckhart

The question of naming the abyss appears as a crucial question, precisely because it leads language to its last resort: to the silence from which it comes, and which is its most secret content. It is then a question of finding the name of the poet capable of saying silence, and thus of identifying the "master of silence."[144] Heraclitus, who thought λόγος in an inaugural way, not only opposed it to Nature's (φύσις) self-hiding (κρύπτεσθαι), but also to the meaning (σημαίνειν) of the "Prince whose oracle is the one in Delphi."[145] Hölderlin devoted himself to listening to these signs coming from the abyss, and he tried to give them a voice in his poetry, which constitutes the historical provenance of all of Nietzsche's thought. But, Heidegger specifies, another thinker stands in this same essantial domain: "Hölderlin too, however, was subject to the power of the Heraclitean thought. A later thinker, Nietzsche, would also come under its power. Indirectly, the commencement of German philosophy with Meister Eckhart fundamentally stood under this power."[146] Meister Eckhart is in fact a crucial thinker: both heir to the mystical thought coming from Pseudo-Dionysius the Areopagite and source of all German speculative philosophy, he is also a poet in that he configures the German language in a decisive way by creating the greatest part of his philosophical vocabulary through his preaching.[147]

The central term of Meister Eckhart's preaching is "deity," *gotheit* in Middle High German, translation of the latin *deitas* with which Eriugena had translated the Dionysian θεότης already used by Saint Paul (Col 2:9). "I say 'one deity' because here nothing is yet flowing out, nor is it touched at all or thought":[148] the term designates the intact because inaccessible depth of God, the divine essance as it unfolds the sovereignty of his rule in a domain that is out of reach for every creature, for all that is not God himself. According to a recurrent metaphor in the *Sermons*, the deity is God "in his dressing room," where he is nude, in his intimacy: God "in that pure, naked substance where he is taking himself bare [. . .] in the dressing room where he is uncovered and naked in himself."[149] The deity is God's intact, untouched, and intangible essance, it is thus what exceeds every human intention: "All that understanding can grasp, all that desire can desire, that is not God. Where understanding and desire end, there is darkness, and there God shines."[150] It is "darkness" not, however, because it is pure and simple absence of light, but because it is "the light that is God which no human faculty can attain. [. . .] If God is to be seen, it has to happen in a light that is God himself." The deity's light is darkness for man's senses, which it saturates with its infinite intensity so that, like Saint Paul on the road to Damascus (Acts 9:8–9), he is blinded by it: therefore, it must be said that "the light that is God shines in the darkness,"[151] in "the hidden darkness of the eternal light of the eternal deity."[152] Because it is beyond natural luminosity and human vision, the deity is unknowable, and unknowable in the precise sense that it is out of reach of all unconcealment: the deity is God "without effects, that is, in his hidden stillness" (*in sîner verborgenen stilheit*),[153] "in his hiddenness" (*in sîne verborgenheit*);[154] it designates "the hidden darkness of the eternal deity" (*diu verborgen vinsternisse der êwigen gotheit*),[155] "the divine purity of the stillness and mystery of God" (*die verborgenheit gotes*).[156] It is that "whose nature is to be hidden";[157] it is thus God *in his very withdrawal*: in it, "He has withdrawn into the first source, to the innermost, to the ground [. . .] where He has been for ever in Himself."[158] The deity, insofar as it is essantially undisclosable, withdrawn into itself, is thus the ultimate darkness *from which* light emerges: "The last end of essance is the darkness or the unknownness of the hidden deity, in which this light shines."[159]

Withdrawn into its concealment, the deity is inaccessible to the understanding and to knowledge: "It is the hidden darkness of the eternal deity, and it is unknown, and it was never known, and it will never be known."[160] The intellect "can never encompass [*begrîfen*] him in the sea of his unfathomableness";[161] to approach the deity is thereby to expressly renounce every concept (*Begriff*), that is, every attempt to grasp it based on its ideas, concepts, categories, or images, which are only ever human things: "Everything which you make the object of your intention which is not God in himself—that can never be so good that it will not be an impediment to the highest truth."[162] Thus, approaching the divine essance does not consist in predicating through concepts or in pronouncing judgments, but, quite the contrary, in disposing of them. The concept in fact is not only insignificant and powerless to approach the deity, it is even an "obstacle," which is to say that it constitutes a power of dissimulation, which "obscures" the deity and "comes between you and the whole of God."[163] Thus, every divine attribute must be renounced, however eminent it may be: "It is its nature to be without nature. To think of goodness or wisdom or power dissembles the essance and dims it in thought. The mere thought obscures essance."[164] Every concept, every attempt to com-prehend, which thus claims to circumscribe the divine essance, in truth encloses it, limits it, de-fines it, and therefore completely misses it: "It all encloses God, whatever we attribute to Him: *anything* we ascribe to Him except pure essance, encloses Him."[165] Far from being able to reveal him, knowledge and comprehension actually constitute veiling powers: "All that the intellect can have of God must be called ignorance rather than knowledge. However much God may reveal Himself in this life, yet it is still as nothing to what He really *is*. Though truth is there, in the ground, it is yet veiled and concealed from the intellect."[166]

For the soul to try to join the deity is therefore to expressly abandon all knowledge, and it is to dive into what Eckhart calls forgetting, an essantial forgetting that precedes all knowing: it is a matter of "com[ing] to a forgetting and an unknowing [*in ein vergezzen und in ein nihtwizzen*]. There must be a stillness and a silence for this Word to make itself heard. We cannot serve this Word better than in stillness and in silence."[167] And indeed, inaccessible to both concept and image, the deity is thereby equally inaccessible to speech. Thus, Eckhart explains that certain prophets who, through revelation, confronted the mystery of God's concealment, that is, "a truth beyond speculation" (*ein unbedahtiu wârheit*),[168] preferred to keep silent: "God was so vast and hidden [*verborgen*] that they could form no conceptual image of it, for whatever they could conceptualise was so unlike what they had seen in God [. . .] They kept silent because they saw the hidden truth and discovered the mystery [*die heimlicheit*] in God, but could find no words for it."[169] The pure immensity of the deity is pure of all differentiation, and if Eckhart sometimes evokes the sea or the ocean of its essance, it must be specified that its surface is rippled with no wave, it thus remains untouched by the articulations and differentiations of speech: it is "the simple ground, [. . .] the quiet desert, into which distinction never gazed [. . .] for this ground is a simple silence, in itself immovable."[170] The deity is "simple silence," and this is why "whoever speaks of God by [using the term] *nothing* speaks of him properly":[171] "silence" is the word proper to divine simplicity, all speech would disrupt its purity. Evoking Cratylus, the disciple of Heraclitus who had given up speaking, Eckhart specifies: "If he could not speak of things, it beseems us all the more to preserve total silence about

Him Who is the source of all things. [. . .] we cannot truly speak of God. What we say of Him, we can but stammer."[172]

Because neither knowledge nor discourse is capable of approaching the deity, no name is commensurate with it: "Thus the unfathomable God is without names, for all the names that the soul gives him it takes from its own knowledge."[173] And indeed, "words cannot give a name to any nature that is above the soul,"[174] which is why it is necessary to recognize "God's ineffability, for God is unnamable and transcends speech in the purity of His ground, where God can have no speech or utterance, being ineffable and wordless."[175] The sermons repeat it tirelessly: "God is nameless [*Got namelôs ist*]. [. . .] God is above all names [*Got ist über alle namen*]."[176] Eckhart can then disqualify the divine names given by the Scriptures themselves: "In scripture God is called by many names. I say that whoever perceives something in God and attaches thereby some name to him, that is not God. God is above names and above nature. [. . .] We cannot find a single name we might give to God." The deity is the pure silence from which every word emerges, and in this sense it can be said that "God is a Word, a Word unspoken";[177] henceforth, every expression, whatever it may be, is inadequate to this silent Word, "no word can declare God."[178] This is the reason why Meister Eckhart rejects the God-spirit identification: "Now we say God is a spirit. That is not so. If God were really a spirit, He would be spoken."[179] Relying upon a tireless reflection on the treatise of the *Divine Names* by Pseudo-Dionysius the Areopagite, Eckhart deepens the theonymic mystery. Thus, in his commentary on Genesis he comes to explain the verse from Judges 13:18: "Why do you ask my name? It is too wonderful." He comments: "In truth, it is wonderful first because it is a name, and yet this name is 'above every name': God 'gave him the name that is above every name' (Phil 2:9). Next, this *name is wonderful* because it is an unnameable name, an unspeakable name and an ineffable name" (*nomen innominabile, nomen indicibile et nomen ineffabile*).[180] Faithful to his desire to "unseal" all the senses of Scripture, Eckhart then redoubles his commentary, by listening to the verse otherwise; here, by having *admirabile* no longer refer to the Name but rather to the question itself: "'Why do you ask my name? That is what is wonderful!': namely, that you ask my name even though I am unnameable. And of course, it is wonderful to ask the name of a thing that cannot be named! In the second place, it is wonderful to ask the name of the one whose nature is to be hidden, according to Isaiah 45:15: 'You are truly a hidden God.'"[181] Therefore it must be recognized that God has no name: "God, who has no name—He has no name—is ineffable."[182] He is strictly speaking the Anonymous: the deity withdraws into its own concealment, but at the same time refuses all naming.

Yet "God"—as well as Θεός in Greek, *Deus* in Latin, and *Gott* in German—

does seem to be a name and a concept. Throughout its entire history and since its Platonic founding, metaphysics has made an "Idea" the cornerstone of ontology, which Aristotle then thought under the concept of "god."[183] Meister Eckhart, however, preaches neither the Idea of the Good nor the god of Aristotle, but the "God of Israel, a God who sees, a God of those who see" (*deus Israel, deus videns, deus videntium*),[184] who is only unveiled to "'a true-seer,' a 'true Israel,' that is, a God-seeing man, for nothing in the deity is hidden from him":[185] his entire preaching presupposes that "the revealing of this is truth" (*diu offenbârunge daz ist wârheit*).[186] Yet Revelation is precisely inseparable from anonymity, and YHWH is the name of the Anonymous. The question of the name is even asked by Moses on Mount Sinai: "If I come to the Israelites and say to them, 'The God of your ancestors has sent me to you,' and they ask me, 'What is his name?' what shall I say to them?" (Ex 3:13). He is then ordered to use these four consonants of the Hebrew alphabet: "Thus you shall say to the Israelites, 'YHWH, the God of your ancestors, the God of Abraham, the God of Isaac, and the God of Jacob, has sent me to you': This is my name forever, and this my title for all generations" (Ex 3:15).[187] The divine name is therefore not a name: it is an abbreviation, an acronym, a hieroglyph, the four unpronounceable letters of a cryptogram that the Jewish tradition—out of respect for Exodus 20:7, "You shall not make wrongful use of the name of YHWH your God, for YHWH will not acquit anyone who misuses his name"[188]—refrains from pronouncing and replaces with *Adonai* ("Lord") or *ha-Shem* ("the Name"). The Tetragrammaton is derived from the revelation of Exodus 3:14: when, in 1302, Eckhart interprets its Latin translation (*Ego sum qui sum*) in the disputation questions at the University of Paris, he understands it precisely as a refusal to respond by someone who wants to remain anonymous: "When someone who wants to conceal his identity and name is asked at night 'Who are you?' he replies, 'I am who I am.' So the Lord, wishing to show that he possesses purity of essance, said 'I am who I am.' He did not say simply 'I am,' but added 'who I am.'"[189]

The name is thus in itself anonymous: a name that refuses all naming, that says nothing other than this withdrawal into anonymity, that says a refusal. It signals toward what hides and withdraws behind a veil. Thus, the Greek translation of Psalm 18 says in the Septuagint: "He made darkness his covering [ἀποκρυφὴν] around him, his canopy thick clouds dark with water" (11), and a verse from the Book of Job (22:14) says similarly: "Thick clouds enwrap [ἀποκρυφὴ] him." YHWH is the one who hides by evading the light, the one who *escapes* (in the most common sense of the Greek ἀποκρυπτειν)[190] the immediacy of vision; he is the "God who hides himself" (οὐκ ᾔδειμεν, Greek translation of Isaiah 45:15): the one of whom there is no εἶδος, of whom we have *no idea*. And if this determination of the Anonymous is crucial, it is because it is the very mode of his Revelation: in the last verses of Exodus (40:34), YHWH manifests himself *by veiling himself*: "Then the cloud covered [ἐκάλυψεν] the tent of meeting, and the glory of the Lord filled the tabernacle." In this way, the name of God signals toward what withdraws outside of the clearing of the visible, it therefore defines nothing, identifies nothing, and ultimately it names nothing: it signals toward a wholly-other that it does not claim to circumscribe in a concept, toward a "place which is nameless."[191] It falls within convention: Henry Suso, a disciple of Eckhart, affirms this in his *Little Book of Truth*: "This nothing is called by common agreement [*nach verhengter wise*] 'God' and is in itself a something essantial to an incomparable degree."[192] The name of God designates a "*je-ne-sais-quoi*" (*neiswaz*):

> Something [*neiswaz*] exists that is universally the first and the simplest, and before which nothing is. Now Dionysius gazed upon this abyssal essance in its nakedness and he states, as do other teachers, that the aforementioned simplest essance is not at all grasped by any name whatever. The science of logic states that a name is supposed to express the nature and the rational concept of the thing named. Now it is obvious that the nature of the aforementioned simple Being is limitless and immeasurable and cannot be grasped by the intellectual powers of any creature.[193]

Situated within this tradition, the name of God is like a porch that extends beyond language, it is a gap, a void within language: in this way, it reveals language's finitude and powerlessness. The word "God" is this word that, on the one hand, signals toward that which is beyond λόγος, and, on the other, reveals the limits of λόγος itself: it does not name [*nomme*], it de-nominates [*dé-nomme*].[194]

By thinking the infinite excess of the deity over the concept at this level of radicality, Meister Eckhart signaled toward an essance transcending Being itself. Indeed, his commentary on "*Ego sum qui sum*" rejects the identification of God and Being ("I am the one who is"), and concludes: "nothing in [God] has the nature of Being."[195] The deity "is" not, its essance prevails beyond concepts and names, beyond distinctions of speech and knowledge, and therefore beyond Being and difference: it designates "essantial beingness [*weselîche istikeit*] in its simple oneness, void of all difference,"[196] "the pure absoluteness of free Being, which has no location [*sunder dâ*], which neither receives nor gives: it is bare 'beingness' which is deprived of all Being and all beingness [. . .] above all Being."[197] Eckhart thus thinks the *finitude of Being* and locates the essantial beyond its limits. Being is the "parvis" (*vorbürge*) of the deity: "When we grasp God in Being, we grasp him in his parvis, for Being is the parvis in which he dwells."[198] The parvis is the outdoor space in front of a cathedral's façade: it can certainly be used as a stage for the performance of "mysteries," a theatrical genre that in the Middle Ages showed the Nativity, the Resurrection, or the life of the saints, however, it remains only a narrow profane place incommensurable with the vast and sanctified interiority of the nave. To say that Being is the "parvis" of the deity is to recognize that it can effectively be a performance space [*milieu de représentation*] for the visible: but this is to affirm that it remains incommensurable with the unfolding of the pure essance on which it is based. Being is finite, in this respect it constitutes the obstacle that veils the infinity of essance. The radicality of the determination of the divine essance leads Eckhart to transgress ontotheology; he addresses this infinite as the One, or "oneness": "oneness [*einsîn*] in eternity."[199] He especially rejects the attributes of metaphysical theology: "The authorities say that God is a being, and a rational one, and that he knows all things. I say that God is neither Being nor rational, and that he does not know this or that."[200] This is why the least improper de-nomination for the deity is "Nothingness" (*niht*), "the divine Nothingness" (*daz götlich niht*),[201] "Nothingness of Nothingness" (*nihtes niht*), "Nothingness, for which there is no name" (*ungenanten nitheit*): "If I say: 'God is a being,' it is not true; he is a being transcending Being and a transcending Nothingness."[202] The term Nothingness does not refer to empty nullity but to a radically other, and originary, modality of essantial unfolding: "God is Nothingness: not in the sense of having no Being. He is neither *this* nor *that* that one can speak of: He is Being above all Being. He is Beingless Being [*Er ist ein wesen weselôs*]."[203] Nothingness is thus originary in that it *precedes* Being, and constitutes the place where God works Being itself: "God works above Being in vastness, where he can roam. He works in Nothingness. Before Being was, God worked. He worked Being when there was no Being."[204]

Beyond λόγος and beyond Being, the deity is thus irreducible to onto-logy—that is, to the Greek guiding hypothesis for the destiny of the West, according to which Being and λόγος are the Same. This destinal decision was only formulated after a long incubation period, by Leibniz, as the Principle of Reason, and it was only thought as such and all the way through by Heidegger in the eponymous course of 1956–57, *Der Satz vom Grund*. In this course, Heidegger confronts the formula of the Principle of Reason with a radically other formula, that of a couplet by Angelus Silesius: "The rose does have no why; it blossoms without reason, / Forgetful of itself, oblivious to our vision." The "without why" is precisely what unfolds its essance above the Principle of Reason; in Angelus Silesius's thought, it qualifies "the deity" (*Gottheit*), which is "a Nothingness and more than Nothingness" (*ein Nichts und Übernichts*):[205] in this respect, Angelus Silesius is a faithful disciple of Eckhart. Indeed, the Meister recognizes that the Principle of Reason is limited, it only concerns the temporal domain, where one thing can always be based on another, which then constitutes its ground and its cause: "All things that are in time have a 'Why.'"[206] But "God acts without why and has no why."[207] The deity is not reason, it is neither cause nor groundwork. All of Meister Eckhart's thinking is to free himself from the metaphysical idol of a "God" produced by the mind: "for if you love God as he is God, as he is Spirit, as he is Person and as he is image—all this must go!"[208] Moreover, whoever loves God as just, as powerful, or as wise, in truth does not love God: he loves justice, power, or wisdom, and "if God were not just—as I have said before—he would care nothing for God," conversely "if the devil were just, he would love him in so far as he was just."[209] To love God for this or that is always to love something other than God; it is to transfer the divine essance into this or that—justice, power, or wisdom—and it is ultimately to sink into idolatry: "when I pray for nothing, then I pray rightly, and that prayer is proper and powerful. But if anyone prays for anything else, he is praying to an idol [*abgot*], and one might say this was sheer heresy."[210] The first exigency therefore consists in freeing oneself from the metaphysical idol of Cause or Groundwork, and that is Meister Eckhart's prayer: "I pray to God that he may make me free of 'God,' for my real Being is above God if we take 'God' to be the beginning of created things."[211]

The deity unfolds its essance above Being and discourse, it exceeds the Principle of Reason and does not constitute a groundwork (*Grund*), and in this sense it must be thought as an abyss (*Ab-grund*): it is "the abyss of the deity" (*abgrund der gotheit*),[212] "the eternal abyss of the divine essence,"[213] "the unfathomable God" (*der gruntlôse got*) that prevails as "the unfathomable ground of the deity" (*der gruntlôsen gotheit*),[214] and with this term it is a matter of approaching "the abyss of the divine essance" (*die abgründicheit götlîches wesens*)[215] in which God knows himself through an "abyssal and thorough knowledge of Himself by Himself" (*ein abgründic durchkennen sîn selbes mit im selber*).[216] Thus, Eckhart inverts the meaning of transcendence, which is not a zenithal transcendence, upward, but an abyssal transcendence, downward; more precisely, the enormity of the chasm precipitates within itself the dimensions of high and low, which can only have meaning in time and space, and thus the *Counsels on Discernment* specify: "The deeper and lower the abyss is, the higher and more immeasurable the exaltation and the heights, and the deeper the fount, the higher it springs; height and depth are the same."[217]

What, then, constitutes the perfection of the soul is being able to "transcend all temporality, all Being and getting into the ground that is groundless" (*der grunt, der gruntlôs ist*).[218] All of Meister Eckhart's preaching consists in urging his listeners to cultivate in their souls this something that "frees from Being,"[219] and thus to undertake this movement of reduction that recedes from beings to nothingness: "in that One we should eternally sink down, out of 'Something' into 'Nothingness'" (*in diesem Einen sollen wir ewig versinken vom Etwas zum Nichts*).[220] It is really a matter of "sinking down" [*s'abîmer*] into this place where I am now only one with the One, and of "sinking" into the abyss. Such a leap into the abyss remains frightening for every mortal, and the Meister himself confided: "Often I feel afraid, when I come to speak of God, at how utterly detached the soul must be to attain to union with Him."[221] There is in fact a risk; in its search for the deity, the soul "plunges into its utter nothingness so distant from its created somethingness in its utter nothingness that it can in no way through its own power come back again to its created somethingness. [. . .] The soul dared to become nothing and cannot on its own return to itself—so far did it go out of itself."[222] But only the acquiescence to this risk can reveal the abyss of the deity—and the Apostle himself justified his testimony by confessing: "Three times I was shipwrecked; for a night and a day I was adrift over the abyss" (2 Cor 11:25).[223] Yet it is not a matter of sinking into an abyss that would be exterior, but into this abyss that the soul itself is in its essance and that constitutes the very place of ipseity. Indeed, only the collapse of the abyss within the density of beings is capable of opening not only the space-time of Being, but also the difference constitutive of existance; only the gaping opened by the chasm of the One gives oneness within the undifferentiated. Ipseity proceeds entirely from this abyss, which is why Eckhart can say that "*Ego*, the word 'I', is proper to none but God in His oneness."[224] The prerequisite for this access to the abyss, then says Eckhart, consists in "totally denying my awareness of self" (*mîn selbes verstandnisses*),[225] that is, in renouncing egoism and the sufficiency of the ego, in order to cultivate the failures [*défaillances*] that reduce it to its essantial fault [*faille*], in agreement with Saint Paul who said: "we also boast in our sufferings" (Rom 5:3). It is therefore no longer a question of enduring these phenomena of faultiness, but of seeking them for themselves, and it is in this sense that Meister Eckhart interprets the evangelical virtues of poverty or humility, as taking on his own fallibility [*faillibilité*] and diving into his own fault: thus "the pinnacle of his abyssal deity responds to the depths of humility."[226] It is then "detachment" that for Eckhart gathers and deepens all these virtues, in that it "reposes in a naked nothingness."[227]

The abyss of the deity is originary in an absolute sense in that it is the origin of "God" himself. Eckhart places the deity "beyond Being and difference," he also places it beyond the Persons of the Trinity as well, and therefore *beyond God* himself: all of his preaching aims to "come to the knowledge of the unknown super-divine God" (*ein bekantnisse des unbekanten übergoteten gotes*).[228] The soul that attempts this access "is not content with the Father or the

Son or the Holy Spirit, or with the three Persons so far as each of them persists in his properties," it does not want the "divine essence" but wants to reach "the source of this essence," which is to say, where "distinction never gazed, not the Father, nor the Son, nor the Holy Spirit. In the innermost part."[229] The deity is this originary that must now be thought as "a non-God, a nonspirit, a nonperson."[230] In the mystery of its concealment, it is what it is. There is now only "God"—as Person—through what makes possible "the effusion" (*ûzfluss*) of Persons outside the deity: that is, creatures. It is in and of itself that the deity is what it is; it is through humanity that it is "God." Not without precaution ("if you do not understand [this truth], do not burden yourself with it"), Eckhart clearly affirms this dependence of "God" with respect to creatures: "before there were any creatures, God was not 'God,' but he was what he was. But when creatures came to be and received their created Being, then God was not 'God' in himself, but he was 'God' in the creatures." And he concluded his sermon in this way: "That God is 'God,' of that I am a cause; if I did not exist, God too would not be 'God'" (*daz got "got" ist, des bin ich ein sache; enwære ich niht, sô enwære got niht "got"*).[231]

However, Eckhart defines man by his soul—in a crucial sense that includes the body since "my body is more in my soul than my soul is in my body."[232] Yet the soul is pure receptivity, pure affectivity, and that is why it is essentially a wife, and not a virgin but a lover: "For if a man were to be a virgin forever, no fruit would come from him. If he is to become fruitful, he must of necessity be a wife. 'Wife' is the noblest word one can apply to the soul, much nobler than 'virgin.'"[233] The soul is thus defined by its "receptivity" (*enpfenclicheit*), "the being of the soul is receptive [*enpfenclich*] to the influence of the divine light";[234] the characteristic of the soul is to "receive and suffer the divine light,"[235] and this suffering is precisely the essantial faultiness that makes the soul sink into the abyss, since "the soul is abyssal in suffering" (*ist diu sêle abgründic an dem lîdenne*).[236] In this there is man's absolute dependence on the deity, to which he owes everything, and which he can only passively endure: how could he be the "cause" of God?

But the deity unfolds its essance as this prodigious and measureless givenness or donation that it continuously makes to the soul, it "gives without expecting any return [. . .] Therefore God's richness is shown in this, that He gives all His gifts for nothing."[237] Moreover, it *is* the gift, "for God does not give, he has never given any gift so that we might have it and then rest upon it; but all the gifts he ever gave in heaven and on earth he gave so that he might give us the one gift that is himself. With all these other gifts he wants to prepare us for the gift that he himself is" (*der gâbe, diu er selber ist*).[238] As he is free, disinterested, and absolute givenness, as he is pure *gift of self-sacrifice* [don de soi], God is love, and that indeed is the very content of Christian Revelation preached in the *Sermons*, and Eckhart even explains the deity's essantial withdrawal by the will to be desired: "He withdraws [*entziuhet*] Himself for no other purpose but to spur [the soul] on and increase her desire."[239] Yet if God is love, if he only effects his essance by giving, then he is dependent on the creature. Depending on whether or not it receives this gift, God does or does not effect his essance. Indeed, the soul can remain closed to divine gifts, and then "the gifts all spoil and turn to nothing."[240] But above all, if God is this pure gift, to turn away from it is to deny what is most divine in him; to reject his gifts is to refuse him that for which he sprang forth out of the unfathomable abyss of the deity. In this way, the creature is the measure of God: "See, thus it is with divine gifts: they must be measured according to him who is to receive them, not according to him who gives them."[241] The creature then has power over God, and Eckhart does not hesitate to admit it: "a God-loving soul conquers [*überwältigt*] God."[242]

Yet this power is that of depriving God of the joy of giving, which is to say of his being and his life: "to rob Him of this joy would be to rob Him at a stroke of His life, His being and his deity."[243] To think God as love is not to deny him infinite power, but it is to put this power at the mercy of consent, that is, of a "Yes!" of the beloved: "'God is love'. Now, my children, I beg you to mark my words. God loves my soul so much that His life and being depend on his loving me, whether He would or no. To stop God loving my soul would be to deprive Him of His deity."[244] "His being depends on his loving me";[245] the finite soul therefore has the power to deprive God of his being and his life, that is, to make him die. The inherent power that the soul has over God is therefore the power to kill him, and this is what Eckhart concludes: "It is God's nature to give, and his essance depends on his giving to us if we are below. If we are not and if we are receiving nothing, we do him violence and kill him [*enpfâhen wir niht, sô tuon wir im gewalt und tœten in*]."[246] He repeats it by commenting on a passage from the Gospel of John: "Know that God loves the soul so powerfully that it staggers the mind. If one were to deprive God of this so that he did not love the soul, one would deprive him of his life and being, or one would kill God [*er tôte got*] if we may say such a thing."[247]

Revelation itself is such a gift: the deity is veiled within itself, it is concealment, darkness, silence, withdrawal, and only reveals itself insofar as it "flows" or "pours" (*ûzgiezen*) out of itself. The One as Nothingness, thus specifies Eckhart, "is originary [*er ursprunclich ist*] and therefore flows out into all things,"[248] and in this way the deity is "the primal source" (*erste ursprunc*),[249] "the divine spring,"[250] the "root from which all things have sprung forth."[251] The deity is untouched and intangible, therefore intact, and unscathed: it is the inexhaustible reserve of every gift. The abyss of the deity is the reserve from which emerges and springs forth (*entspringen*, *urspringen*, *ûzquellen*) every source, and this in accordance with the meaning of the word "abyss" in the Old Testament, where it designates an inexhaustible reserve of fresh water hidden deep in the earth and feeding the springs [*sources*], for example in Psalm 78: "As from the Abyss He made streams come out of the rock, and caused waters to flow down like rivers" (15–16).[252] Revelation is then the source that springs to light from this dark abyss: and following the word of Saint Paul, according to which "in him the whole fullness of deity dwells [τὸ πλήρωμα τῆς θεότητος] bodily" (Col 2:9), Eckhart recognizes in Jesus of Nazareth the very source of the "divine stream" (*götliche vluz*).[253] Indeed, the inaccessible and undisclosable depth of the deity could not be revealed in knowledge, but only in non-knowledge; neither in speech, but only in silence; neither in a concept, but only in suffering; neither in dogma (insofar as God "erased the record," Saint Paul asks [Col 2:14 and 20], "Why do you submit to dogmas?");[254] nor even in a book, if not the "book of Life" which no one "was able to open [. . .] or look into"[255] and which will only be unsealed at the end (Apoc. 5:3):[256] it is only revealed in the "mediating Person"[257] of Christ, who makes manifest the unapparent and in that is the mystery: he is, says the Meister, "an image of His concealed deity."[258]

It must then be observed that the figure of Christ in Christian thought corresponds exactly to that of the "poet," which Heidegger elaborated from Hölderlin, and in which he saw the condition of possibility for an "other Beginning." The work "allows truth to arise [*entspringen*]," and this is why the poet—which is to say, even more essantially, the prophet—is the founder of truth; because he stands in the middle between men and gods, the prophet is even a "demigod," and insofar as he listens to and passively endures all that wells up from the origin, he is defined by the suffering of his passion: "His hearing stands firm before the frightfulness of the fettered origin. Such hearing that stands firm is suffering [*Leiden*]. Suffering, however, is the Being of the demigod."[259] Jesus is such a prophet, a suffering servant who endured the passion right to the end, who thus draws from the abyss of concealment to make a gift of it for mortals, with this decisive, distinctive trait that his work is nothing exterior to himself—and especially not a "message" or "wisdom" or "values"—but his life and body, offered in a chalice gathering (Col 2:9) and pouring (Jn 1:16) the originary fullness of essance: "the temple of his body" (Jn 2:21) then receives what springs forth from it, and in doing so establishes another truth by making his body this "temple work that first structures and simultaneously gathers around itself the unity of those paths and relations in which birth and death, disaster and blessing, victory and disgrace, endurance and decline acquire for the human being the shape of its destiny."[260] Christ is thus "the first outburst" (*der êrste ûzbruch*), but as he receives everything from the abyss of the deity and therefore cannot serve as a groundwork, he presents himself as Son, and the Son in turn can name the deity with the name Father: "The first outburst and the first effusion God runs out into is His fusion into His Son, who flows back into the Father."[261] In this way, the Son precedes the Father—like every son, who baptizes his father by calling him "Papa," and that is in fact the Aramaic term (*abba*: Mk 14:36) used by Jesus to name God. What makes Christ a prophet (Lk 24:19) is precisely the name "Father" as the naming of the deity ("I made Your Name known to them": Jn 17:26), and at the same moment he reveals the abyss of the originary as the true fatherland of humanity. Using Hölderlin to contemplate "the enigma" of the origin, Heidegger defined "the full concept of that which has purely sprung forth" by specifying: "It comprises two things in one: (1) the origin as such (that is, that from which there springs forth that which springs forth), and (2) that which has sprung forth itself, the way it *is* as that which has sprung forth."[262] This is how Meister Eckhart understands the enigma of consubstantiality: the Father and the Son "are one in God and the only difference is that between outpouring and outpoured."[263]

The ultimate end of essance, said Meister Eckhart, is "the darkness or the unknownness of the hidden deity, in which this light shines":[264] Christ is then this "light of the world" (φῶς τοῦ κόσμου: Jn 8:12) originating in the originary darkness, he is the source of "the Spirit of truth" (τὸ πνεῦμα τῆς ἀληθεία: Jn 14:17) emerging from in-truth, the clearing unfolding from the mystery of the undisclosable. This truth is no longer established in the denial of the mystery, but quite the opposite in its proclamation: "That the Son is said to be born of the Father," thus said Eckhart, "is due to the fact that the Father, as a father, is revealing to him his secrets."[265] The very opposite of the "*not*-naming of the covering-over" that constitutes "the fundamental essence of Greek thinking,"[266] it names this concealment of the Father's name. If, therefore, the abyss of the deity is the inexhaustible resource that is "the sea of his unfathomableness,"[267] Christ is the source through which this underground sea springs forth and pours "the river of the water of Life, bright as crystal" (Apoc. 22:1), that is, the Holy Spirit "spilling over with an overabundant fullness of sweetness and richness, pouring into all receptive hearts."[268] That the Spirit is such a river is recognized by the Gospel of John (7:38–39): "As the Scripture has said, 'Out of the believer's heart shall flow rivers of living water.' Now he said this about the Spirit, which believers in him were to receive." The deity is the originary given the name of the Father, the Son is the source, and the Holy Spirit is the river that flows from it: "The origin of the Holy Spirit is the Son [*Ursprunc des heiligen geistes ist der sun*]. If it were not for the Son there would be no Holy Spirit. The Holy Spirit cannot have his outflowing or his blossoming forth anywhere but from the Son."[269] This river, specifies Eckhart, is "love, the Holy Spirit

[that] springs and flows from the Son,"[270] and love is then the essance of this truth, which flows from the Father through the Son: "The Father and the Son 'exhale' [*geistent*] the Holy Spirit when the Holy Spirit is exhaled [*gegeistet*]; this is essential and spiritual [*wesenlich und geistlich*]."[271]

The relation to such an origin then consists in "staying there," in "abiding" (Jn 15:9) in the flow of this Spirit: it is an "endurance" [*tenir bon*] (ὑπομονή: Lk 21:19; Rom 5:3; Apoc. 13:10), which seeks to maintain itself in this abode arranged as close as possible to the origin and oriented toward the origin, and thus to stand there by turning around toward the origin rather than turning away from it, and to safeguard what flows from this abyss. This standing within the abode opened by the outpouring of the Spirit is in its essance fidelity to a unique event that took place "once for all" (ἅπαζ: Heb 9:26–28); "enduring" there consists in keeping holy, safe, and sound [*garder sain(t) et sauf*] what revealed itself there. The abode thus opened *is* a safeguard, and insofar as this safeguard is fidelity, it is faith: but this faith is what Heidegger called an "originary faith" understood as an "*abiding in the essance of truth*" [se-tenir-dans-l'essance de la vérité] and irreducible to all "deeming true" [*tenir-pour-vrai*][272]—and that is how in 1920 he defined Christian faith in his reading of 1 Thessalonians, as a "faithful *endurance* grounded in Christian factical life. [. . .] *Faith*! πιστεύειν not mere deeming (as true) of a fact!"[273] To stand and persevere there is to commemorate the death of God on the Cross, and thus to live in a sacred mourning, that is, in "the remembrance of mourning [that] remains near to what has been taken from it and seems to be distant."[274] This remembrance that continually comes back to mind is anamnesis (ἀνάμνησις: Lk 22:19), which is a continued parousia, and through this remembrance truth is established as safeguard: this truth, then, is not attested to by demonstrations, arguments, deductions, or experiments, but by testimony (Jn 21:24), the verification proper to the safeguard of the absent.

By gathering in this safeguard, human beings can then establish a new—radically new—community. "This originary community," said Heidegger, "does not first arise through the taking up of reciprocal relations—only society arises in this way. Rather, community *is* through *each individual's* being bound in advance to something that binds and determines every individual in exceeding them. Something must be manifest that is neither the individual taken alone nor community as such."[275] There is only community as long as a common point is manifest that gathers the individuals, that is, through the phenomenology immanent to the dialogue in and through which this common point is manifest: "The unity of a conversation consists in the fact that in the essantial word there is always manifest that One and the Same on which we agree, on the basis of which we are united and so are authentically ourselves."[276] Far from being formal, the question of λόγος, that is, of the originary essance of language and its logic, founds human communities and determines the modalities of their being-in-common, and that is why every community is founded upon a primordial poetry that constitutes its common heritage [*patrimoine*] and its common references. But language is "dangerous," because "by its very essence it bears decline within it,"[277] in that it bears within it the risk of falling into beings, and therefore of fetishism: the risk is that the community will no longer gather except through its common aim of "the most common of all" (τὸ κοινότατον), that is, an Idea (ιδέα) that "constitutes the 'Universal'" in relation to which each member of the community will only be a "particular":[278] a fetishism characteristic of the Greek institution of metaphysics, which subjects the dialogue constitutive of human communities to the speculative dialectic of this Universal's self-determination.[279] The incarnation of the λόγος then disqualifies the abstract universality of this Idea in favor of the fleshly singularity of one person, who thus becomes all in one the principle of the community and the mediator between all its members: "For where two or three are gathered in my name, I am there among them" (Mt 18:20). The community is thus united by "love of the brothers and sisters" (1 Thes 4:9), a community of "friends" (Jn 15:15), who "have all things in common" (Acts 2:44),[280] and whose logic of exchange is reciprocal love (Jn 15:17). The Holy Spirit, which is no longer noetic (νοῦς) but pneumatic (πνεῦμα) spirit, not theory and logic but breath and respiration, is in this way another destiny, and its coming is another Beginning: thus "everything old has passed away; everything has become new" (2 Cor 5:17),[281] and the apocalypse is this event whereby "the one who is seated on the throne" proclaims: "See, I am making all things new" (Apoc. 21:5).[282]

The question of naming the abyss of originary Nothingness therefore receives an answer in the thought of Meister Eckhart, whose cardinal importance Heidegger recognized: this abyss is that of the deity, from which occurs the naming of the Father by the Son who opens the abode of the Holy Spirit. Only a new configuration is in a position to escape the destiny of nihilism, and Heidegger defined the way of salvation out of the danger as the establishment of a "wholly other truth," understood as the arrangement of a region of the unconcealed *for* the depth of concealment, that is, as the safeguard of the mystery, and makes the "passing by" of the last god the essantial trembling capable of making possible the other beginning of another history, specifying that "passing by is precisely the kind of presence belonging to the gods: the fleeting character of a scarcely graspable beckoning that, in the flash of its passing over, can indicate all bliss and all terror."[283] Jesus's preaching was such a passing by, in which God was only present for "a little while" (Jn 7:33) and announced: "you do not always have me" (Jn 12:8). It must then be observed that the passing by was—literally[284]—a trembling and an earthquake (σεισμὸς: Mt 27:54 and Apoc. 16:18), and another beginning of another history, by opening the space of the safeguard of the mystery and the time of commemoration proper to sacred mourning.

In the epoch of onto-logical totalization, the essantial question is that of the hole that opens this stifling totality to the vastness that it dissimulates: it is the search for a way (ὁδός) out toward a radical exteriority (ἐζ), it is the quest for ex-odus (ἔζοδος). Since Parmenides, all metaphysical thought has closed the "way" (ὁδός)[285] of Nothingness: since Saint Paul, all of Christian thought sees in Christ such a "way" (ὁδός: Jn 14:6), a "gate" (Jn 10:9) between the originary abyss and the world that has emerged from it: between the deity and humanity, since "humanity and the deity are One personal being in the person of Christ";[286] between eternity and time, since "because nature works in time and space, the Son and the Father are different";[287] between the deity that is not "touched at all"[288] and the λόγος of life that we have "touched with our hands" (1 Jn 1:1); between "things that are not" (τά μὴ ὄντα) and "things that are" (τά ὄντα) (1 Cor 1:28); and finally between the "Being [. . .] that God works in all creatures"[289] and "the simple ground," the "quiet desert" that is "the source of this Being."[290] In this way, Christ *incarnates exodus*, he is the "mediating Person,"[291] the mediation between Being and originary Nothingness, and mediation *as person*. In Greek as in Latin (πρόσωπον, *persona*), the word "person" first designates the mask worn by tragic actors. The mask is a symbol, the symbol of the ambivalence between Being and Nothingness, speech and silence, truth and mystery, and that is why Heidegger saw in Dionysus, the masked god, the "distinctive" demigod: "in being, he at the same time is not and in not being, he is. Being, however, for the Greeks means 'presence'—παρουσία. In presencing, this demigod is absent, and in absencing he is present. The symbol of the one who is absent in presencing and present in absencing is the mask. The mask is the distinctive symbol of [. . .] the originary relatedness to one another of Being and Nothingness (presence and absence)."[292] It then becomes possible to think Christ in this way, whose very life is parousia (παρουσία), the entry into presence of absence, and far from being accidental, this encounter of Dionysus and Christ is found at the heart of the completion of the thought of Western destiny. Hölderlin, all of whose poetry is the search for a mediator, for a "reconciler" between the divine and the human, actually saw in Christ and Dionysus two "brothers," who "stand at all times, one next to the other, as on the edge of an abyss [*als an einem Abgrund*]";[293] identified the one who "reconciles Day with our Night-time" both with the "Son of the Highest" and with the god crowned with a "wreath wound out of ivy";[294] and finally made Christ the one in whom "the mystery of the vine"[295] is consummated. Nietzsche himself, thinker of the death of God who only ever lived awaiting his resurrection, saw the limit of Greek thought for conceiving such a mediation and considered the Son as a bridge above the abyss: "The *tension* between God conceived of as ever purer and farther and man conceived of as ever more sinful—one of humanity's greatest shows of force. God's love for the sinner is miraculous. Why didn't the Greeks have such a tension between divine beauty and human ugliness? Or between divine knowledge and human ignorance? The bridges that span these two abysses would be new creations which remain to be invented (Angel? Revelation? Son of God?)."[296] His thought then crystallizes in waiting for a god, Dionysus, constantly thought in his intimate relation to Christ, and he came to define the man of the future as "the Roman Caesar with Christ's soul."[297] Commenting on this passage, Heidegger saw in this recapitulation the most secret content of the eschatology of Beyng:

> We must not pass over these words in too great a hurry—especially since they bring to mind other words, spoken even more deeply and more secretly, in one of Hölderlin's late hymns: there Christ, who is "of still another nature," is called the brother of Heracles and Dionysus—so that there is announced here a still unspoken gathering of the whole of Western destiny, the gathering from which alone the Occident can go forth to meet the coming decisions—to become, perhaps and in a wholly other mode, a land of dawn, an Orient.[298]

The Adieu

Heidegger's entire path gathers in the thought of an "other Beginning," which only the passing by of a "last god" would be able to bring about, by establishing, beyond the Greek experience itself, a "wholly other truth," defined by the safeguard of the mystery. From the perspective opened on Christianity by the position proper to our epoch—that is, from the end of metaphysics, which recognizes the *finitude* of its truth and its architectonic foundation upon the Principle of Reason—it becomes apparent that the Christic title granted to Jesus (that is, the fundamental and destinal hypothesis: Jesus = Christ, which Saint Paul formulated in a decisive way in his epistles) is an inaugural event in the same way as the onto-logical Appropriation (that is, the fundamental and destinal hypothesis: εἶναι = λόγος, which Parmenides formulated in a decisive way in his *Poem*): to say that Jesus is Christ is to say that he is a Beginning, and quite simply to recognize the naming of the originary as Father and the essence of truth as mourning, commemoration, and safeguard, that is, as historical fidelity and as memorial; it is to confront the Principle of Reason with a "Prince of life" (Acts 3:15).[299] It is then possible to object to Heidegger that the "other Beginning," precisely as he conceived it, has already taken place: and in fact an "other Beginning" can only occur outside of the temporality constitutive of the history of the first Beginning. The other history does not take over from the first on the same timeline, but unfolds otherwise, in and as another temporality, albeit in the catacombs of the first, in a mysterious, occult, and clandestine way. This other history, that of the safeguard of the sacred and the naming of the Holy, is sacred history, and since then these two histories, said Saint Augustine, "are entangled in the present age."[300]

The exigency of thinking nevertheless remains lucidity, and so it is important to specify the relationship between these two histories today. Yet the crucial event of the twentieth century—the cross of our time[301]—is their apocalyptic conflict in the event of Auschwitz, the peak of a process of exterminating sacred history by a totalitarian machinery of extermination obeying only its own logic, that is, the eradication of every trace of alterity through the closure of the totality in on itself: and it would be to endorse Nazi racism to deny that the Jews were assassinated as Jews.[302] And the fact is that the "God of Israel" did not "awake to punish all the Nations" (Ps 59:5), even though his faithful were "accounted as sheep for the slaughter" (Ps 44:22). As such, this event is the destruction of every theodicy, that is, the end of the justification of evil in history by its integration into a divine plan, which thus maintained divine providence in the face of evidence of immediate suffering. But the Shoah is the Unjustifiable. "The end of theodicy," it must be said with Emmanuel Levinas, is "perhaps the most revolutionary fact of our twentieth-century consciousness." Indeed, this century piled sufferings upon sufferings in an uninterrupted succession of destructions, massacres, tortures, subjugations, and senseless humiliations, which appear, not as residues of barbarism called to be overcome by the progress of "culture" as Renan still believed, but as the very effect of the historiological process, which here reveals its essance and its internal logic: nihilism. Such a suffering could not without obscenity be integrated into a divine plan of any kind, and even less into the sacred history of Israel. "The disproportion between suffering and every theodicy was shown at Auschwitz with a glaring, obvious clarity," continued Levinas, specifying that "this drama of Sacred History has had among its principal actors a people that has forever been associated with that history, whose collective soul and destiny would be wrongly understood as limited to any sort of nationalism, and whose historic deeds, in certain circumstances, still belong to the Revelation (be it as apocalypse)."[303]

The twentieth century therefore demands this crucial *aggiornamento* of renouncing the idea of a God who is lord of history and abandoning the thesis of a divine providence; it demands as well the duty to think what is revealed in the apocalypse of Auschwitz. In a lecture held in Germany in 1984 under the title "The Concept of God after Auschwitz," Hans Jonas observed that "no saving miracle occurred. Through the years that 'Auschwitz' raged God remained silent";[304] he took notice of this disqualification of "theodicy,"[305] and tried to rethink the relationship between God and world history. He then develops a myth of "God's being in the world," which is the opposite of a pantheistic immanentism since it is about affirming that the space-time of the human world can only be granted by a *withdrawal* and an *abstention* as the only way to *give rise* to a history: "Only with creation from nothing do we have the oneness of the divine principle combined with that self-limitation that then permits (gives 'room' to) the existence and autonomy of a world. Creation was that act of absolute sovereignty with which it consented, for the sake of self-determined finitude, to be absolute no more—an act, therefore, of divine self-restriction" (*ein Akt der göttlichen Selbstentäußerung*).[306] It is thus the abyssal absenting of the One that clears the way for the space-time of the universe: "In the beginning, for unknowable reasons, the ground of Being, or the Divine, chose to give itself over to the chance and risk and endless variety of becoming. And wholly so: entering into the adventure of space and time, the deity [*die Gottheit*] held back nothing of itself."[307] In this thought of creation—deeply dependent upon Heidegger—the very advent of Being can only occur through an originary renunciation: "in order that the world might be, and be for itself, God renounced his Being, divesting himself of his deity [. . .] God committed his cause in effacing himself for the world."[308] Such a renunciation includes the renunciation of omnipotence, and Hans Jonas emphasizes the contradiction of the concept of absolute power, since such a power would have nothing external to it upon which to focus its power: "absolute power then, in its solitude, has no object on which to act,"[309] it is completely unable to exercise its power and is identified with impotence. The idea that creation is inseparable from the renunciation of power, which otherwise would crush and smother its own creature under the weight of its infinite sovereignty, involves "the idea of a God who for a time—the time of the ongoing world process—has divested himself of any power to interfere with the physical course of things."[310] The creative act is thus a letting-go, an aban-donment that abandons things to their course so that they can take place; it can be conceived as an act of delegation, since during this time of universal history—which is finite, even if it lasts the billions of years that contemporary astrophysicists grant to the universe—God "has left something for other agents to do," and since he has thus taken a risk, he is "an endangered God, a God who runs a risk."[311] The radical divestment and consent to impotence, this risk and this danger, thus make him, specifies Jonas, a "*suffering God*,"[312] whose suffering is coextensive with the time of the world.

This conception of creation necessarily involves the long process of evolution, since creation is nothing other than the pure opening of a field of possibilities, and since it is thus from the outset "safe in the slow hands of cosmic chance." The slow emergence of life then leads to perception, sensation, suffering, and finally to the "advent of man" when it "passes the threshold" of consciousness and freedom: freedom, the very thing given by the sovereignly free act of divine self-restriction. The deity then passes "into man's precarious trust, to be completed, saved, or spoiled by what he will do to himself and the world"[313]—and for man it is indeed a question of *safeguarding* the deity, and perhaps of completing it, but also, and this is the entire risk taken, of corrupting it. Thus, in this process "the deity comes to experience itself" (*kommt die Gottheit zur Erfahrung ihrer selbst*); this slow process is one of "a hesitant emergence of transcendence from the opaqueness of immanence,"[314] and in this sense Jonas affirms that "with the appearance of man, transcendence awakened to itself and henceforth accompanies his doings with the bated breath of suspense, hoping and beckoning,"[315] so that it must be concluded that "having given himself whole to the becoming world, God has no more to give: it is man's now to give to him."[316]

Hans Jonas subtitles his text "A Jewish Voice," and indeed, he addresses the Shoah from the point of view of the history of Israel, where Auschwitz appeared as "the most monstrous inversion of election into curse," and asks: "What God could let it happen?"[317] The point of view that he proposes, that of a God who only fully discovers who he is through the history of the world, a history whose every new dimension "means another modality for God's trying out his hidden essance [*sein verborgenes Wesen zur erproben*] and discovering himself [*sich selbst zu entdecken*] through the surprises of the world-adventure,"[318] can in fact be read as a powerful meditation on the Hebraic formula of Revelation (Ex 3:14), which, translated literally, does not say: "I am the one who is," or "I am who I am," but: "I am who I will be" or "I will be who I will be,"[319] in the future: which assumes that the question will only be able to receive a full answer at the end—at the time of the apocalypse, therefore.

But the thought of God's divestment and of his renunciation of power is of course the very heart of the Incarnation such as it was thought as kenosis, as an act of self-emptying. Indeed, Saint Paul says that Christ "emptied himself" (ἑαυτὸν ἐκένωσεν: Phil 2:7) by renouncing divine power: Christian Revelation is nothing other than this self-restriction, when God "humbled himself" (ἐταπείνωσεν: Phil 2:8), when he also "became poor" (ἐπτώχευσεν: 2 Cor 8:9), and expressly renounced "authority" over "all the kingdoms of the world" (Lk 4:5–8), to make radical and pathetic impotence the very mode of his revelation. Thought and deepened by the Church Fathers, kenosis is then conceived precisely as this extreme divestment of divinity, this renunciation of absoluteness, glory, and omnipotence in order to have a body of flesh: it is this self-renunciation which is then quite simply the gift of self-sacrifice and Revelation.

God's consent to the most extreme weakness—which occurs from the newborn body to the tortured body—is the very heart of Christianity; by evoking "the Lamb that was slaughtered from the foundation of the world" (Apoc. 13:8),[320] the Apocalypse of John reveals that this sacrifice is the very act of creation. It is thus creation itself that is the fruit of kenosis, and it is this idea that Hans Jonas develops: the universe as history, and history as kenosis, self-divestment by the divinity, and this absolute self-renunciation as the very essance of the deity.[321] To think kenosis all the way through is then not only to think Being as nothing, which Heidegger did, and not only to think Being as emptiness (τὸ κενόν), as the Pythagoreans already did,[322] but to think it as *God's* emptiness: an emptiness in which there is not God, but quite simply an emptiness hollowed out by God's own self-emptying, and granted by his kenosis. Far from the "metaphysics of Exodus,"[323] which identifies God with Being (more exactly with the highest being), totally smuggles Greek ontotheology into Hebraic Revelation, and thus *veils* the revealed by the concept, it is a matter of thinking Being as God's absence, the event of Being as God's ab-stention, and of sensing God's presence as hyperessantial Nothingness—which therefore arrives fully only in death, and at the end of the world.

Hans Jonas sees in the cosmic chance of spinning matter and undulating life "a hesitant emergence of transcendence from the opaqueness of immanence," a process in which "the deity comes to experience itself":[324] from this perspective, the history of humanity within nature is a slow *rise into appearing* of transcendence. In this history, the Jewish people, a wandering people who were unable to settle permanently in immanence, are the ones who not only accessed infinite transcendence, but saw in it their true fatherland and the very principle of their gathering in community. The history of the people of Israel is thus the process of the Infinite's appearing, and this process as an ex-odus—that is, literally, a way out toward a radical exteriority. By accepting the responsibility to take on the messianic title that this history announced, Jesus of Nazareth incarnated it, and he became the Prince of Israel, the Prince of sacred history who always rejected the profane kingdom (Jn 18:36–37), and whose very death was an "exodus" (ἔξοδος: Lk 9:31).[325] By taking the risk that was "out of his mind" (Mk 3:21) to go, as Hölderlin said of the poet, "bareheaded beneath God's thunder-storms, / To grasp the Father's ray, no less, with [his] own two hands,"[326] he thus came forward to find himself, at this given moment in the history of Israel, at the precise perspective point where, suddenly, the Infinite revealed itself as such—as divestment and renunciation of power, giving abstention: aban-donment (Mt 27:46). He thus made of his person "the icon of the invisible God" (Col 1:15),[327] that is, its anamorphosis,[328] this manifestation that, on the one hand, depends on the precise perspective point occupied by the *I*, and that, on the other hand, only occurs from the moment when this *I* lets itself be dictated by the conditions of manifestation. The status of only Son designates precisely the uniqueness of this point when Revelation takes place through obedience, "for whatever the Father does, the Son does likewise" (Jn 5:19), and when the One is no longer revealed simply by the uniqueness of an elected people (the Jews), but by the singularity of one of its sons, the "Son, the Beloved" (Mt 3:17). If kenosis is the very essance of world history, then the person of Jesus of Nazareth is its recapitulation in the singularity of one flesh, when the deity, which had gotten totally lost in its own creation, finds itself again and has the fully conscious experience of itself: in love lived as the gift of self-sacrifice until death. Christ thus becomes, in love lived "to the end" (Jn 13:1), in his becoming poor (2 Cor 8:9) and humbling himself (Phil 2:8), in the passivity of his suffering (Mk 8:31), his anguish and sadness[329] as well (Mt 26:37–38), the fault-iness where the fault of the originary abyss is revealed.

The fissuring of transcendence from the field of immanence is an "earthquake" (Mt 27:54); it also has the violence of war and struggle: "Do not think that I have come to bring peace to the earth; I have not come to bring peace, but a sword" (Mt 10:34). But this struggle must be understood as the "originary struggle," the πόλεμος that defines the coming of λόγος, and in which, said Heidegger, "clefts, intervals, distances and joints open themselves up,"[330] that is, when the opacity of the earth fissures to suddenly let in the ray of light that reveals the abyss of originary hyperclarity: the sword stroke that has not "come to bring peace to the earth [. . .] but rather division" (Lk 12:51), and that tears natural immanence to let divine transcendence surge in—and it is important to recall that such a transcendence is abyssal; it could not be reduced to the unilateral (and therefore limited) dimension of height, but refers to an unfathomable abyss in the enormity of which the field of immanence is nothing more than a "platform in the center of chasms."[331]

The coming of λόγος, its dialogue and struggle with φύσις, the tearing of the density of the earth, this is what defines history. The characteristic of metaphysical rationality is to present λόγος as abstract and objective universality, and to present it as a groundwork: history is thereby the process of actualizing this λόγος, that is, the self-grounding of the Abstract-Universal; it is a totalizing process where truth fully occurs only when all the subtleties of its logic, all of its concepts and categories are made completely explicit, and it therefore is fully only at the end, in the form of the encyclopedic recapitulation of a scientific system, which furthermore remains incomprehensible to any finite existant. Thus, everyone is submitted and subjected to the dialectic of the self-development of the Concept; everyone is waiting for his own truth and the very meaning of his life, which will only be granted to him by this Universal that remains the sole aim of the process and to which he can only defer; the Totality is Ground-and-Reason (*Grund*), and everyone is therefore only an individuation of this Totality. The terminal thinker of this rationality could thus affirm that "Reason cannot stop to consider the injuries sustained by single individuals, for particular ends are submerged in the universal end":[332] it would then be possible to approach the incarnate λόγος as a reason that does stop to consider the injuries sustained by single individuals, a λόγος who says: "Truly I tell you, just as you did it to one of the least of these who are members of my family, you did it to me" (Mt 25:40 and 45), and who comes to "wipe every tear from their eyes" (Apoc. 21:4). Metaphysical rationality, where meaning and truth are delegated to an objective totality that becomes the very Being in relation to which individual existances are only empirical and secondary manifestations, is thus confronted with a rationality that recognizes in existance itself, in its exodus toward death, the fullness of meaning.[333] It is a matter of confronting the abstract and universal λόγος of metaphysics, defined by the neutrality of an anonymous Concept presented as an unshakeable foundation, with a singular and faulty λόγος, a λόγος of the abyss (*Abgrund*), which relegates the totality itself to a derivative position: as Hölderlin had rigorously conceived it, to recognize that "it is from the abyss indeed that we have begun" is thereby to recognize "the apriority of the individual over the Whole,"[334] which is to refuse to make the Totality its own foundation and to reduce everyone to one of its functions, in order rather to center it on the singular fault that gapes toward the abyss of the One, from which each one proceeds uniquely.

From this point of view, then, no finite existance has anything whatsoever to expect from any sort of "progress," which is only ever the process of its totalization, the self-development of the Same, its laborious and redundant self-explication in which all things are valued equally. Enclosed within its own immanence, "the creation was subjected to vanity" (τῇ ματαιότητι ὑπετάγη: Rom 8:20),[335] and if boredom, sadness, and melancholy remain essential for all thinking, it is precisely for the lucidity that they provide regarding the vanity of all things. This lucidity reveals that the Totality does not manage to give meaning, nor to fill the fault of existance that it nevertheless claims to integrate without remainder as one of its moments; it reveals that the Same does not manage to ground itself. Only a free gift of the Other can tear the Same away from its vanity: this gift is love, and indeed, only the (unforeseeable) encounter with the pure alterity (irreducible to the dialectic of the Same) of an embodied singularity (insoluble within the anonymity of the Universal) can justify my existance and save it from its vanity. If the Christian λόγος is defined in its essance as love—and not as logic, dialectics, mathematics, logistics, and other redundancies—it is precisely because it is the unforeseeable event of the advent, in a singular flesh, of the Wholly Other within the Same, because it thus reveals that love alone gives meaning. Once this *declaration* has taken place, then it is imprescriptible and irreversible: in this way meaning and truth have already been given, in all their fullness, "once for all" (ἐφάπαζ: Rom 6:10). And indeed, no historiological progress is imaginable concerning love, since it is entirely present in the least movement, "supernatural,"[336] of true charity. Love alone saves from vanity, and only as long as it is safeguarded in its supernaturalness and recognized in its absoluteness, and not profaned by its barbaric reduction to self-serving calculations and transference neuroses, when it is not being reduced to organic secretions.[337] It is just as important not to reduce it to sentimentality or self-indulgence, when on the contrary it is the annihilation of all sufficiency and constitutes an irreducible subversion of the Totality, contests the legitimacy of all order, and short-circuits the Universal and its dialectic by the one-to-one relationship: it is *insofar as* he brings love that Jesus, "this holy anarchist,"[338] brings the sword.

History, as the slow and laborious appearance of transcendence from immanence, the succession of peoples confusedly rising to this point of anamorphosis, finds its consummation in this necessarily unique point where the vertical of transcendence and the horizontal of immanence *cross*, this point of contact between the Same and the Other. If the time of the world is the enigmatic emergence, by an infinity of degrees, of singularity from the impersonal neutrality of nature, then time culminates in the most singular person of history, Jesus of Nazareth, who in this respect is "the fullness of time" (τὸ πλήρωμα τοῦ χρόνου: Gal 4:4). Of all these degrees, he is then the peak, he is, as Nietzsche himself had seen, "nature's masterpiece,"[339] who becomes "the head" (ἡ κεφαλὴ: Col 1:18) of creation, and in his life was thus able "to recapitulate all things" (ἀνακεφαλαιώσασθαι τὰ πάντα: Eph 1:10).[340] This singularity is, in every sense of the word, the *apotheosis* of universal history, the unique event when it is condensed and revealed in its most proper content, that is, when history itself is recapitulated. Thus, when Irenaeus of Lyons in the second century develops the Pauline thought of recapitulation, he specifies that "the Lord is He who has recapitulated in Himself all nations dispersed from Adam downwards, and all languages and generations of men [. . .] He recapitulated in Himself the long line of human beings" (τὴν μακρὰν τῶν ἀνθρώπων ἱστορίαν εἰσ ἀυτὸν ἀνεκεφαλαιώσατο).[341]

Thus, "the other history" can be conceived, not as another stage or another series of epochs on the same timeline, but as *another recapitulation* of one and the same event—the event of history as such, the advent of the word within the eternal silence of infinite space—from another principle, which in truth is no longer a principle, sovereign and omnipotent, but a Prince, poor and humble of heart. To the onto-logical hypothesis that delegates meaning and truth to a Universal at work in history, the Christo-logical hypothesis states that the singular and faulty flesh is the unique and abyssal principle, and thus highlights that every attempt to rely on any sort of "progress" is "vanity and a chasing after wind" (Eccl. 1:14), because "all streams run to the sea, but the sea is not full" (Eccl. 1:7). Henceforth, if the truth, and "all the truth" (Jn 16:13), has already occurred "once for all" (Rom 6:10) in all its fullness, then "all is now finished" (Jn 19:28).[342] The peak of history, the revelation of the singularity of the Wholly-Other inasmuch as his love saves us from vanity, has already been achieved, and now it is precisely only a matter of safeguarding the memory of him: now it can only be a matter, as Hölderlin says in "Patmos," of existing in "the loved one's shadow," and thus of "dwell[ing] in loving Night and in fixed, / Ingenuous eyes to preserve / Abysses of wisdom."[343]

To stand in this loving fidelity is then to dwell in the "mildness of an *intimacy* proper to that *divinization* of the god of gods," and it thus becomes possible to consider the "last god" (*der letzte Gott*), which according to Heidegger raises to the highest level "the essance of the uniqueness of the Godhead." The passing by of the last god is the trembling that assigns our existance to the "grounding of truth," in that sense it is "the most profound Beginning rather than a cessation": it is the other Beginning of the other history. Heidegger constantly approached the question of the divine through Hölderlin, and he understands the relation to the god as standing "at the same time in departure and in arrival, in sorrow *and* in joy." His reading nevertheless remains rooted in the project of making the pure essance of an eclipsed Greece arise and flourish, and this in an unwavering rejection of Judaism:[344] this is why he tries to develop a figure of the divine that is "wholly other than the Christian god." It is then to the Earth that he grants the possibility that it "will raise love and death to their highest level and will integrate them into fidelity to the god."[345] Such a reading of Hölderlin, related to the poetico-political project of Stefan George and his circle, is nevertheless biased—even in bad faith. If the search for the reconciliation of the human and divine had led Hölderlin to look for this union in Greece, his meditation on tragedy in fact leads him to recognize a failure there: it is then Christ who comes, as a "beggar," to accomplish what the Greek gods, Heracles and Dionysus above all, had not been able to achieve. Because Christ really lived and really suffered death, where the martyrdom of Dionysus remained purely mythological, and because "Christ's consent comes from himself," he is the god who by his coming "accomplishes / What the others lacked for / The presence of the divine to be complete,"[346] and he accomplishes it precisely because he incarnates it in his body: he is the one "to whom beauty most adhered, so that / A miracle was wrought in his person and / The Heavenly had pointed at him."[347] Christ is then "the Only One," who recapitulates all the figures of the divine, he is the recapitulating god, "the god of gods" (*der Götter Gott*) whom the poet praises in this way: "May all be one in you. [. . .] No one, like you, counts for all the others."[348] That is why, concludes Hölderlin, "Christ is the end," he is the "last" (*der letzte*)[349] of the gods: the last because he comes after all the Greek gods, because he incarnates and consummates all the figures of the divine, but also because after this consummation without remainder, the deity withdraws into the abyss of its absence. Indeed, Christ comes when "the Highest / Himself averts his face,"[350] and it is precisely his mission to "convey the trace of the gods now departed / Down to the godless below into the midst of their gloom."[351] He is the last god because he is the god of God's absenting, of God's withdrawal, perhaps even of his abdication, who "broke / The straightly beaming, the sceptre, / Divinely suffering,"[352] that is, the god who comes precisely to announce his renunciation of authority over the kingdom of this world (Lk 4:5–8 and Jn 18:36–37). Christ is the last god because he is the coming into presence of absence, who in kenosis reveals the abyss of an originary withdrawal, then himself withdraws; he thereby inaugurates the time of mourning and twilight:

> When the Father had turned his face from the sight of us mortals
> And all over the earth, rightly, they started to mourn,
> Lastly a Genius had come, dispensing heavenly comfort,
> He who proclaimed the Day's end, then himself went away.[353]

In Christ, God thus comes to pass as a departure (*Abschied*). But the departure is not an end, it is a Beginning, because this separation or detachment (*Abgeschiedenheit*) is an inexhaustible offering: "The Beginning that takes place from detachment is an abyss of gifting," and the Beginning is then "the taking-into-oneself of the departure towards the abyss."[354] Christ is then the Beginning as the departure of God and departure toward God, he is the event of the *à-Dieu*: he is the Adieu. And indeed it is possible to define Christian faith just as Heidegger thought the relation to the last god, this acceptance of an adieu, "in sorrow *and* in joy" which "will raise love and death to their highest level and will integrate them into fidelity to the god."[355] Such a faith is the most originary, and it opens up to a poetics of truth, because "the adieu [*Abschied*] is pure poetizing, a poetizing more initial than all the poetry of the 'poet' and every thought of the 'thinker.'"[356] It must also be recognized that the last god has already passed by, and that this passing by is imprescriptible: the Adieu has already taken place, and an adieu only ever takes place once and for all. Everything is accomplished, the peak of time is crossed, there is nothing more to wait for,[357] but only to commemorate, in sacred mourning and loving melancholy. As Rimbaud said of the genius "that we, standing amid rage and troubles, see passing in the storm-rent sky," and in whom he saw "love, perfect and reinvented measurement, wonderful and unforeseen reason": "He won't descend from a heaven again, he won't accomplish the redemption of women's anger and the gaiety of men and all of that sin: for it is now accomplished, with him being, and being loved."[358]

Epilogue

To think apocalyptically is to think from the point of view of the ultimate (ἔσκατον): not teleologically, from the point of view of the end (τέλος), but eschatologically, from the point of view of *after* the end. Such a point of view is forced upon every finite existant, whose essance unfolds temporally until its death: only a recapitulatory point of view is capable of circumscribing it in its being; a man can only be de-fined after his end, "changed to Himself at last by eternity,"[1] and eschatological thinking then consists in everyone asking himself what he *will have been*, what he *will have made* of his life, and in adopting on himself this final judgment that speaks from the ultimate, the ἔσκατον. But our epoch demands transferring this eschatological perspective to history, humanity, life, and the universe, whose finitude is now manifested from all sides. History had a beginning [*début*], it was preceded by hundreds of millennia of prehistory: it will have an end; the human species had a beginning, which only occurred after millions of years of animal evolution: it will have an end; life emerged on planet earth after billions of years of minerality, it had a beginning: it will have an end; and one major scientific revolution of the twentieth century was the thesis—still unthinkable for Einstein—of a universe in becoming, whose beginning it is possible to date, and also to foresee its end. It is thus a trait proper to our epoch to place all things within the horizon of the end, and to demand of the end itself the eschatological perspective. For millennia, the cosmos gave itself as an eternal Whole, albeit under the cyclical form of its own return; the eschatological perspective was then heterogeneous, offered by messengers of God who, like Philippulus the Prophet,[2] could always be considered crazy: but now it is the world itself, from its immanent rationality, that unfolds only in anticipation of its own end. Therefore, the horizon of the possible is now the horizon of the end, and to the thought of this *possibility*, our epoch furthermore demands taking into account its *imminence*. Indeed, contemporary technology possesses the means to annihilate all life on earth—through its chemical and nuclear potential—and climatology, in some of its predictive models, raises the possibility of an imminent collapse of the biosphere threatening terrestrial life in the short term.[3] And, even more disturbing if possible, all of humanity seems only to desire this end, and is only motivated by the will to *get it over with*. Man never knew what he was, but he always knew how to preserve a mystery and a promise in this enigma: but now *he no longer believes in it*, and consents wholeheartedly and unqualifiedly to his reduction to the rank of a herd animal. Man is tired,[4] with an ancient tiredness, and now seeks only to forget himself and run away from himself, in any pharmacopoeia, even the most narcotic, and any entertainment, even the most grotesque, to the point of seeking to leave the earth in order to lose himself in the interplanetary void, to the point of planning his own genetic mutation, to the point of putting his whole heritage up for sale in sales[5] that organize its total liquidation, where *everything must go*. Humans have long understood themselves as intermediaries between animal and divine, but now they consent to have been only intermediaries between nature and machine, and it is to their own disappearance that they are resigned today. Is a "genuine revolution of the whole of Being and knowledge"[6] going to occur to ward off these threats, are we "in the very twilight of the most monstrous transformation of the whole earth and of the time of the historical space in which it is suspended?"[7]—this is what thought is not in a position to know, and what it is not intended to organize.

It is only a matter of thinking, but precisely from this eschatological point of view, which tries to think λόγος from the silence that succeeds it—from the epi-logue, therefore—and thus to *think in the future anterior*: what *will have been* the event of speech and thought, what *will have been* human history within the universe once planet earth becomes sterile and deserted again and still slides around its orbit for millions of years before being evaporated in the expansion of the sun? Humanity certainly emerges from nature, but the fact remains that within nature it is the advent of something that is not natural at all, that in it springs forth a light that illuminates nature in its totality and (in the sciences) lights up its smallest corners, but also a power that (in technology) dominates it, turns against it, and can destroy it: in the eternal silence of infinite space humanity is a *blaze* that we must try to think as such. Humanity makes non-being emerge within beings, that is, Being and nothing, it makes meaning [*sens*] emerge in the whole panic of primordial senselessness [*insensé*], and that is why we must conceive the human being "not as one among the other things on the Earth that creep and fly, but as the meaning of the Earth, in the sense that with and through the existant each and every being first arises as such a being, closes itself off (comes under command), succeeds and fails, and returns again to the origin."[8] And it is precisely because the event of human history is the advent of meaning that one can hardly come to terms with its absurdity: or at least, highlighting the emptiness of all signification, that is, of meaning as "vanity of vanities" (Eccl 1:2) is precisely what reveals the unfathomable abyss from which it proceeds, and reveals meaning itself as lack, and as empty.

According to the word of Hegel often recalled by Heidegger, *Wesen ist was gewesen ist*, "essance is the gathering of what has been," and it is the very content of the thinking of our epoch to be recapitulatory. But the whole question is then to know what is the *principle* of recapitulation, or what is its *prince*, its leader or its head, since *recapitulatio*, built on *caput*, as well as ἀνακεφαλαίωσις, on κεφαλή, literally means gathering on a single head, a single leader. To this question Hegel, which is to say metaphysics, answers: it is the Idea, which recapitulates itself encyclopedically, and this speculative logic was verified in contemporary totalization, the effective gathering of all that is into the planetary totality of technology, and the dissolution in the *spectrality* of cyberspace. Our epoch is, in fact, the systematic and automatic recapitulation of all the scattered nations, of all languages and all the generations of men in the same abstract and universal space-time that reduces everything to a quantity of ideal value: that is, in Capital, a word equally derived from *caput*, "the head." The contemporary re-capit-ulation is capit-alization.

Our epoch is that of the triumph of Capital and the onto-logical totalization that submits the entire planet to technical rationality and finally integrates it into Machinery: it is thereby the triumph of calculative thinking and its functionaries, it recapitulates knowledge and thought themselves, which have become a vast reserve fund for "research," in an apparatus in which "the scholar disappears and is replaced by the researcher engaged in research programs. [...] From an inner compulsion, the researcher presses forward into the sphere occupied by the figure of, in the essential sense, the technologist."[9] The destiny of philosophy, knowledge, art, and religion then becomes "culture," that is, the available stock of "cultural products," and fundamentally cultural capital. In this way our epoch is the domination of "specialists" to whom it recklessly grants the power to state the very meaning of history, and to give the impression that the conquering rationality that has conquered everything is recapitulation in-and-for-itself: that it is the Universal. Yet the eschatological question is to know who has the keys to define the very meaning of humanity's irruption within nature, *who is right* [qui a raison] in the recapitulation of meaning: who is the head, and the prince. Apocalyptic thinking then allows the elitist sufficiency of specialists to be sent back into the insignificance of its inanity, and it is in this sense that Hans Urs von Balthasar interprets the verse from the Apocalypse of John (5:2) that asks: "Who is worthy to open the scroll and break its seals?"

> Who can decipher the meaning of the universe, its nature, its history? What philosophy can explain the beginning, the middle, and the end, and break its seven seals? To this question a terrifying silence responds: "But no one on earth or under the earth was able to open the scroll or to read it." In the middle of this distraught silence burst the cries of the visionary: "And I began to weep bitterly because no one was found worthy," because no one has the strength, even if he has the courage, to solve the enigma of the world. These cries reveal more to us and are more precious than all the dry eyes of the philosophers or other sages of this world, who manipulate the seals however they see fit, who recommend to us a solution, a "way" to slip through the seals or to simply deny their existence.[10]

In the eternal silence of infinite space, humanity is an essantial interruption, which opens a fault in the continuum of immanence where transcendence occurs from a word that through this fissuring introduces meaning. It is the abyss of this fault that reveals lucidity *regarding meaning itself*, which sees that "all is vanity and a chasing after wind. [. . .] For in much wisdom is much vexation, and those who increase knowledge increase sorrow" (Eccl 1:14–18): the Qoheleth thus grasped in the vanity of history as such, in the vanity of all labor and every work, the emptiness of an absence and the experience of a haunting lack of the essantial that could only be filled by an infinite love. The ultimate key to the fissuring of this fault in the field of immanence is then divine kenosis *as* fault-iness, in the singular person of the poorest, who endures, takes on, and recapitulates this infinite by an acquiescence, itself infinite, to the mystery, whose abyss he thus unveils.

But the destiny of the West is the panicked flight before the abyss of this infinite, the impossibility of enduring it and taking it on, its history is the continuous transfer of this infinite into thingness and objectivity, a transfer completed today in globalized techno-capitalist Machinery. In this way, it is annihilation of the infinite, in the sense that it denies it and takes it for nothingness, but also in the sense that it transfers it into non-Being, and makes it into a pure annihilating power: Machinery is extroverted infinitude, it is the attribution of the infinite to beings. "Man," continued Balthasar, "has had enough of being mortal, and he always invents new atomic bombs to blow up his finitude and acquire the infinite by any means necessary," and in this way he risks "lighting the match that, one day, by the explosion of all creation, would send the finite into the infinite."[11] The search for the infinite that characterizes European modernity and that is unleashed in the possibilities, themselves infinite, of technology is in truth only the refusal of the originary infinite and the idolatry of an objectified infinite that only promises annihilation, and that at the same time covers and veils the abyss: the blinding clarity that contemporary rationality makes prevail throughout the whole universe and the immensity of space thus exhibited, because they are enough to strike thought with terror, dissimulate the very possibility of the originary infinite; and thus the universe veils the One. Contemporary existance, that of the functionary of technology, is then entirely dedicated to fleeing melancholy, avoiding solitude, eradicating silence, despising the sacred, renouncing the past, denying death, tracking down and anesthetizing all phenomena of faultiness: it is the distraught denial of the abyss of its own distress. But as Heidegger said: "In the face of this abyss one can try to shut one's eyes. One can erect one illusion after another. The abyss does not retreat."[12]

Apocalyptic thinking can only give the key to the abyss. "That key is charity."[13] Today it must be content with rejecting "the wisdom of the princes of this epoch, who are doomed to perish" (1 Cor 2:6),[14] it reveals to one and all: "For you say, 'I am rich, I have prospered, and I need nothing.' You do not realize that you are wretched, pitiable, poor, blind, and naked" (Apoc. 3:17). It leaves nothing to be done apart from standing resolutely in eschatological imminence, and our epoch thus demands from itself the eschatological community that defined early Christianity: a new people who leave history because they gather in the end time; not the end of time, but a time that "has grown short" or "contracted" (ὁ καιρὸς συνεσταλμένος ἐστίν: 1 Cor 7:29) by the knowledge that "the end of all things is near" (1 Pt 4:7), that is, a time that expects nothing more from time, which has always already rejected all historiological progress in order to place itself in the parvis of eternity. Such a community is always difficult to establish and maintain, and in principle since an eschatological community is essentially aporetic and exodic; it can in no way be identified with any politics whatsoever and could only be *underground*;[15] moreover, it always remains exposed to the apparatus's atomizing power, and to the effective violence of real nihilism; it especially does not constitute any "solution" to the technological danger. But the tension of eschatological imminence nevertheless gives all its weight to the crucial phenomena of death and love, it thus gives a setting and a provisional morality that Ernst Jünger defined perfectly in a text where he addressed the surge of contemporary nihilism under the monstrous figure of totalitarianism:

> In our deserts there are also oases where wilderness flourishes. Isaiah had recognized this at the time of an analogous upheaval. These are the gardens to which Leviathan has no access, around which he prowls with fury. In the

first place, there is death. Today, as always, those who do not fear death are infinitely superior to the greatest of temporal powers. [. . .] The second power of the depths is Eros. Wherever two beings love each other, they gain ground on Leviathan, they create a space that he does not control. Eros will always win the day, as the true messenger of the gods, over all the fictions of the Titans.[16]

Notes

PREFACE

1 In French, *revenir* can mean "to return," "to come back," "to be sent back," or "to amount to"—Trans.

CHAPTER ONE

1 René Descartes, Preface to the French edition of *Principles of Philosophy*, in *The Philosophical Writings of Descartes*, trans. J. Cottingham, R. Stoothoff, and D. Murdoch, 3 vols. (Cambridge: Cambridge University Press, 1984–91), 1:180; AT 9:3.

2 Descartes, *Discourse on the Method*, AT 6:61 [*Philosophical Writings*, 1:142].

3 Preface to the French edition of *Principles of Philosophy*, AT 9:3 [*Philosophical Writings*, 1:180].

4 *Discourse on the Method*, AT 6:10 [*Philosophical Writings*, 1:115].

5 "Meditation III," in *Meditations on First Philosophy*, AT 9:38 [*Philosophical Writings*, 2:32].

6 "Meditation II," AT 7:29 [*Philosophical Writings*, 2:19].

7 *Discourse on the Method*, AT 6:39 [*Philosophical Writings*, 1:131].

8 "Meditation V," AT 9:71 [*Philosophical Writings*, 2:49].

9 All Heidegger citations are from Martin Heidegger's *Gesamtausgabe* (GA), followed by the corresponding citation in the available English translation, given in brackets. GA 10:8 [*The Principle of Reason*, trans. Reginald Lilly (Bloomington: Indiana University Press, 1991), 6]. Translation altered—Trans.

10 GA 7:234 [*Early Greek Thinking*, trans. David Farrell Krell and Frank A. Capuzzi (New York: Harper & Row, 1975), 78].

11 GA 14:81 [*On Time and Being*, trans. Joan Stambaugh (New York: Harper & Row, 1972), 66].

12 GA 13:84.

13 GA 9:361 [*Pathmarks*, ed. William McNeill (New York: Cambridge University Press, 1998), 274].

14 GA 8:45 [*What Is Called Thinking?*, trans. J. Glenn Gray (New York: Harper & Row, 1968), 43].

15 This is obviously not the case for Descartes, where the *ego* immediately opens up to the infinity of God.

16 Levinas, *On Escape*, trans. Bettina Bergo (Stanford, CA: Stanford University Press, 2003), 50.

17 The sufficiency characteristic of humanism found its unforgettable formulation in Ernest Renan, who confessed in 1848: "I, as a man of culture, do not find any evil in myself, and I am impelled spontaneously towards what seems to me the most noble. If all others had as much culture as myself, they would all, like myself, be incapable of doing an evil act." Ernest Renan, *The Future of Science*, trans. Albert D. Vandam and C. B. Pitman (London: Chapman & Hall, 1891), 333.

18 GA 13:62.

19 GA 9:113 [*Pathmarks*, 90].

20 GA 9:112 [*Pathmarks*, 88].

21 GA 9:115 [*Pathmarks*, 91].

22 GA 9:114 [*Pathmarks*, 90].

23 GA 9:306–7 [*Pathmarks*, 233].

24 GA 79:17–18 [*Poetry, Language, Thought*, trans. Albert Hofstadter (New York: Harper & Row, 1971), 178].

25 SZ, 262 [*Being and Time* (hereafter BT), trans. John Macquarrie and Edward Robinson (New York: Harper Press, 1962), 307].

26 GA 20:440 [*History of the Concept of Time: Prolegomena*, trans. Theodore Kisiel (Bloomington: Indiana University Press, 1985), 318].

27 GA 20:437–38 [*History of the Concept of Time: Prolegomena*, 316–17].

28 SZ, 254 [BT, 298].

29 Cesare Pavese, *The Business of Living: Diaries 1935–1950*, trans. A. E. Murch with Jeanne Molli (New Brunswick, NJ: Transaction Publishers, 2009), 345.

30 Alphonse de Lamartine, "L'isolement," in *Méditations poétiques*, in *Oeuvres poétiques complètes*, ed. M.-F. Guyard (Paris: Gallimard, Bibliothèque de la Pléiade, 1963), 3.

31 To the typology of common-law phenomena studied by Husserl, Jean-Luc Marion (in *Being Given: Toward a Phenomenology of Givenness* [Stanford, CA: Stanford University Press, 2002]) has added the saturated phenomenon, defined by an irreducible excess of intuition over the intention of meaning. Perhaps we could symmetrically consider the case of an irreducible faultiness of intuition, which would not be simply the experience of a disappointment of intention in the face of a momentary shortage of intuition (where the shortage concerns only the intention in question), but proof of a vertigo before the abyss of a radical absence, a vertigo that then reveals the *ego* and existance itself as a gaping void that nothing could ever fill, and also reveals the constitutive emptiness of meaning: thus, the charge of the vanity of all things is a destruction of signification as such, and not the simple lack of filling one signification among others. Mourning, the amorous lack, and radical boredom would be the privileged examples of such phenomena of faultiness [*phénomènes de défaillance*].

32 Blaise Pascal, *Pensées*, Laf. §597 (Br. §455) [*Pensées*, trans. A. J. Krailsheimer (New York: Penguin Books, 2005), 201].

33 François-René Chateaubriand, *Atala/René*, trans. Irving Putter (Berkeley: University of California Press, 1952), 96 and 98]. Translation altered—Trans.

34 GA 29/30:115 and 218 [*The Fundamental Concepts of Metaphysics: World, Finitude, Solitude*, trans. William McNeill and Nicholas Walker (Bloomington: Indiana University Press, 1995), 77 and 145].

35 GA 50:102 [*Introduction to Philosophy: Thinking and Poetizing*, trans. Phillip Jacques Braunstein (Bloomington: Indiana University Press, 2011), 11].

36 GA 50:153 [*Introduction to Philosophy: Thinking and Poetizing*, 57].

37 GA 14:79 [*On Time and Being*, 64].

38 GA 39:173 [*Hölderlin's Hymns: "Germania" and "The Rhine,"* trans. William McNeill and Julia Ireland (Bloomington: Indiana University Press, 2014), 158].

39 Following the spelling proposed by Emmanuel Levinas: "We write essance with *a* to designate by this word the verbal sense of the word *to be*: the effectuation of Being, the *Sein* distinct from the *Seiendes*"; "We write essance with an *a* in order to express thereby the act or the event or the process of *esse*, the act of the verb 'to be' (*être*)" (*Of God Who Comes to Mind*, trans. Bettina Bergo [Stanford, CA: Stanford University Press, 1998], 195 and 203). This spelling is the most capable of conveying Heidegger's thought: "But what does *essance* mean here? We are not adopting the idea of 'essentialities' from the word. In the name *essance* [*Wesen*] we perceive what occurs essantially [*das Wesende*]" (GA 6.2:310 [*Nietzsche, Volumes 3 and 4*, trans. Joan Stambaugh, David Farrell Krell, and Frank A. Capuzzi, ed. David Farrell Krell (San Francisco: HarperSanFrancisco, 1991), 4:206].

40 GA 10:90 [*The Principle of Reason*, 61].

41 GA 10:131 [*The Principle of Reason*, 88]. Translation altered—Trans.

42 GA 6.2:489.

43 GA 11:60 [*Identity and Difference*, trans. and introd. Joan Stambaugh (Chicago: University of Chicago Press, 2002), 51].

44 GA 39:109 [*Hölderlin's Hymns: "Germania" and "The Rhine,"* 99].

45 GA 9:314 [*Pathmarks*, 240].

46 GA 38:81 [*Logic as the Question concerning the Essence of Language*, trans. Wanda Torres Gregory and Yvonne Unna (Albany: State University of New York Press, 2009), 69].

47 GA 38:84 [*Logic as the Question concerning the Essence of Language*, 71].

48 GA 7:25 [*The Question concerning Technology*, trans. William Lovitt (New York: Harper & Row, 1977), 25].

49 GA 10:135 [*The Principle of Reason*, 91].

50 GA 10:131 [*The Principle of Reason*, 88].

51 GA 14:50 [*On Time and Being*, 41].

52 GA 10:135 [*The Principle of Reason*, 91].

53 GA 38:168–69 [*Logic as the Question concerning the Essence of Language*, 140]. Translation altered—Trans.

54 GA 12:230 [*On the Way to Language*, trans. Peter D. Hertz (New York: Harper & Row, 1971), 112].

55 GA 9:313 [*Pathmarks*, 239].

56 Descartes, "Meditation II," AT 7:25 and AT 9:19 [*Philosophical Writings*, 2:17].

57 Heidegger, GA 39:73 [*Hölderlin's Hymns: "Germania" and "The Rhine,"* 66–67].

58 GA 8:19 [*What Is Called Thinking?*, 16].

59 To this primordiality of language is opposed, in Heidegger's own work (in his debate with Husserl and the notion of "lifeworld"), the recognition of the primordiality of the "workworld" (*Werkwelt, Arbeitswelt*). The 1934 course entitled *Logic as the Question concerning the Essence of Language* (GA 38) then proves to be crucial in that it precisely articulates both of them: its aim takes up again the Husserlian project of a genealogy of logic, which bases it on language, but in order to immediately make language the essance of a historical community, and finally defines it as a community of work. Language is originarily immanent to the community of work, it is the dialogue of Being-with-one-another and of Being-for-one-another made necessary for all community work, and this articulation of the meaning immanent to each people is prior to all sound-uttering: "The being-gathered-together of production is at

play in the gathering (λέγειν) of the discussion and of the cognizance that discusses what is or is not suitable. This is that *talking to oneself* which for the most part goes on silently or as a commentary which gets lost in the work and is often seen only from outside as a bunch of disconnected words. Producing is intrinsically a talking to oneself and letting oneself talk. To tell oneself something does not just mean to form words but to want to proceed in a certain way, that is, to have already gone there in advance" (GA 33:146 [*Aristotle's Metaphysics θ 1–3: On the Essence and Actuality of Force*, trans. Walter Brogan and Peter Warnek (Bloomington: Indiana University Press, 1995), 124]. The crucial point here is, on the one hand, that Being only unfolds its essance as common essance (*das gemeine Wesen*) to a community (*Gemeinwesen*), and, on the other hand, that this one essance is manifest in the exchange (dialogue) that then constitutes its immanent phenomenology.

60 GA 4:39 [*Elucidations of Hölderlin's Poetry*, trans. Kieth Hoeller (Amherst, MA: Humanity Books, 2000), 56–57]. Translation altered—Trans.

61 GA 5:366 [*Off the Beaten Track*, ed. and trans. Julian Young and Kenneth Haynes (New York: Cambridge University Press, 2002), 276].

62 SZ, 384 [BT, 436]. Translation altered—Trans.

63 GA 38:157 [*Logic as the Question concerning the Essence of Language*, 130]. Translation altered—Trans.

64 GA 38:155–56 [*Logic as the Question concerning the Essence of Language*, 129].

65 GA 38:156–57 [*Logic as the Question concerning the Essence of Language*, 130]. Translation altered—Trans.

66 GA 69:8 [*The History of Beyng*, trans. William McNeill and Jeffery Powell (Bloomington: Indiana University Press, 2015), 8].

67 GA 65:48 [*Contributions to Philosophy (Of the Event)*, trans. Richard Rojcewicz and Daniela Vallega-Neu (Bloomington: Indiana University Press, 2012), 39].

68 GA 38:57 [*Logic as the Question concerning the Essence of Language*, 50]. Translation altered—Trans.

69 GA 34:145 [*The Essence of Truth: On Plato's Cave Allegory and Theaetetus*, trans. Ted Sadler (London: Continuum, 2002), 104].

70 GA 34:86 [*The Essence of Truth: On Plato's Cave Allegory and Theaetetus*, 63].

71 GA 12:251 [*On the Way to Language*, 134].

72 GA 5:60 [*Off the Beaten Track*, 46]. Translation altered—Trans.

73 GA 5:27–28 [*Off the Beaten Track*, 20–21].

74 GA 5:310 [*Off the Beaten Track*, 232–33].

75 GA 5:61–62 [*Off the Beaten Track*, 46].

76 To be the most lucid is not to be the most clairvoyant, nor is it to be visionary [*extralucide*].

77 GA 6.2:32 [*Nietzsche*, 4:10], emphasis added.

CHAPTER TWO

1 "The Cairo Hymns to Amun-Rê [Papyrus Boulaq XVII]," from the epoch of Amenhotep II (1430 BCE), in *Hymns, Prayers, and Songs: An Anthology of Ancient Egyptian Lyric Poetry*, trans. John L. Foster, ed. Susan Tower Hollis (Atlanta: Scholars Press, 1995), 58–59.

2 Thales is the first to have determined the ecliptic and to have established a solstice cycle: tradition attributes to him the writing of a "nautical astronomical guide."

3 The difference in regimes of phenomenality based on the relation to the sun is illustrated well

by Hergé in the scene of the eclipse that concludes [the "Tintin" cartoon story] *Prisoners of the Sun*, trans. Leslie Lonsdale-Cooper and Michael Turner (Boston: Little, Brown & Co., 1975), 58–59.

4 GA 65:147 [*Contributions to Philosophy (Of the Event)*, 115].

5 GA 65:127 [*Contributions to Philosophy (Of the Event)*, 100].

6 Compare Niels Bohr, *Essays 1958–1962 on Atomic Physics and Human Knowledge* (New York: John Wiley & Sons, 1963), 4: "While, within the scope of classical physics, the interaction between object and apparatus can be neglected or, if necessary, compensated for, in quantum physics this interaction thus forms an integral part of the phenomenon. Accordingly, the unambiguous account of proper quantum phenomena must, in principle, include a description of all relevant features of the experimental arrangement."

7 GA 6.2:19 [*Nietzsche*, 3:180]. Translation altered—Trans.

8 GA 66:32 [*Mindfulness*, trans. Parvis Emad and Thomas Kalary (London: Continuum, 2006), 24].

9 GA 65:109 [*Contributions to Philosophy (Of the Event)*, 87].

10 GA 79:104 [*Bremen and Freiburg Lectures*, trans. Andrew J. Mitchell (Bloomington: Indiana University Press, 2012), 99].

11 GA 7:13 [*The Question concerning Technology*, 12]. We translate *entbergen, Unverborgenheit, Verborgenheit, Verbergung* by "to unconceal," "unconcealment," "concealment," "concealing," and reserve "to unveil," "unveiling" for *enthüllen, Enthüllung.*

12 GA 8:25 [*What Is Called Thinking?*, 22].

13 GA 65:109 [*Contributions to Philosophy (Of the Event)*, 87].

14 Hölderlin, *Hyperion: or, the Hermit in Greece*, GSA 3:153 [*Hyperion and Selected Poems*, ed. Eric L. Santner (New York: Continuum, 1990), 129].

15 GA 6.2:146 [*Nietzsche*, 4:116].

16 GA 7:94 [*The End of Philosophy*, trans. and introd. Joan Stambaugh (Chicago: University of Chicago Press, 2003), 106–7].

17 GA 5:292 [*Off the Beaten Track*, 219].

18 GA 5:294 [*Off the Beaten Track*, 220].

19 GA 79:35 [*Bremen and Freiburg Lectures*, 33].

20 GA 5:292 [*Off the Beaten Track*, 219].

21 *SZ*, 188 [*BT*, 233].

22 Thus, Günther Anders will reproach Heidegger for ignoring "the reality of industrialization, democracy, the scope of the contemporary world," and for not asking himself "which modes of production [. . .] which property relations" constitute the They ("Nihilismus und Existenz," in *Die Stockholmer Neue Rundschau* (Frankfurt/Main: Suhrkamp, 1949), 99 and 109).

23 *SZ*, 126 [*BT*, 164].

24 GA 69:83 [*The History of Beyng*, 71].

25 GA 66:319 [*Mindfulness*, 283].

26 GA 9:317 [*Pathmarks*, 242].

27 GA 10:45 [*The Principle of Reason*, 29].

28 GA 79:38 [*Bremen and Freiburg Lectures*, 36].

29 As Ernst Jünger said in 1983: "All change, whether it comes from the right or the left, from above or below, from the West or the East, brings us closer to the abyss. There are many opinions, many parties, but *only one* slippery slope," in *Soixante-dix s'efface III. Journal 1981–1985* (Paris: Gallimard, 1993), 245.

30 GA 79:3 [*Bremen and Freiburg Lectures*, 3].

31 GA 40:40–41 [*Introduction to Metaphysics*, trans. Gregory Fried and Richard Polt (New Haven: Yale University Press, 2014), 41–42].

32 GA 7:167 [*Bremen and Freiburg Lectures*, 3].

33 GA 79:37 [*Bremen and Freiburg Lectures*, 35].

34 GA 16:521 [*Discourse on Thinking*, trans. John M. Anderson and E. Hans Freund (New York: Harper & Row, 1966), 48]. Heidegger wrote these lines in 1959; in 2013, "Americans over 18 years old spend on average 5 hours and 19 minutes per day on the Internet and 4 hours and 31 minutes in front of the television" (*La Croix*, August 14, 2013). Bergson in *Creative Evolution* ([New York: Random House, 1944], 156 and following) establishes the difference between intelligence and instinct based on the difference between instrument and organ: the instrument then proves to be superior to the organ in its very imperfection, that is, in its unsuitability, which will open the field of consciousness, while the organ "blocks sight" and encloses it within the narrow circle of a function. Bergson thus defines the animal, not by an "absent consciousness," but by a "nullified consciousness." The spread of screens and the tangentially infinite growth of available content are such that everyone can immediately obtain customized content: thus the screen "blocks sight" and imposes the "nullified consciousness" of the animal—and the hypnotic state in which hours are sunk during screen usage refers well to this nullified consciousness. The relation to the screen is moreover only the most visible manifestation of this meticulous and constant (cybernetic) adaptation of Machinery to the behavior of each of us, which thus works continuously toward our equalization.

35 GA 40:41 [*Introduction to Metaphysics*, 42].

36 GA 13:211.

37 GA 12:150 [*On the Way to Language*, 58].

38 GA 8:242 [*What Is Called Thinking?*, 238].

39 GA 9:317 [*Pathmarks*, 242–43].

40 GA 79:51 [*Bremen and Freiburg Lectures*, 48].

41 GA 7:95 [*The End of Philosophy*, 107].

42 GA 65:121 [*Contributions to Philosophy (Of the Event)*, 96].

43 GA 7:94 [*The End of Philosophy*, 107].

44 GA 14:72 [*On Time and Being*, 58].

45 GA 16:674 [*The Heidegger Reader*, ed. Günter Figal (Bloomington: Indiana University Press, 2009), 328].

46 GA 6.2:146 [*Nietzsche*, 4:117].

47 GA 65:120 [*Contributions to Philosophy (Of the Event)*, 95].

48 GA 69:63 [*The History of Beyng*, 54–55].

49 Letter to Elisabeth Blochmann, March 3, 1947, in Martin Heidegger and Elisabeth Blochmann, *Briefwechsel, 1918–1969*, ed. Joachim W. Storck (Marbach am Neckar: Deutsche Schillergesellschaft, 1989), 93.

50 GA 29/30:315 [*The Fundamental Concepts of Metaphysics: World, Finitude, Solitude*, 215].

51 GA 6.2:16 [*Nietzsche*, 3:177].

52 GA 65:127 [*Contributions to Philosophy (Of the Event)*, 100].

53 GA 69:202 [*The History of Beyng*, 171].

54 GA 6.2:20 [*Nietzsche*, 3:181].

55 GA79:36, 25, and 33–34, respectively [*Bremen and Freiburg Lectures*, 34–35, 24, 32].

56 GA 7:97 [*The End of Philosophy*, 110].

57 GA 79:25–26 [*Bremen and Freiburg Lectures*, 25–26].

58 Bernanos, *Essais et écrits de combat II*, ed. M. Estève (Paris: Gallimard, Bibliothèque de la Pléiade, 1995), 1042. In 1944, when the political totalitarianisms were not yet defeated, Bernanos perceived that the coming victory would not resolve anything, because the essential thing was no longer ideology, but technology: "The regimes once opposed by ideology are now closely united by technology," he observed, "the techniques of governments at war only differ by negligible features, justified by habits. It is always a matter of ensuring total mobilization for total war, pending total mobilization for total peace" (981). At the same moment as Heidegger, Bernanos thus described "the invasion of Machinery, [. . .] an entirely new phenomenon" (1023), which demands the "serial formation of a docile humanity, increasingly docile, as economic organization, competitions, and wars demand a more meticulous regulation" (991). The concept of Machinery therefore overflows the strict setting of factories and instrumental apparatuses: Machinery mobilizes the totality of humanity, of which it organizes the entirety of behaviors and thoughts, hence the difficulty in making a critical discourse about technology audible, since every addressee of this discourse is formatted and disciplined by it—hence, in Bernanos, a quite understandable recourse to insult: "Don't you see that the civilization of machines demands from you a discipline that becomes more strict each day? It demands it in the name of progress, which is to say in the name of a new conception of life imposed on minds by its enormous machinery of propaganda and publicity. Fools! Understand that the civilization of machines is itself a machine, all of whose movements must be more and more perfectly synchronized!" (1047). By affirming that "the civilization of machines is itself a machine," Bernanos gives the most precise definition of Machinery, which is none other than the gigantic global equipment where all devices are connected in order to guarantee the perfection of its functioning. It is therefore humanity's universal servility toward Machinery that carries with it the threat of annihilation: "If our species ends by disappearing one day from this planet thanks to the growing efficiency of technologies of destruction," thus wrote Bernanos, "it is not cruelty that will be responsible for our extinction, but rather docility" (1056).

59 GA 79:29 [*Bremen and Freiburg Lectures*, 28].

60 GA 69:81 [*The History of Beyng*, 69].

61 GA 7:95 [*The End of Philosophy*, 108].

62 GA 7:167 [*Bremen and Freiburg Lectures*, 4].

63 GA 79:25 [*Bremen and Freiburg Lectures*, 25].

64 GA 9:158 [*Pathmarks*, 123]. Translation altered—Trans.

65 *SZ*, 132 [*BT*, 171].

66 GA 9:159 [*Pathmarks*, 123]. Translation altered—Trans.

67 GA 6.2:356 [*Nietzsche*, 4:246].

68 GA 6.2:351 [*Nietzsche*, 4:242].

69 GA 9:158 [*Pathmarks*, 123].

70 GA 7:91 [*The End of Philosophy*, 104].

71 GA 7:96 [*The End of Philosophy*, 108–9].

72 GA 6.2:356 [*Nietzsche*, 4:246].

73 GA 7:70–71 [*The End of Philosophy*, 85, 87].

74 GA 6.2:337 [*Nietzsche*, 4:229].

75 Günther Anders, *L'obsolescence de l'homme. Sur l'âme à l'époque de la deuxième révolution industrielle* (Paris: Ivréa/L'Encyclopédie des nuisances, 2002), 338.

76 What the term "nihilism" itself suggests. The word derives from the latin *nihil*, which is itself a compound word, built from the negation (*ne-*) of *hilum*, "the hilum," which is the minuscule

scar left on the tegument of a bean by the rupture of the funicle that holds it in its pod. Latin used the word *hilum* to designate an insignificant thing or a negligible quantity (for example, Cicero: *neque proficit hilum*, "he advances not one inch," *Tusculan Disputations* 1.10), in English: a nothing. Whereas the word "nothing" [*"rien"*] is the negation of the thing (*res non*), the word *nihil* is the negation of the nothing. Nihilism is the annihilation of negativity and the total affirmation of positivity, that is, "the complete *dissolution* of negativity into the positivity of the absolute" (GA 68:14 [*Hegel*, trans. Joseph Arel and Niels Feuerhahn (Bloomington: Indiana University Press, 2015), 11]): the "extreme omission" of Being thus "aids and abets the advance of the purely actual—of those popularly acclaimed realities—which prides itself on being what it is, while at the same time presuming itself to be the measure for deciding that only what is effectual—what is palpable and makes an impression, what is experienced and its expression, what is useful and its success—should pass as being" (GA 6.2:340 [*Nietzsche*, 4:231–32]). Positivism and nihilism, it's all the same [*c'est du pareil au même*].

77 GA 68:15 [*Hegel*, 12].

78 GA 7:27 [*The Question concerning Technology*, 26].

79 GA 16:669 [*The Heidegger Reader*, 325].

80 GA 79:65 [*Bremen and Freiburg Lectures*, 62].

81 GA 7:93, 95 [*The End of Philosophy*, 106, 108].

82 GA 7:52 [*The Question concerning Technology*, 170].

83 GA 41:95 [*What Is a Thing?*, trans. W. B. Barton Jr. and Vera Deutsch (Chicago: Henry Regnery Co., 1967), 94].

84 GA 65:164 [*Contributions to Philosophy (Of the Event)*, 128].

85 GA 7:51 [*The Question concerning Technology*, 169].

86 GA 65:120 [*Contributions to Philosophy (Of the Event)*, 95].

87 GA 79:104–5 [*Bremen and Freiburg Lectures*, 99]. Translation altered—Trans.

88 GA 41:73 [*What Is a Thing?*, 73].

89 GA 41:90 [*What Is a Thing?*, 89].

90 GA 41:104 [*What Is a Thing?*, 104].

91 GA 41:73 [*What Is a Thing?*, 73].

92 GA 41:108 [*What Is a Thing?*, 107–8].

93 GA 10:175–76 [*The Principle of Reason*, 120].

94 GA 10:177 [*The Principle of Reason*, 121].

95 The neologism *amêmement* was proposed by François Fédier in his translation of §238–42 of the *Beiträge zur Philosophie* (*Po&sie* 81 [Paris, 1997]:8 and following) to render *Ereignis*. Here it designates the Greek Event in and through which: Being and λόγος = the Same [*le Même*].

96 GA 10:158 [*The Principle of Reason*, 105–6]. Translation altered—Trans.

97 GA 79:65 [*Bremen and Freiburg Lectures*, 62].

98 GA 65:132 [*Contributions to Philosophy (Of the Event)*, 104].

99 GA 55:3 [*Heraclitus: The Inception of Occidental Thinking and Logic: Heraclitus' Doctrine of the Logos*, trans. S. Montgomery Ewegen and Julia Goesser Assaiante (London: Bloomsbury Academic, 2018), 3].

100 GA 66:194 [*Mindfulness*, 171].

101 GA 9:236 [*Pathmarks*, 181].

102 GA 6.2:312 [*Nietzsche*, 4:208].

103 GA 68:15 [*Hegel*, 12].

104 GA 54:79 and 167 [*Parmenides*, trans. Andrew Schuwer and Richard Rojcewicz (Bloomington: Indiana University Press, 1992), 54 and 113].

105 GA 10:80 [*The Principle of Reason*, 53].
106 GA 7:75 [*The End of Philosophy*, 90].
107 GA 4:177 [*Elucidations of Hölderlin's Poetry*, 201].
108 GA 11:60–61 [*Identity and Difference*, 50–51]. "Cybernetics" is a marginal note from Heidegger, added to the volume of the *Gesamtausgabe*.
109 GA 7:76 [*The End of Philosophy*, 90].
110 GA 8:57 [*What Is Called Thinking?*, 54].
111 GA 8:164 [*What Is Called Thinking?*, 160].
112 GA 7:69 [*The End of Philosophy*, 85].
113 GA 15:437–38 ["Zurich Seminar"]. It is moreover what marks the limit of the "serenity" or "letting-be" (*Gelassenheit*) that Heidegger advises in the face of technology, a serenity that "promise[s] us a new ground and foundation upon which we can stand and endure in the world of technology without being imperiled by it" (GA 16:527–28 [*Discourse on Thinking*, 54–55): first because, in the age of globalized capitalism and the absolute unleashing of machination, this reserve position safe from "being imperiled" could only affect a tiny minority of the privileged; then because the devastation reaches such an extent that it is not certain that this shelter "upon which we can stand and endure" could last for long; finally and above all because this position in no way thwarts a process of devastation that it precisely "lets be." By this serenity, Heidegger furthermore specified, it is a matter of being able to "affirm the unavoidable use of technical devices, and also deny them the right to dominate us, and so to warp, confuse, and lay waste our nature": which assumes that everyone *still* has some leeway regarding the use of machines, and especially that we are *already* freed from our fascination for them, which is not the case for those (most of us) who are subjected to the production apparatus and to the propaganda of the consumption apparatus. "Serenity" can only be a provisional morality for times of need, and not a way out of the danger zone.

CHAPTER THREE

1 Plato, *Republic* VI.508a [*Plato: Complete Works*, ed. John M. Cooper (Indianapolis: Hackett Publishing Co., 1997), 1128].
2 Aristotle, *De Interpretatione* I.16a [*The Complete Works of Aristotle*, ed. Jonathan Barnes, 2 vols. (Princeton: Princeton University Press, 1984), 1:25].
3 Thomas Aquinas, *Questiones de veritate* q.1.a.1 [*The Disputed Questions on Truth*, trans. Robert W. Mulligan, 3 vols. (Chicago: H. Regnery Co., 1952–54), 1:6].
4 Descartes, Letter to Mersenne, October 16, 1639, AT 2:597 [*The Philosophical Writings of Descartes*, trans. John Cottingham, Robert Stoothoff, and Dugald Murdoch, 3 vols. (Cambridge: Cambridge University Press, 1984–91), 3:139].
5 Kant, *Critique of Pure Reason*, AK 3:79 [*Critique of Pure Reason*, trans. Paul Guyer and Allen W. Wood (New York: Cambridge University Press, 1998), 195].
6 Parmenides, *Poem*, respectively, fragments DK B VIII, 43, 31, and 29; VI, 2 and 3; VII, 2; VIII, 17 [*Early Greek Philosophy, Volume 5: Western Greek Thinkers, Part 2*, ed. and trans. André Laks and Glenn W. Most (Cambridge, MA: Harvard University Press, 2016), 49, 47, 43, 45]. Translation altered—Trans.
7 Compare Charles Mugler, *Dictionnaire historique de la terminologie optique des Grecs* (Paris: Klincksieck, 1964), 241: "λανθάνειν—Verbal expression often synonymous with the passives of καγύπτειν, κρύπτειν, and their compounds, indicating that an object goes unnoticed behind opaque objects or under the cover of night."

8 Homer, *Iliad* XII.390 [Homer, *The Iliad*, trans. Robert Fagles (New York: Penguin Books, 1990), 338].

9 Plato, *Republic* IV.427d [*Plato: Complete Works*, 1059].

10 GA 54:25 [*Parmenides*, 17].

11 Democritus, fragment DK B 131 [*Early Greek Philosophy, Volume 7: Later Ionian and Athenian Thinkers, Part 2*, ed. and trans. André Laks and Glenn W. Most (Cambridge, MA: Harvard University Press, 2016), 355].

12 GA 54:26 [*Parmenides*, 18].

13 Plato, *Phaedrus* 248b [*Plato: Complete Works*, 526].

14 GA 9:191 [*Pathmarks*, 146].

15 GA 34:10–11 [*The Essence of Truth: On Plato's Cave Allegory and Theaetetus*, 7–8].

16 Anaximander, fragments DK B 1–3 [*Early Greek Philosophy, Volume 2: Beginnings and Early Ionian Thinkers, Part 1*, ed. and trans. André Laks and Glenn W. Most (Cambridge, MA: Harvard University Press, 2016), 282–85].

17 We translate *Un-wesen* and *Un-wahrheit* by "in-truth" and "in-essance" to stress that it is simultaneously a matter of the adversarial element of essance and truth (*in-* as negative prefix) as well as the element "in" which essance and truth unfold (*in-* as locative prefix).

18 GA 9:193 [*Pathmarks*, 148].

19 GA 9:193–94 [*Pathmarks*, 148].

20 GA 7:212–13 [*Early Greek Thinking*, 71].

21 GA 5:48 [*Off the Beaten Track*, 36].

22 GA 9:194 [*Pathmarks*, 148].

23 Anaxagoras, DK B 14 [*Early Greek Philosophy, Volume 6: Later Ionian and Athenian Thinkers, Part 1*, ed. and trans. André Laks and Glenn W. Most (Cambridge, MA: Harvard University Press, 2016), 73].

24 GA 14:80 [*On Time and Being*, 65].

25 Heraclitus, fragments DK B 90, 30, 31, and 66 [*Early Greek Philosophy, Volume 3: Early Ionian Thinkers, Part 2*, ed. and trans. André Laks and Glenn W. Most (Cambridge, MA: Harvard University Press, 2016), 179]. Translation altered—Trans.

26 Fragment DK B 64 [*Early Greek Philosophy*, 3:177].

27 GA 39:135 and 173 [*Hölderlin's Hymns: "Germania" and "The Rhine,"* 120 and 158].

28 GA 70:79.

29 GA 68:48 [*Hegel*, 39].

30 GA 68:29 [*Hegel*, 22].

31 GA 4:63 [*Elucidations of Hölderlin's Poetry*, 85].

32 GA 5:33 [*Off the Beaten Track*, 25].

33 Heraclitus, fragment DK B 103 [*Early Greek Philosophy*, 3:163].

34 GA 68:45 [*Hegel*, 36]. The topology of Beyng therefore requires distinguishing (1) non-Being [*le non-être*] = the highest being (i.e., the being, other than Being, that becomes estranged from its essance) = the ground (*Grund*); (2) the nothing [*le rien*] = non-being [*le non-étant*] = Being (*Sein*); and (3) Nothingness = the originary = the depths, or abyss (*Abgrund*) = Beyng (*Seyn*). Taken in this last sense, "Nothingness is neither negative nor a 'goal.' Instead, it is the essantial trembling of Beyng itself and therefore *is* more than any being" (GA 65:266 [*Contributions to Philosophy (Of the Event)*, 209]; "*the Beyng-historical concept of 'Nothingness'*—the abyss as the essance of Beyng [*der Ab-grund als Wesen des Seyns*]" (GA 66:312 [*Mindfulness*, 278]. Translation altered—Trans.

35 Heraclitus, fragments DK B 123 (and DK B 93) [*Early Greek Philosophy*, 3:155 and 157].

36 GA 6.2:319 [*Nietzsche*, 4:214]. "Ab-stention" here translates *das Ausbleiben* (literally: to stay away, to fail to appear), to be understood as a "holding oneself back," "standing in absence."

37 GA 9:194 [*Pathmarks*, 148].

38 GA 16:528 [*Discourse on Thinking*, 55].

39 GA 6.2:334 [*Nietzsche*, 4:226].

40 GA 65:78 [*Contributions to Philosophy (Of the Event)*, 63].

41 GA 39:119 [*Hölderlin's Hymns: "Germania" and "The Rhine,"* 108].

42 GA 14:17–18 [*On Time and Being*, 13].

43 GA 54:112 [*Parmenides*, 76]. Compare Jean-François Marquet, "Mort, mystère et oubli dans la pensée de Heidegger," in *Restitutions. Études d'histoire de la philosophie allemande* (Paris: Vrin, 2001), 281.

44 GA 4:165 [*Elucidations of Hölderlin's Poetry*, 190].

45 Charles Baudelaire, "The Death of the Poor," in *The Flowers of Evil*, trans. William Aggeler (Fresno, CA: Academy Library Guild, 1954), 443.

46 GA 79:18 [*Bremen and Freiburg Lectures*, 17].

47 GA 4:55 [*Elucidations of Hölderlin's Poetry*, 77].

48 It could even be possible that mourning is the essance of phenomenality such as it was thought by Husserl. The phenomenon is the correlation of an ideal signification with an intuitive filling-in: but if every ideality proceeds from an archaic originary intuition of which it is only the remnant [*survivance*], then the work of mourning (as idealizing internalization of the lost object) is the very establishment of idealities; their maintenance in (and as) the interiority of the subject is the memory and the safeguard of this absence. The quest for the verification of ideality by an intuitive filling-in is the search for the return to presence (parousia) of this initial death. Derrida gave precious indications in this direction in "*Fors*: The Anglish Words of Nicolas Abraham and Maria Torok," trans. Barbara Johnson, foreword to Nicolas Abraham and Maria Torok, *The Wolf Man's Magic Word: A Cryptonymy* (Minneapolis: University of Minnesota Press, 1986), xi–xlviii, and in *Specters of Marx: The State of the Debt, the Work of Mourning and the New International* (New York: Routledge, 1994). Philosophy itself is perhaps nothing other than the mourning of an originary wisdom.

49 GA 65:350 [*Contributions to Philosophy (Of the Event)*, 277].

50 GA 8:21 [*What Is Called Thinking?*, 19].

51 GA 69:222 [*The History of Beyng*, 187].

52 GA 65:340 [*Contributions to Philosophy (Of the Event)*, 269].

53 GA 9:194 [*Pathmarks*, 149].

54 GA 11:59 [*Identity and Difference*, 50].

55 GA 66:96 [*Mindfulness*, 80]. Translation altered—Trans.

56 GA 66:201–2 [*Mindfulness*, 177]. Translation altered—Trans.

57 GA 9:195 [*Pathmarks*, 149].

58 Arthur Rimbaud, "Clearance," in *Illuminations*, trans. John Ashbery (New York: W.W. Norton and Company, 2011), 125. On Rimbaud's work as a poetics of excess, see Jérôme Thélot, *La poésie excédée. Rimbaud* (Les Cabannes: Fissile, 2008).

59 GA 39:240–41 [*Hölderlin's Hymns: "Germania" and "The Rhine,"* 218–19].

60 GA 55:137 [*Heraclitus*, 104].

61 GA 39:64 [*Hölderlin's Hymns: "Germania" and "The Rhine,"* 59].

62 GA 66:128 [*Mindfulness*, 108].

63 GA 6.2:319 [*Nietzsche*, 4:214]. Translation altered—Trans.

64 GA 68:46 [*Hegel*, 37].

65 GA 66:187–88 and 192–93, respectively [*Mindfulness*, 166 and 170].
66 GA 4:63 [*Elucidations of Hölderlin's Poetry*, 85]. Translation altered—Trans.
67 GA 4:146 [*Elucidations of Hölderlin's Poetry*, 167].
68 GA 65:422 and 430, respectively [*Contributions to Philosophy (Of the Event)*, 334 and 340].
69 GA 4:77 [*Elucidations of Hölderlin's Poetry*, 98].
70 GA 4:171 [*Elucidations of Hölderlin's Poetry*, 195].
71 GA 4:93 [*Elucidations of Hölderlin's Poetry*, 117].
72 GA 39:3–4 [*Hölderlin's Hymns: "Germania" and "The Rhine,"* 3].
73 GA 5:64 [*Off the Beaten Track*, 48].
74 GA 39:247 [*Hölderlin's Hymns: "Germania" and "The Rhine,"* 225]. Translation altered—Trans.
75 GA 4:76 [*Elucidations of Hölderlin's Poetry*, 97].
76 GA: 68:14 [*Hegel*, 11].
77 GA 9:196 [*Pathmarks*, 150].
78 GA 54:38–39 [*Parmenides*, 26].
79 GA 9:199 [*Pathmarks*, 152].
80 GA 9:196 [*Pathmarks*, 150].
81 GA 9:197 [*Pathmarks*, 150].
82 GA 9:196 [*Pathmarks*, 150].
83 GA 5:337 [*Off the Beaten Track*, 253–54].
84 GA 9:197–98 [*Pathmarks*, 150–51].
85 GA 65:132 [*Contributions to Philosophy (Of the Event)*, 104].
86 GA 34:120 [*The Essence of Truth: On Plato's Cave Allegory and Theaetetus*, 87].
87 GA 65:119 [*Contributions to Philosophy (Of the Event)*, 94].
88 GA 65:115 [*Contributions to Philosophy (Of the Event)*, 91].
89 GA 65:125 [*Contributions to Philosophy (Of the Event)*, 99]. Translation altered—Trans.
90 GA 69:71 [*The History of Beyng*, 61].
91 GA 34:146 [*The Essence of Truth: On Plato's Cave Allegory and Theaetetus*, 105]. Translation altered—Trans.
92 GA 7:75 [*The End of Philosophy*, 90].
93 GA 45:197 [*Basic Questions of Philosophy*, trans. Richard Rojcewicz and André Schuwer (Bloomington: Indiana University Press, 1994), 169]. Translation altered—Trans.
94 GA 65:21 (*Contributions to Philosophy (Of the Event)*, 19].
95 Letter to Elisabeth Blochmann, April 12, 1938, in *Briefwechsel*, 91.
96 GA 45:159 [*Basic Questions of Philosophy*, 138].
97 GA 39:140 [*Hölderlin's Hymns: "Germania" and "The Rhine,"* 124].
98 GA 65:57 [*Contributions to Philosophy (Of the Event)*, 46].
99 GA 66:47 [*Mindfulness*, 39].
100 GA 79:72 [*Bremen and Freiburg Lectures*, 68].
101 GA 7:29 [*The Question concerning Technology*, 28].
102 GA 40:42 [*Introduction to Metaphysics*, 43]. Translation altered—Trans.
103 GA 65:186 [*Contributions to Philosophy (Of the Event)*, 146].
104 GA 5:335 [*Off the Beaten Track*, 253].
105 GA 14:63, 88, and 90, respectively [*On Time and Being*, 53, 71, and 73].
106 GA 65:338 [*Contributions to Philosophy (Of the Event)*, 268].
107 GA 65:356 [*Contributions to Philosophy (Of the Event)*, 281].
108 GA 65:90 [*Contributions to Philosophy (Of the Event)*, 72].
109 GA 65:246 [*Contributions to Philosophy (Of the Event)*, 194].

110 GA 65:350 [*Contributions to Philosophy (Of the Event)*, 277].
111 GA 65:348 [*Contributions to Philosophy (Of the Event)*, 275].
112 GA 5:348 [*Off the Beaten Track*, 262].
113 GA 5:286 [*Off the Beaten Track*, 233].
114 GA 9:198 [*Pathmarks*, 151].
115 GA 79:26 [*Bremen and Freiburg Lectures*, 25]. Compare Damien Le Guay, *Qu'avons-nous perdu en perdant la mort?* (Paris: Cerf, 2003) and *La mort en cendres. La crémation aujourd'hui* (Paris: Cerf, 2012). Le Guay calls into question the "zero degree of the funeral" reached by contemporary societies, and shows that "individuals think, in their lifetime, that they are redundant to the point of accepting, once dead, that they will end up as final waste." An article published in *Le Monde*, October 30, 2012, described the contemporary forms of death management and concluded: "No funeral homes, no religious ceremonies, no burials . . . What was until recently the greatest of indignities in the West, reserved for witches or the worst miscreants, is becoming a social norm." The disappearance of the cult of the dead and funerary rites is *much more* than a step backward for civilization.
116 GA 4:24 [*Elucidations of Hölderlin's Poetry*, 43]. Here we (awkwardly) translate *entschleiern* with "unmask," in order to reserve "unveil" for *enthüllen*.
117 GA 54:93 [*Parmenides*, 63].
118 GA 65:227 [*Contributions to Philosophy (Of the Event)*, 179].
119 GA 7:34 [*The Question concerning Technology*, 33].
120 GA 6.2:20 [*Nietzsche*, 3:181].
121 GA 68:46 [*Hegel*, 37].
122 GA 6.2:333 [*Nietzsche*, 4:226].
123 GA 6.2:334 [*Nietzsche*, 4:227]. Translation altered—Trans.
124 GA 6.2:347 [*Nietzsche*, 4:239].
125 A reference to Jacques Derrida's notion of différance—Trans.
126 GA 5:33 [*Off the Beaten Track*, 25].
127 GA 6.2:332 [*Nietzsche*, 4:225].
128 GA 6.2:350–51 [*Nietzsche*, 4:241–42]. Translation altered—Trans.
129 GA 6.2:355–56 [*Nietzsche*, 4:245–46].
130 GA 8:10 [*What Is Called Thinking?*, 9].
131 GA 14:50 [*On Time and Being*, 41].
132 GA 39:173 [*Hölderlin's Hymns: "Germania" and "The Rhine,"* 158].
133 GA 11:59 [*Identity and Difference*, 50].
134 GA 54:2 [*Parmenides*, 1].
135 GA 7:71 [*The End of Philosophy*, 86].
136 GA 5:327 [*Off the Beaten Track*, 246].
137 This concept has been established in recent philosophical discourse, first and foremost in the work of Günther Anders, who noticed as early as 1956 that "modern man is in a situation of apocalyptic danger" (*L'obsolescence de l'homme. Sur l'âme à l'époque de la deuxième révolution industrielle*, 264) and devoted himself to thinking "the technological apocalypse" (*L'obsolescence de l'homme 2. Sur la destruction de la vie à l'époque de la troisième révolution industrielle* [Paris: Éditions Fario, 2011], 274), but also in that of Hans Jonas, who was similarly confronted with the "apocalyptic potential of our technology" and tried to devise an ethics for a time when "power has become self-acting, while its promise has turned into threat, its prospect of salvation into apocalypse" (*The Imperative of Responsibility*, trans. Hans Jonas with David Herr [Chicago: University of Chicago Press, 1984], 202 and 141). Starting from *La mobilisation*

totale ([Paris: Gallimard, 1990], 139), Ernst Jünger evoked "an apocalyptic world, the sight of which would freeze the heart of the most intrepid"; more recently, Peter Sloterdijk defined our time as the "apocalypse of reality" ("La politique de Heidegger. Reporter la fin de l'Histoire," in G. Bensussan and J. Cohen, eds., *Heidegger. Le danger et la promesse* [Paris: Kimé, 2006], 153), and noted that "it is neither our fault, nor to our credit if we live in an epoch where the apocalypse of humanity is an everyday thing" (*La domestication de l'être* [Paris: Mille et Une Nuits, 2000], 106); Slavoj Žižek has shown how "the global capitalist system is approaching an apocalyptic zero-point" (*Living in the End Times* [New York: Verso, 2010], x); and Philippe Muray has observed with his unfailing clairvoyance that "it is every day or nearly so that the apocalypse strikes and destroys, it is every day that we have abundant proof of the ongoing mutation of humanity" ("Apocalypse," in *Causes toujours* [Paris: Descartes & Cie, 2013], 107).

CHAPTER FOUR

1 Modern thought itself has been confronted with "Monstrosity" (GA 79:29 [*Bremen and Freiburg Lectures*, 28]), and to that end it has had recourse to the names of the Beast: first in Hobbes, who calls the State "Leviathan," but also in Marx, who addresses Capital as "Moloch" (for example, *A Contribution to the Critique of Political Economy*, MEW 13:40 [CW 29:294]); in Nietzsche, who sees nihilism as a "sacrifice in front of the Moloch of abstraction" (KSA 6:177 [*The Anti-Christ, Ecce Homo, Twilight of the Idols, and Other Writings*, trans. Judith Norman, ed. Aaron Ridley and Judith Norman (Cambridge: Cambridge University Press, 2005), 10]); in Husserl, who defines modern political danger by the coming of the "Moloch of the idea of power" (Hua 27:117); in Anders as well, who defines Machinery as "Behemoth" (*Le temps de la fin* [Paris: L'Herne, 2007], 62–63); Bernanos, who evokes "the technological Moloch" (*Essais et écrits de combat II*, 991), or Jünger, who wrote: "The communications System, one of the idols of the modern era, is a Moloch" (*Soixante-dix s'efface. Journal 1965–1970*, trans. Henry Plard [Paris: Gallimard, 1984], 340). There is a secret connection between the visions of the *Apocalypse* and our epoch, which Cioran noted in *Drawn and Quartered*: "What was envisioned on Patmos we shall see with our own eyes one of these days, we shall distinctly perceive that sun 'black as sackcloth of hair,' and that moon of blood, those stars falling like figs, that sun 'departing as a scroll when it is rolled together.' Our anxiety echoes that of the Seer, whom we are closer to than were our forebears, including those who wrote on him [. . .] The semiliterate Evangelist saw more clearly than his learned commentator, adherent of modern superstitions" (*Drawn and Quartered* [New York: Arcade Publishing, 2012], 90).

2 Modern criticism distinguishes, in the New Testament, between authentic and pseudepigraphic texts. This distinction rests, however, upon a hermeneutic fully based on the regime of truth—objectivism, scientism, and positivism—that it is here a question of leaving: "With the completion of modernity history [*Geschichte*] capitulates to historiology [*Historie*], which is of the same essential stamp as technology," thus wrote Heidegger (GA 6.2:19 [*Nietzsche*, 3:180]). The quest for an "other truth" therefore demands receiving the New Testament corpus as is, albeit on a provisional and methodical basis, since fixing a "canon of truth" (κανῶν τῆς ἀληθείας: Irenaeus of Lyons, *Against Heresies*, 1.9.4; PG 7, 545) is involved in the inaugural configuration of a truth.

3 Homer, *Iliad* 5.23 [*The Iliad*, trans. Robert Fagles, 165] and *Odyssey* 5.352 [*The Odyssey*, trans. Emily Wilson (New York: W.W. Norton, 2018), 191].

4 Compare Mugler, *Dictionnaire historique de la terminologie optique des Grecs*, 214.

5 GA 14:88 [*On Time and Being*, 71].

6 GA 65:229 [*Contributions to Philosophy (Of the Event)*, 180–81].

7 Giorgio Agamben begins his book *The Time That Remains: A Commentary on the Letter to the Romans*, trans. Patricia Dailey (Stanford, CA: Stanford University Press, 2005) by affirming that between Paul's Epistles and our epoch there is a sort of secret encounter that we must not miss at any cost. And this is indeed what contemporary philosophy bears witness to, with Bernard Sichère in *Le jour est proche. La révolution selon Paul* (Paris: Desclée de Brouwer, 2003); Slavoj Žižek in *The Fragile Absolute: Or, Why Is the Christian Legacy Worth Fighting For?* (New York: Verso, 2000); Alain Badiou in *Saint Paul: The Foundation of Universalism*, trans. Ray Brassier (Stanford, CA: Stanford University Press, 2003). Let us recall that the philosophical interpretation of the Epistles of Saint Paul in the 1920–21 course entitled *The Phenomenology of Religious Life* (GA 60 [*The Phenomenology of Religious Life*, trans. Matthias Fritsch and Jennifer Anna Gosetti-Ferencei (Bloomington: Indiana University Press, 2004)]) is a point of departure for Heidegger's path.

8 Compare Pascal (second letter to Mlle de Roannez, October 1656): "All things cover some mystery. All things have veils that cover God" (in *Blaise Pascal: Thoughts, Letters, Minor Works*, ed. Charles W. Eliot [New York: P. F. Collier & Son Co., 1910], 349), and Chateaubriand, who suggested that temporality itself, as finitude, is this veil: "Oh, but there is more to life than that! If, from the shores of this world, we do not discern divine things clearly, we should not be surprised. Time is a veil between ourselves and God" (*Memoirs from Beyond the Grave: 1768–1800*, trans. Alex Andriesse [New York: New York Review Books, 2018], 432).

9 Compare Oscar Cullmann, *Christ and Time: The Primitive Christian Conception of Time and History*, trans. Floyd V. Wilson (Philadelphia: Westminster Press, 1964).

10 Eudemus, DK B 34.

11 Compare Victor Goldschmidt, *Le système stoïcien et l'idée de temps* (Paris: Vrin, 1953).

12 These are precisely the arguments that led Celsus to reject the Incarnation on behalf of the theory of the eternal return: "because things happen in cycles, what is happening now [. . .] happened before and will happen again" (*On the True Doctrine: A Discourse Against the Christians*, trans. R Joseph Hoffman [New York: Oxford University Press, 1987], 82).

13 For a thorough philosophical thematization of the truth proper to Christianity, one can only refer to Michel Henry, *I Am the Truth: Toward a Philosophy of Christianity* (Stanford, CA: Stanford University Press, 2002).

14 Nietzsche, KSA 3:13 [*Daybreak: Thoughts on the Prejudices of Morality*, trans. R. J. Hollingdale, ed. Maudemarie Clark and Brian Leiter (Cambridge: Cambridge University Press, 1997), 2].

15 Nietzsche, KSA 5:12 [*Beyond Good and Evil: Prelude to a Philosophy of the Future*, trans. Judith Norman, ed. Rolf-Peter Horstmann and Judith Norman (Cambridge: Cambridge University Press, 2002), 2–3].

16 Compare, for example, John Chrysostom ("ἀληθὴς φιλοσοφία": *Ad. pop. Antoich.* 19.1 [PG 49:189] and *Adv. opp. vitæ monast.* 3.19 [PG 47:382]).

17 Plato, *Phaedo* 99c [*Plato: Complete Works*, 85].

18 Plato, *Republic* VI.508a [*Republic*, trans. C. D. C. Reeve (Indianapolis: Hackett Publishing Co., 2004), 203].

19 Plato, *Republic* VI.509b [*Republic*, trans. Reeve, 205]. This is why the Incarnation remains inconceivable for metaphysics, which makes λόγος a universal and objective reality (οὐσία) laid as a foundation, precisely because it ignores and represses all that relates to the faulty finitude of the flesh. Thus the Greco-Roman philosophers, loyal to Plato who denied "the

body's folly" (*Phaedo* 67a [*Plato: Complete Works*, 58]) and distinguished "the divine Beauty" from the beauty "polluted by human flesh or colors or any other great nonsense of mortality" (*Symposium*, 212a [*Plato: Complete Works*, 494), attacked Christianity on this precise point, by opposing the perfection of the celestial sphere to this miserable thing that is the human body. Compare, for example, Porphyry's *Against the Christians*, ed. R. Joseph Hoffman (Amherst, NY: Prometheus Books, 1994), 86–87: "Even if someone among the Greeks were silly enough to think that gods dwelled in statues, his idea would be more sensible than that of a man who believes that the Divine Being entered into the womb of the virginal Mary to become her unborn son—and then was born, swaddled, [hauled off] to the place of blood and gall, and all the rest of it"; or Celsus, *On the True Doctrine: A Discourse Against the Christians*, trans. R. Joseph Hoffman (New York: Oxford University Press, 1987), 77–78: "God is that which is beautiful and happy and exists within himself in the most perfect of all conceivable states. This means that God is changeless. A god who comes down to men undergoes change—a change from good to bad; from beautiful to shameful; from happiness to misfortune; from what is perfect to what is wicked. Now what sort of a god would choose a change like that?"

20 Heidegger, GA 5:60 [*Off the Beaten Track*, 45].

21 Parmenides, *Poem*, fragment DK B I, 10 [*Early Greek Philosophy*, 5:33].

22 Aeschylus, *The Libation Bearers* 811 [*Aeschylus*, ed. and trans. Alan H. Sommerstein, 3 vols. (Cambridge, MA: Harvard University Press, 2008), 2:315].

23 Parmenides, *Poem*, fragments DK B I, 9 and 11 [*Early Greek Philosophy*, 5:33–35].

24 Parmenides, *Poem*, fragments DK B VIII, 17–18 [*Early Greek Philosophy*, 5:45].

25 Parmenides, *Poem*, fragment DK B VI, 2 [*Early Greek Philosophy*, 5:41]. Translation altered—Trans.

26 Heraclitus, fragment DK B 123 [*Early Greek Philosophy*, 3:154].

CHAPTER FIVE

1 Compare Nietzsche, KSA 5:127–28 [*Beyond Good and Evil*, §203, 92]: "The *total degeneration of humanity* down to what today's socialist fools and nitwits see as their 'man of the future'—as their ideal!—this degeneration and diminution of humanity into the perfect herd animal (or, as they say, into man in a 'free society'), this brutalizing process of turning humanity into stunted little animals with equal rights and equal claims is no doubt *possible*! Anyone who has ever thought this possibility through to the end knows one more disgust than other men." Philippe Muray has meticulously documented this degeneration, which demands disgust as the essantial mood of thought: but just as much shame.

2 GA 8:31 [*What Is Called Thinking?*, 30].

3 GA 7:93 and 70 [*The End of Philosophy*, 106 and 85].

4 Nietzsche, KSA 4:380 [*Thus Spoke Zarathustra*, trans. Adrian Del Caro, ed. Adrian Del Caro and Robert B. Pippin (Cambridge: Cambridge University Pres, 2006), 248].

5 An article published in the journal *Nature* in November 2012 shows that 70 percent of the planet's trees are threatened with dieback; the rapid acidification of sea waters (by absorbing CO_2), together with the overexploitation of halieutic reserves (by industrial fishing) and the formation of vast dead zones at the mouth of major rivers (where fertilizer and pesticides spill out) threaten the oceanic ecosystem with imminent collapse; according to a study in the English medical journal *The Lancet* from December 2012, atmospheric pollution already causes 3.2 million deaths per year (compared to 800,000 in 2000); according to Edward O. Wilson

(*The Future of Life* [New York: Vintage Books, 2002]), at least half of all the species alive on earth will have disappeared before the end of the century, and so on. Pascal Bruckner's essay (*The Fanaticism of the Apocalypse: Save the Earth, Punish Human Beings* [Malden, MA: Polity Press, 2013]) has the sole merit of clearly showing "the blindness in the face of the apocalypse" in which Günther Anders (*L'obsolescence de l'homme*, 308) had seen the nodal point of contemporary ideology.

6 GA 79:4 [*Bremen and Freiburg Lectures*, 4]. Compare Günther Anders, *Le temps de la fin* (Paris: l'Herne, 2007).

7 GA 16:528 [*Discourse on Thinking*, 56].

8 Karl Marx, *Neue Rheinische Zeitung*, April 1850, MEW 7:272 [CW 10:316].

9 GA 16:525 [*Discourse on Thinking*, 52].

10 GA 69:23 [*The History of Beyng*, 22].

11 GA 66:194 [*Mindfulness*, 171].

12 The apocalyptic event is in itself revolutionary, in the sense that Marx conceived it. The Apocalypse of John is a symbolic poem in which mythological figures designate historiological powers: the Beast symbolizes imperial political power, and the Great Whore economic power (compare, for example, Richard Bauckham, *The Theology of the Book of Revelation* [New York: Cambridge University Press, 1993], 35–36). The apocalyptic moment occurs when the Great Whore "who corrupted the earth with her fornication" (19:2) rides the Beast (17:3) and exercises its "authority over every tribe and people and language and nation" (13:7). The crisis (κρίσις) is then the time "for destroying those who destroy the earth" (11:18), and for judging the Whore: "he has avenged on her the blood of his servants" (19:2). Marx himself compared Capital to the Beast, and cites several times (for example, *Capital*, MEW 23:101 [*Capital, Volume 1*, trans. Ben Fowkes (New York: Penguin Books, 1981), 181]) the same two verses of the Book of Revelation: "These are united in yielding their power and authority to the Beast" (17:13); and "no one can buy or sell who does not have the mark, that is, the name of the Beast or the number of its name" (13:17). Compare Hugo Assmann, "Marx et l'usage des symboles bibliques," in Hugo Assmann and Franz Hinkelammert, *L'idolâtrie de marché. Critique théologique de l'économie de marché* (Paris: Cerf, 1993), 327 and following.

13 GA 77:110 [*Country Path Conversations*, trans. Bret W. Davis (Bloomington: Indiana University Press, 2010), 71].

14 Philippe Lacoue-Labarthe, *Heidegger, Art, and Politics: The Fiction of the Political* (Hoboken, NJ: Blackwell, 1990), 35.

15 GA 7:75 [*The End of Philosophy*, 90].

16 GA 5:353 [*Off the Beaten Track*, 266].

17 GA 79:51 [*Bremen and Freiburg Lectures*, 48].

18 Thus Rimbaud, when he observes in *A Season in Hell* (*Arthur Rimbaud: Complete Works*, 239): "I can see that my troubles come from not realizing soon enough that this is the Western World," recognizes immediately that "the mind is in control, it insists that I remain in the West."

19 GA 65:132 [*Contributions to Philosophy (Of the Event)*, 104].

20 GA 39:173 [*Hölderlin's Hymns: "Germania" and "The Rhine,"* 158].

21 GA 40:172 [*Introduction to Metaphysics*, 181].

22 GA 70:79.

23 GA 40:172 [*Introduction to Metaphysics*, 182]. Translation altered—Trans.

24 Pascal, *Pensées*, Laf. §114 (Br. §558) [*Pensées*, 29].

25 GA 40:170 [*Introduction to Metaphysics*, 179–81].

26 GA 53:89 [*Hölderlin's Hymn "The Ister,"* trans. William McNeill and Julia Davis (Bloomington: Indiana University Press, 1996), 72].

27 GA 39:200 [*Hölderlin's Hymns: "Germania" and "The Rhine,"* 182–83].

28 GA 51:80 [*Basic Concepts*, trans. Gary E. Aylesworth (Bloomington: Indiana University Press, 1993), 68].

29 GA 39:74 [*Hölderlin's Hymns: "Germania" and "The Rhine,"* 67].

30 GA 51:82 [*Basic Concepts*, 70].

31 GA 53:94 [*Hölderlin's Hymn "The Ister,"* 77].

32 GA 66:47 [*Mindfulness*, 39]. Translation altered—Trans.

33 GA 8:45 [*What Is Called Thinking?*, 42].

34 GA 10:71 [*The Principle of Reason*, 48]. Translation altered—Trans.

35 GA 66:47 [*Mindfulness*, 39]. Translation altered—Trans.

36 GA 79:70 [*Bremen and Freiburg Lectures*, 66]; Meister Eckhart, DW 5:198 [*Meister Eckhart: The Essential Sermons, Commentaries, Treatises, and Defense* (trans. and ed. Edmund College and Bernard McGinn [New York: Paulist Press, 1981], 250–51].

37 GA 14:70–71 [*On Time and Being*, 57].

38 GA 65:436 [*Contributions to Philosophy (Of the Event)*, 344].

39 GA 5:353 [*Off the Beaten Track*, 266].

40 To take the title of the trilogy that Hans Urs von Balthasar published in the 1930s, *Apokalypse der deutschen Seele* (Salzburg/Leipzig: Verlag Pustet, 1937–39).

41 GA 65:90 and 229 [*Contributions to Philosophy (Of the Event)*, 72 and 181].

42 GA 6.2:355 [*Nietzsche*, 4:245].

43 GA 5:60 [*Off the Beaten Track*, 45].

44 GA 40:166 [*Introduction to Metaphysics*, 175].

45 GA 5:64 [*Off the Beaten Track*, 47–48].

46 GA 40:166 [*Introduction to Metaphysics*, 175].

47 Rimbaud, "Cities [II]," and "Childhood," in *Illuminations*, 79 and 31.

48 GA 40:168 [*Introduction to Metaphysics*, 180]. Translation altered—Trans.

49 GA 5:63 [*Off the Beaten Track*, 47–48]. Translation altered—Trans.

50 GA 40:200 [*Introduction to Metaphysics*, 213].

51 GA 40:168 [*Introduction to Metaphysics*, 178].

52 Rimbaud, "Cities [II]," in *Illuminations*, 79. Translation altered—Trans.

53 GA 40:181 [*Introduction to Metaphysics*, 191]. Translation altered—Trans.

54 GA 5:63 [*Off the Beaten Track*, 47].

55 GA 40:140 [*Introduction to Metaphysics*, 146].

56 GA 40:140 [*Introduction to Metaphysics*, 146].

57 GA 5:65 [*Off the Beaten Track*, 49].

58 GA 39:99 [*Hölderlin's Hymns: "Germania" and "The Rhine,"* 89–90].

59 Rimbaud, Letter to Paul Démeny, May 15, 1871, in *Rimbaud: Complete Works, Selected Letters*, trans. Wallace Fowlie (Chicago: University of Chicago Press, 2005), 377.

60 GA 40:172 [*Introduction to Metaphysics*, 182].

61 Heraclitus, fragments DK B 64 and 66 [*Early Greek Philosophy*, 3:177 and 179.

62 Rimbaud, Letter to Paul Démeny, May 15, 1871, in *Rimbaud: Complete Works, Selected Letters*, 377.

63 "Lucifer" means etymologically "the one who carries the light," "the one who brings clarity" (from the Latin *lux*, *lucis*, "light," and *ferre*, "to bring").

64 GA 66:135 [*Mindfulness*, 115]. Compare Jean-François Marquet, "Quinze regards sur la métaphysique," in *Heidegger*, ed. Maxence Caron (Paris: Cerf, 2006), 536–37. Translation altered—Trans.

65 GA 9:333 [*Pathmarks*, 254].

66 GA 39:69 [*Hölderlin's Hymns: "Germania" and "The Rhine,"* 63]. Translation altered—Trans.

67 GA 38:168 [*Logic as the Question concerning the Essence of Language*, 140].

68 GA 38:170 [*Logic as the Question concerning the Essence of Language*, 141–42].

69 GA 40:170 [*Introduction to Metaphysics*, 180].

70 Rimbaud, Letter to his family, August 4, 1888, in *Rimbaud: Complete Works, Selected Letters*, 437.

71 GA 39:55–56 [*Hölderlin's Hymns: "Germania" and "The Rhine,"* 53]. Translation altered—Trans.

72 GA 29/30:270–71 [*Fundamental Concepts of Metaphysics*, 182–83].

73 GA 39:62 [*Hölderlin's Hymns: "Germania" and "The Rhine,"* 58].

74 GA 4:46 [*Elucidations of Hölderlin's Poetry*, 63]. Translation altered—Trans.

75 GA 5:64 [*Off the Beaten Track*, 48].

76 GA 5:62–63 [*Off the Beaten Track*, 47]. Translation altered—Trans.

77 GA 5:60 [*Off the Beaten Track*, 45].

78 GA 10:139 [*The Principle of Reason*, 93].

79 GA 39:196 [*Hölderlin's Hymns: "Germania" and "The Rhine,"* 179].

80 Heraclitus, fragment DK B 75 [*Early Greek Philosophy*, 3:263]. The fragment is reported to us by Marcus Aurelius (*Meditations* 6.42), who explained it in this way: "We are all fellow-workers towards the fulfilment of one object, some of us knowingly and intelligently, others blindly; just as Heraclitus, I think, says that *even when they sleep men are workers* and fellow-agents in all that goes on in the world" (*Marcus Aurelius*, ed. and trans. C. R. Haines [Cambridge, MA: Harvard University Press, 2014], 153). Hence one see that Marx's call comes from afar: it is the wake-up call for those who are asleep.

81 Rimbaud, "Scenes," in *Illuminations*, 141.

82 Letter to Paul Démeny, May 15, 1871, in *Rimbaud: Complete Works, Selected Letters*, 377.

83 Letter to Paul Démeny, May 15, 1871, in *Rimbaud: Complete Works, Selected Letters*, 379.

84 GA 4:114 [*Elucidations of Hölderlin's Poetry*, 136].

CHAPTER SIX

1 Parmenides, *Poem*, fragment DK B VIII, 29 [*Early Greek Philosophy*, 5:47]. Translation altered—Trans.

2 Parmenides, *Poem*, fragment DK B VIII, 17 [*Early Greek Philosophy*, 5:45].

3 GA 55:365 [*Heraclitus*, 273].

4 GA 65:369 [*Contributions to Philosophy (Of the Event)*, 291–92]. Translation altered—Trans.

5 GA 9:319 [*Pathmarks*, 243].

6 GA 6.2:332 [*Nietzsche*, 4:225].

7 GA 14:50 [*On Time and Being*, 41].

8 GA 55:365 [*Heraclitus*, 273].

9 GA 65:229 [*Contributions to Philosophy (Of the Event)*, 181].

10 GA 7:234 [*Early Greek Thinking*, 78].

11 GA 6.2:353 [*Nietzsche*, 4:243–44].

12 GA 9:408 [*Pathmarks*, 309].

13 GA 6.2:319–20 [*Nietzsche*, 4:215].

14 GA 4:30 [*Elucidations of Hölderlin's Poetry*, 48].

15 GA 39:250–51 [*Hölderlin's Hymns: "Germania" and "The Rhine,"* 227].

16 Rimbaud is undoubtedly, with Hölderlin, the purest of apocalyptic poets: compare Jean-Pierre Richard, *Poésie et profondeur* (Paris: Seuil, 1955), 209; and Marc Eigeldinger, "L'Apocalypse dans les *Illuminations*," in *Revue d'histoire littéraire de la France* 2 (1987): 182 and following.

17 Rimbaud, "Historic Evening," in *Illuminations*, 147.

18 In historiological epochs, religion was the most powerful force of reducing sufficiency and laying bare the essantial faultiness in existance. Céline said it impeccably:

> practical superiority of the great Christian religions was that they did not try to sugar-coat the pill. They did not try to throw dust in the eyes; they were not looking for voters; they never felt the need of ingratiating themselves; they did not wiggle their tails in an effort to please. They just seized Man in his cradle, and broke the bad news to him, without reservation. They told him: 'You little shapeless stinker you, you can never be anything but filth. By birth you are nothing but *merde*. Do you hear me, you? That's the evidence, that's the principle of everything. . . . However, maybe . . . maybe . . . in scrutinizing the matter more closely . . . you have got one little chance of winning a bit of a pardon for being as you are—so filthy, so excremental, so unbelievable. . . . That is, if you can hold your chin up in the face of all the sorrows, all the afflictions, all the ordeals, miseries and tortures you will have to face during your lifetime, whether it be long or short. Always with perfect humility! Life, you louse, is just one long bitter ordeal! Don't get out of breath! Don't expect noon to come at two o'clock! Just try to save your soul, that is something in itself! Maybe at the end of this calvary of yours, if you get to be a regular fellow, a hero in keeping your trap shut, you may be saved by these principles. . . . But even that is not a sure thing . . . one little hair's breadth less filthy when you come to croak than when you were born . . . and the darkness may be easier to breathe in than the daybreak was. . . . But don't take too much for granted! That's the whole story! Watch your step! Don't speculate on first and last things! For a turd that is the maximum! . . .' That was seriously spoken. By real Church Fathers! (*Mea Culpa* [*Mea Culpa & The Life and Work of Semmelweis*, trans. Robert Allerton Parker (New York: Howard Fertig, 1979), 19–20])

19 GA 5:294 [*Off the Beaten Track*, 221].

20 GA 55:209 [*Heraclitus*, 159].

21 Pascal (*Pensées*, Laf. §179/Br. §256 [*Pensées*, 55]) noticed it already in the France of Louis XIV: "There are few true Christians. I mean even as regards faith. There are plenty who believe, but out of superstition."

22 What the helplessness of Pope Benedict XV had brought to light during World War I, with his having condemned the war in an encyclical from November 1, 1914, having evoked in May 1915 "the horrible butchery that disgraces Europe," and having declared on May 4, 1916, "the suicide of Europe."

23 Kant, AK 6:94 [*Religion and Rational Theology*, trans. Allen Wood and George di Giovanni (Cambridge: Cambridge University Press, 1996), 130].

24 Philippe Muray, *L'empire du Bien* (Paris: Les Belles Lettres, 1991).

25 GA 5:76 [*Off the Beaten Track*, 58].

26 Léon Bloy, *Au seuil de l'Apocalypse (Journal 1913–1915)* (Paris: Mercure de France, 1915), 316 (entry of May 21, 1915).

27 GA 5:269 [*Off the Beaten Track*, 200].

28 GA 5:295 [*Off the Beaten Track*, 221]. Dietrich Bonhoeffer had the lucidity to admit this even within theology, recognizing that "as a working hypothesis for morality, politics, and the natural sciences, God has been overcome and done away with, but also as a working hypothesis for philosophy and religion [. . .] The return to that [system] is only a counsel of despair, a sacrifice made only at the cost of intellectual integrity." This then made the task to "really live in that godless world and not try to cover up or transfigure its godlessness somehow with religion." And because he admitted that "we are approaching a completely religionless age; people as they are now simply cannot be religious anymore," Bonhoeffer formulated the project, no longer to free Christianity only from metaphysics, but also from religiosity, and to "judge even the Western form of Christianity to be only a preliminary stage of a complete absence of religion. [. . .] If religion is only the garb in which Christianity is clothed—and this garb has looked very different in different ages—what then is religionless Christianity?" (*Letters and Papers from Prison*, 478, 480, and 362–63).

29 It is also the effect of the Copernican Revolution that Pascal observed: "nature is such that it points at every turn to a God who has been lost, both within man and without" (*Pensées*, Laf. §471/Br. §441 [*Pensées*, 152]).

30 GA 7:27 [*The Question concerning Technology*, 26].

31 Compare Emmanuel Levinas ("De la phénoménologie à l'éthique," *Esprit* 234 [July 1997]: 126): "To believe is not a verb that must be used in the first person singular. No one can truly say *I believe*—or *I do not believe*—that God exists. Concerning the existence of God, it is not a matter of an individual soul pronouncing logical syllogisms. His existence cannot be proved. The existence of God, the *Sein Gottes*, is sacred history itself."

32 GA 54:166–67 [*Parmenides*, 112].

33 GA 39:80 [*Hölderlin's Hymns: "Germania" and "The Rhine,"* 73–74].

34 Only the functionaries of contemporary nihilism still take Nietzsche for an atheist. Compare Heidegger: "Whoever says in all seriousness 'God is dead,' and like Nietzsche devotes his life to this predicament, is no atheist. Such is the opinion only of those who relate to and treat their God in the same way as a pocketknife. When the pocketknife is lost, it is indeed gone. But to lose God means something else, and not only because God and a pocketknife are intrinsically different things. Thus atheism is altogether a strange state of affairs; for many who sit in the cage of a traditional religious belief that has so far failed to astound them, because they are either too cozy or too smart for that are more atheistic than the great skeptics. The necessity of renouncing the gods of old, the enduring of this renunciation, is the *safeguarding* of their divinity." GA 39:95 [*Hölderlin's Hymns: "Germania" and "The Rhine,"* 86].

35 Nietzsche, "Letter to my friend, in which I recommend that he read my favorite poet," KGW 1.2:338–41 [*Selected Letters of Friedrich Nietzsche*, trans. and ed. Christopher Middleton (Indianapolis: Hackett Publishing Co., 1996), 4–6].

36 Hölderlin, "Patmos," lines 7, 46, 19, 25–26, 54–56, 70–71, 74–75, 80, 3–4; GSA 2.1:165 [*Friedrich Hölderlin: Selected Poems and Fragments*, trans. Michael Hamburger, ed. Jeremy Adler (New York: Penguin Books, 1998), 231–35]. Translation altered—Trans.

37 "Germania," lines 9–11 and 83–86; GSA 2.1:151 [*Friedrich Hölderlin: Selected Poems and Fragments*, 189–91 and 195].

38 Heidegger, GA 39:6 [*Hölderlin's Hymns: "Germania" and "The Rhine,"* 5].

39 Hölderlin, "The Rhine," lines 38–39; GSA 2.1:143 [*Friedrich Hölderlin: Selected Poems and Fragments*, 199]. Translation altered—Trans.

40 "The Blind Singer," lines 34 and 45–46; GSA 2.1:55 [*Friedrich Hölderlin: Selected Poems and Fragments*, 89–91]. Translation altered—Trans.

41 "The Rhine," lines 177, 171, 122, 127–29, and 48; GSA 2.1:143–48 [*Friedrich Hölderlin: Selected Poems and Fragments*, 205, 203, and 199]. Translation altered—Trans.

42 "As on a holiday . . . ," line 25; GSA 2.1:118 [*Friedrich Hölderlin: Selected Poems and Fragments*, 175]. Translation altered—Trans.

43 "The Rhine," lines 146 and 220; GSA 2.1:146–48 [*Friedrich Hölderlin: Selected Poems and Fragments*, 205 and 209]. Translation altered—Trans.

44 "As on a holiday . . . ," line 21; GSA 2.1:118 [*Friedrich Hölderlin: Selected Poems and Fragments*, 173].

45 "Homecoming," lines 79–80; GSA 2.1:98 [*Friedrich Hölderlin: Selected Poems and Fragments*, 165].

46 "Heidelberg," line 16; GSA 2.1:14 [*Friedrich Hölderlin: Selected Poems and Fragments*, 51].

47 "Apriority of the individual (second version)," GSA 2.1:250. Reproduction of the manuscripts and reconstruction of the sketches in *Cahier de l'Herne Hölderlin*, ed. Jean-François Courtine (Paris: Éditions de l'Herne, 1989), 108 and following.

48 Rimbaud, *A Season in Hell*, in *Rimbaud: Complete Works, Selected Letters*, 297.

49 Hölderlin, *Hyperion: or, the Hermit in Greece*, GSA 3:80–83 [*Hyperion and Selected Poems*, 66, 67, 4, and 65]. Aristotle himself, in the *Politics* (7.7.1327b20–23 [*The Complete Works of Aristotle*, 2:2107]), situates the Greeks *between* Europe and Asia: "Those who live in a cold climate and in Europe are full of spirit, but wanting in intelligence and skill; and therefore they retain comparative freedom, but have no political organization, and are incapable of ruling over others. Whereas the natives of Asia are intelligent and inventive, but they are wanting in spirit, and therefore they are always in a state of subjection and slavery. But the Hellenic race, which is situated between them, is likewise intermediate in character, being high-spirited and also intelligent." It is therefore important to distinguish Europe from the West [*l'Occident*]: the West is the decline (*occidens*) of Europe, its twilight.

50 "Bread and Wine," lines 24–25; GSA 2.1:91 [*Friedrich Hölderlin: Selected Poems and Fragments*, 151].

51 "Homecoming," lines 5–8; GSA 2.1:96 [*Friedrich Hölderlin: Selected Poems and Fragments*, 161].

52 Heraclitus, fragment DK B 51 [*Early Greek Philosophy*, 3:161]. Translation altered—Trans.

53 Winckelmann (*Reflections on the Imitation of Greek Works in Painting and Sculpture* [1755], trans. Elfriede Heyer and Roger C. Norton [La Salle, IL: Open Court, 1987]) imposes the image of a Greece that is the fatherland of the ideal and the rational, of moderation and measure, populated by impassive sages walking slowly along pathways paved with marble. But this classicism ignores all of Greek art and is only familiar with late works, even Roman imitations. Thus the dull Apollo Belvedere, in which Winckelmann, Goethe, and Hegel agree to recognize the pinnacle and the quintessence of Hellenism, has nothing Greek about it: it is the Roman copy in marble of a late bronze from the Hellenistic epoch. If Winckelmann devotes pages to it that quickly became famous, it is because he gives exactly what the classics were looking for in Greece, namely, a pure form, bloodless and fleshless. When archeology exposed Europeans to authentically Greek works, there was disbelief and even dismay: the marble sculptures that Lord Elgin had brought back from the Parthenon were thus at first considered to be a Roman fraud from Hadrian's time; Goethe was nearly frightened by the intimidating size of the temples of Paestum. But it is Charles Maurras's reaction (*Anthinéa d'Athènes à Florence* [Paris:

Honoré-Champion, 1901]) that is the most significant. Between 1886 and 1889 a group of votive statues of maidens—the Kore—was discovered on the Acropolis, having been buried in 480 BCE to protect them from the Persians; these statues, among which figures the lovely "sulky" Kore, undoubtedly constitute a pinnacle of Greek art. Maurras, steeped in Ernest Renan's *Prière sur l'Acropole*, discovered them in 1896 during his trip to Athens; he was then literally horrified by these statues, which break so drastically with the canons of classicism: "Their slanted eyes, as in Mongolian faces, their nostrils, their strange brow, this uniform and indefinite smile on cheeks shining like ivory caused me a kind of Grief that scared me off. [. . .] Alas! I said, who will take these Chinese away from me?" Maurras's terms are highly significant: to see in these young Athenians "Mongolians" and "Chinese" is to be stunned by the presence of the Eastern even within what was taken for the sanctuary of the Western, and it is to be scandalized by a "contagion from Asia" defined by "the madness of the East and the taste for rage proposed to tired sprits."

54 Hölderlin, "Remarks on 'Antigone,'" GSA 5:266 [*Friedrich Hölderlin: Essays and Letters on Theory*, trans. Thomas Pfau (Albany: State University of New York Press, 1988), 110].

55 "Bread and Wine," line 32; GSA 2.1:91 [*Friedrich Hölderlin: Selected Poems and Fragments*, 151].

56 Letter to Friedrich Wilmans, September 28, 1803, GSA 6.1:434 [*Friedrich Hölderlin: Essays and Letters*, trans. and ed. Jeremy Adler and Charlie Louth (New York: Penguin Books, 2009), 215].

57 "The Ground for Empedocles," GSA 4.1:153–54 [*Essays and Letters on Theory*, 53].

58 Letter to Böhlendorff, December 4, 1801, GSA 6.1:425 [*Essays and Letters on Theory*, 149–50].

59 *Hyperion: or, the Hermit in Greece*, GSA 3:77 [*Hyperion and Selected Poems*, 63].

60 *Hyperion: or, the Hermit in Greece*, GSA 3:83 [*Hyperion and Selected Poems*, 68].

61 Heraclitus, fragment DK B 8 [*Early Greek Philosophy*, 3:167].

62 Hölderlin, *The Perspective from Which We Have to Look at Antiquity*, GSA 4.1:221–22 [*Essays and Letters on Theory*, 39–40].

63 "Remarks on 'Antigone,'" GSA 5:269–70 [*Essays and Letters on Theory*, 113–14].

64 "Bread and Wine," line 122; GSA 2.1:94 [*Friedrich Hölderlin: Selected Poems and Fragments*, 157].

65 Letter to Böhlendorff, December 4, 1801, GSA 6.1:425 [*Essays and Letters on Theory*, 149]. Translation altered—Trans.

66 Letter to Böhlendorff, December 4, 1801, GSA 6.1:425 [*Essays and Letters on Theory*, 149].

67 ". . . Do you think it should happen . . . ," lines 2–6; GSA 2.1:228.

68 "The Rhine," lines 96–104; GSA 2.1:145 [*Friedrich Hölderlin: Selected Poems and Fragments*, 201].

69 "Voice of the People," lines 4 and 8; GSA 2.1:51 [*Friedrich Hölderlin: Selected Poems and Fragments*, 83].

70 "Remembrance," lines 38–41; GSA 2.1:189 [*Friedrich Hölderlin: Selected Poems and Fragments*, 253].

71 "The Fettered River," lines 1–3; GSA 2.1:67 [*Friedrich Hölderlin: Selected Poems and Fragments*, 103].

72 "The Rhine," lines 91–94; GSA 2.1:145 [*Friedrich Hölderlin: Selected Poems and Fragments*, 201].

73 "Greece (third version)," lines 23–24; GSA 2.1:257 [*Friedrich Hölderlin: Selected Poems and Fragments*, 319].

74 *Hyperion: or, the Hermit in Greece*, GSA 3:87 [*Hyperion and Selected Poems*, 72].

75 Letter to Böhlendorff, December 4, 1801, GSA 6.1:426 [*Essays and Letters on Theory*, 150].

76 Letter to his mother, February 14, 1791, GSA 6.1:64 [*Essays and Letters on Theory*, 120]. Translation altered—Trans.

77 *Hyperion: or, the Hermit in Greece*, GSA 3:153 [*Hyperion and Selected Poems*, 128–29].

78 Rimbaud, "Cities [I]," in *Illuminations*, 87.

79 Hölderlin, *Hyperion: or, the Hermit in Greece*, GSA 3:31 and 23 [*Hyperion and Selected Poems*, 130 and 16].

80 Letter to Böhlendorff, December 4, 1801, GSA 6.1:426 [*Essays and Letters on Theory*, 150].

81 *The Perspective from Which We Have to Look at Antiquity*, GSA 4.1:221 [*Essays and Letters*, 246].

82 Letter to his brother, August 21, 1794, GSA 6.1:131 [*Essays and Letters*, 31].

83 Rimbaud, Letter to Georges Izambard, August 25, 1870, in *Oeuvre-Vie*, 105 [*Rimbaud: Complete Works, Selected Letters*, 363]. *Patrouillotisme* is a pun on the French words for "patriot," *patriote*, and "patrol," *patrouille*—Trans.

84 Nietzsche, KSA 5:180 [*Beyond Good and Evil*, 132] ("patriots" translates *Vaterlanderei*).

85 Hölderlin, "Remarks on 'Antigone,'" GSA 5:271 [*Essays and Letters on Theory*, 114–15]. Translation altered—Trans.

86 "The Fettered River," lines 3–6; GSA 2.1:67 [*Friedrich Hölderlin: Selected Poems and Fragments*, 103].

87 "The Rhine," lines 182–83; GSA 2.1:147 [*Friedrich Hölderlin: Selected Poems and Fragments*, 207]. Translation altered—Trans.

88 "Bread and Wine," lines 31–34; GSA 2.1:91 [*Friedrich Hölderlin: Selected Poems and Fragments*, 151].

89 "Germania," lines 90–93; GSA 2.1:150–51 [*Friedrich Hölderlin: Selected Poems and Fragments*, 195].

90 "As on a holiday . . . ," lines 56–60; GSA 2.1:119 [*Friedrich Hölderlin: Selected Poems and Fragments*, 177].

91 Heraclitus, fragments DK B 93 and 32 [*Early Greek Philosophy*, 3:157 and 159]. Translation altered—Trans.

92 Hölderlin, "Bread and Wine," lines 37, 40, 74, and 113–14; GSA 2.1:91–93 [*Friedrich Hölderlin: Selected Poems and Fragments*, 153, 155, and 157]. Translation altered—Trans.

93 "At the Source of the Danube," lines 82–83; GSA 2.1:128–29 [*Friedrich Hölderlin: Selected Poems and Fragments*, 183.

94 "Bread and Wine," line 22; GSA 2.1:90 [*Friedrich Hölderlin: Selected Poems and Fragments*, 151].

95 Letter to Böhlendorff, November 1802, GSA 6.1:432 [*Essays and Letters on Theory*, 152].

96 "As on a holiday . . . ," line 20; GSA 2.1:118 [*Friedrich Hölderlin: Selected Poems and Fragments*, 173]. Translation altered—Trans.

97 "Homecoming," lines 79–80; GSA 2.1:98 [*Friedrich Hölderlin: Selected Poems and Fragments*, 165].

98 "Germania," lines 17 and 2–3; GSA 2.1:150–51 [*Friedrich Hölderlin: Selected Poems and Fragments*, 189–91].

99 "Greece (third version)," lines 26–27; GSA 2.1:257 [*Friedrich Hölderlin: Selected Poems and Fragments*, 319]. Translation altered—Trans.

100 "Remembrance," lines 38–40; GSA 2.1:189 [*Friedrich Hölderlin: Selected Poems and Fragments*, 253].

101 "Homecoming," lines 85–86 and 99–101; GSA 2.1:98 [*Friedrich Hölderlin: Selected Poems and Fragments*, 165]. Translation altered—Trans.

102 "Germania," line 6; GSA 2.1:149 [*Friedrich Hölderlin: Selected Poems and Fragments*, 189]. Translation altered—Trans.

103 "Patmos," lines 99 and 117–19; GSA 2.1:168 [*Friedrich Hölderlin: Selected Poems and Fragments*, 235 and 237]. Translation altered—Trans.

104 Heidegger, GA 4:47 [*Elucidations of Hölderlin's Poetry*, 64].

105 GA 16:528 [*Discourse on Thinking*, 55–56].

106 GA 4:178 [*Elucidations of Hölderlin's Poetry*, 202].

107 GA 16:671 [*The Heidegger Reader*, 326].

108 GA 65:17 [*Contributions to Philosophy (Of the Event)*, 16].

109 GA 39:95 [*Hölderlin's Hymns: "Germania" and "The Rhine,"* 86]. Translation altered—Trans.

110 GA 11:77 [*Identity and Difference*, 72]. Translation altered—Trans.

111 GA 65:263, 411, and 437 [*Contributions to Philosophy (Of the Event)*, 207, 325–26, and 345].

112 GA 4:169–70 [*Elucidations of Hölderlin's Poetry*, 194].

113 GA 39:189–90 [*Hölderlin's Hymns: "Germania" and "The Rhine,"* 173]. Translation altered—Trans.

114 GA 55:24 [*Heraclitus*, 20].

115 GA 7:185 [*Poetry, Language, Thought*, trans. Albert Hofstadter (New York: Harper & Row, 1971), 182]. Translation altered—Trans.

116 Hölderlin, "The Poet's Vocation," lines 45–48 and 64; GSA 2.1:47–48 [*Friedrich Hölderlin: Selected Poems and Fragments*, 81 and 83].

117 GA 39:232 [*Hölderlin's Hymns: "Germania" and "The Rhine,"* 212]. Translation altered—Trans.

118 GA 33:146 [*Aristotle's Metaphysics θ 1–3: On the Essence and Actuality of Force*, 125].

119 GA 39:218 [*Hölderlin's Hymns: "Germania" and "The Rhine,"* 199].

120 GA 51:64 [*Basic Concepts*, 54]. Translation altered—Trans.

121 GA 11:63 [*Identity and Difference*, 54–55].

122 GA 66:241 [*Mindfulness*, 213]. Translation altered—Trans.

123 GA 70:157. On the situation of the divine in the topology of Beyng, compare Jean-François Marquet, "L'Être et le dieu. Notes sur quelques pointes de la *Seynsgeschichte* de Heidegger," *Revue de métaphysique et de morale* 52 (2006): 457–67.

124 GA 4:147–48 [*Elucidations of Hölderlin's Poetry*, 169].

125 GA 4:68 [*Elucidations of Hölderlin's Poetry*, 90]. Translation altered—Trans.

126 Hölderlin, "Mnemosyne (first version)," lines 13–15; GSA 2.1:194 [*Hyperion and Selected Poems*, 273].

127 GA 4:69 [*Elucidations of Hölderlin's Poetry*, 90–91].

128 GA 39:111 [*Hölderlin's Hymns: "Germania" and "The Rhine,"* 101].

129 Perhaps the Earth can be thought otherwise in the topology of Beyng. Indeed, it is important to distinguish two essantial modalities of λήθη: on the one hand, beings that stand in latency and constitute the reserve from which ἀλήθεια draws and thus makes them evident [*patent*] (pre-ontic λήθη), and, on the other hand, Beyng's self-withdrawal that frees the space-time of ἀλήθεια (pre-ontological Λήθη, "the essantially undisclosable"). In the vocabulary of Heraclitus, and from the central "fire" that illuminates the Clearing, it is necessary to distinguish, on the one hand, what stands beyond the "circumference of a circle" (κύκλου περιφέρια; DK B 103 [*Early Greek Philosophy*, 3:163]), and, on the other, what hides within itself (κρύπτεσθαι; DK B 123) and is thus hollowed out in the center of the circle. If the *world* is thought as the region of the clearing, then the *Earth* would be the density and opacity of "the totality of beings that remain enveloped within themselves" (GA 39:173 [*Hölderlin's Hymns: "Germania" and "The Rhine,"* 158]) that Beyng comes "to fissure": the *abyss* that opens in these "clefts of Beyng" (GA 39:135 [*Hölderlin's Hymns: "Germania" and "The Rhine,"* 120]) is therefore not the Earth, it is

the mystery that it is a question of naming. Thus Heidegger, instead of overcoming the Greek Beginning, would only have prolonged Heraclitus's decision to give the abyss of χάος the name φύσις.

130 Hölderlin, "Germania," lines 97–98; GSA 2.1:152 [*Friedrich Hölderlin: Selected Poems and Fragments*, 195]. Translation altered—Trans.

131 GA 4:59–61 [*Elucidations of Hölderlin's Poetry*, 82–83]. Translation altered—Trans.

132 GA 5:33 [*Off the Beaten Track*, 25].

133 In French, *terre* can mean both "earth" and "land"—Trans.

134 GA 66:93 [*Mindfulness*, 78]. Translation altered—Trans.

135 GA 39:181–82 [*Hölderlin's Hymns: "Germania" and "The Rhine,"* 165].

136 GA 4:92 [*Elucidations of Hölderlin's Poetry*, 115].

137 GA 39:258 and 216 [*Hölderlin's Hymns: "Germania" and "The Rhine,"* 233 and 197]. This rerooting therefore cannot be understood either biologically ("All too frequently we continue to think all history in the categories of the natural sciences, in particular biology and the sociology that is determined from there"; GA 39:228 [*Hölderlin's Hymns: "Germania" and "The Rhine,"* 207]) or geographically ("The Earth of the homeland here is not a mere space delimited by external borders, a realm of nature, or a locality constituting a possible arena for this or that event to be played out there"; GA 39:104–5 [*Hölderlin's Hymns: "Germania" and "The Rhine,"* 95]): it is what determines the relation to the divine ("The Earth, as this Earth of the homeland, is nurtured for the gods. Through such nurturing it first becomes homeland, yet as such it can once again fall into decline and sink to the level of a mere place of residence, which accordingly goes hand in hand with the advent of godlessness"; GA 39:104–5 [*Hölderlin's Hymns: "Germania" and "The Rhine,"* 95]), and its purpose is to wait for the last god. But precisely in this, Heidegger missed exile and diaspora as a community's mode of being, which thus released from all rootedness finds its fatherland in God: a trait proper to the Jewish people, a landless people who were made to wander under the sky, which is also found in medieval mysticism. Compare, for example, Angelus Silesius (*The Cherubinic Wanderer*, trans. Willard R. Trask [New York: Pantheon, 1953], 44): "He who was born nowhere, who to no one is known, / Even in Hell shall find his fatherland and home."

138 GA 65:403 [*Contributions to Philosophy (Of the Event)*, 319].

139 A critique that Günther Anders had addressed to Heidegger in person as early as the 1920s: "I reproached him for having left aside man's dimension as a nomad, a traveler, a cosmopolitan, for in fact having represented human existence as merely vegetal, as the existence of a being that would be rooted in one place and would not leave it. [. . .] I thus reproached him for not even granting man the mobility of an animal, in any case for not treating this mobility as an existential, but for treating man as fundamentally a rooted being, like a plant" (*Et si je suis désespéré, que voulez-vous que j'y fasse?* [Paris: Allia, 2010], 17–18).

140 Levinas, *Difficult Freedom*, trans. Séan Hand (Baltimore: Johns Hopkins University Press, 1990), 232; and Levinas, *Totality and Infinity*, trans. Alphonso Lingis (Pittsburgh: Duquesne University Press, 1969), 46.

141 The problem of Heidegger's relation to Nazism could be addressed philosophically in this way: first by recognizing that Heidegger is the ultimate thinker of the West, who brought to light the unthought essance of its destiny—nihilism—saw that it led to the "enormity of total annihilation" (GA 40:18 [*Introduction to Metaphysics*, 17), and formulated the need for an "other Beginning," but then by observing that to define this other Beginning—and although he recognized in 1934 that "we today do not even know the adversary yet, so that we run the

danger of inadvertently making common cause with the adversary, instead of attacking him" (GA 38:8–9 [*Logic as the Question concerning the Essence of Language*, 7)—he did little more than extend the project of a poetic mythology and a Germanic religion developed in Germany in the nineteenth century and systematized by Stefan George at the beginning of the twentieth century, and understood National Socialism as the setting to work of this project. His thought is the apocalypse of metaphysics: it is the crucial work of our time, including to think Nazi annihilism (as the release of a hitherto repressed nihilism, and as "unleashing the Inhuman which we did not immediately recognize in its cunning and to which we have so recklessly handed over the power play," Letter to Elisabeth Blochmann, March 3, 1947, in *Briefwechsel*, 92). Therefore, it is important—as for every philosopher—to distinguish between, on the one hand, the problems identified and concepts developed by Heidegger, and, on the other hand, the use that he himself made of these concepts to treat these problems, a use in this case profoundly dependent on the crisis of the German ideology.

142 Heine, *Sämtliche Werke. Düsseldorfer Ausgabe*, 8.1:118 [*On the History of Religion and Philosophy in Germany*, trans. Howard Pollack-Milgate, ed. Terry Pinkard (New York: Cambridge University Press, 2007), 116]. Translation altered—Trans.

143 Heine, *Sämtliche Werke. Düsseldorfer Ausgabe*, 8.1:77–78 [*On the History of Religion and Philosophy in Germany*, 76]. It is remarkable that Ernst Jünger, in a text written in 1950 in homage to Heidegger, makes a diagnosis ultimately very close to Heine's: "We are still in conflict with nihilism: for the moment, it is undoubtedly both more wise, and more noble, to side with the Churches rather than their assailants. After all, if avowed cannibalism and ardent animal worship were not established to the cheers of the masses, this is owed to the Church. [. . .] To repress the Churches would be either to deliver the masses completely over to technological collectivism and its exploitation, or else to throw them into the arms of sectarians and charlatans" (*Passage de la ligne*, trans. Henri Plard [Paris: Christian Bourgois, 1970], 81–82).

144 Rimbaud, "Childhood," in *Illuminations*, in *Rimbaud: Complete Works, Selected Letters*, 313.

145 Heraclitus, fragment DK B 93 [*Early Greek Philosophy*, 3:157]. Translation altered—Trans.

146 GA 39:133–34 [*Hölderlin's Hymns: "Germania" and "The Rhine,"* 118].

147 Compare Ernst Benz, *The Mystical Sources of German Romantic Philosophy*, trans. Blair R. Reynolds and Eunice M. Paul (Eugene, OR: Pickwick Publications, 1983).

148 Meister Eckhart, Sermon 21, DW 1:514 [*Meister Eckhart: Teacher and Preacher*, ed. Bernard McGinn, with Frank Tobin and Elvira Borgstadt (New York: Paulist Press, 1986), 281].

149 Sermon 40, DW 2:274 [*Meister Eckhart: Teacher and Preacher*, 300].

150 Sermon 42, DW 2:303–4 [*Meister Eckhart: Sermons and Treatises*, 2:236].

151 Sermon 71, DW 3:214 and 223 [*Meister Eckhart: Teacher and Preacher*, 320–21 and 323].

152 Sermon 51, DW 2:476 [*Meister Eckhart: Sermons and Treatises*, 2:254].

153 Sermon 80, DW 3:382 [*Meister Eckhart: Teacher and Preacher*, 333].

154 Sermon 90, DW 4.1:68.

155 Sermon 22, DW 1:389 [*Meister Eckhart: The Essential Sermons*, 196].

156 Sermon 77, DW 3:335 [*Meister Eckhart: Sermons and Treatises*, 2:37].

157 Commentary on Genesis, §300; OLME 1:638.

158 Sermon 51, DW 2:470 [*Meister Eckhart: Sermons and Treatises*, 2:251].

159 Sermon 15, DW 1:253 [*Meister Eckhart: The Essential Sermons*, 192].

160 Sermon 22, DW 1:389 [*Meister Eckhart: The Essential Sermons*, 196].

161 Sermon 7, DW 1:123 [*Meister Eckhart: Teacher and Preacher*, 254].

162 Sermon 16b, DW 1:274 [*Meister Eckhart: Teacher and Preacher*, 278].

163 Sermon 5b, DW 1:93 [*Meister Eckhart: The Essential Sermons*, 184].

164 Sermon 31, DW 2:120 [*The Complete Mystical Works of Meister Eckhart*, trans. and ed. Maurice O'C. Walshe (New York: Crossroad Publishing Co., 2009), 259].

165 Sermon 54b, DW 2:569 [*Meister Eckhart: Sermons and Treatises*, 2:22].

166 Sermon 104, DW 4.1:594–95 [*Meister Eckhart: Sermons and Treatises*, 1:31]. Translation altered—Trans.

167 Sermon 102, DW 4.1:419 [*Meister Eckhart: Sermons and Treatises*, 1:20–21]. The difficulty with recognizing that such a non-knowing is not nothing, neither a shortcoming nor a capitulation of reason, is what Heidegger said (GA 39:184 [*Hölderlin's Hymns: "Germania" and "The Rhine,"* 168]): "The historical existance of the Western world is unavoidably and irrevocably one of *knowing*. [. . .] Because our existance is a knowing one—which is not to be taken as synonymous with rational calculation—there can, therefore, no longer be a *purely poetic* becoming of existance for us; neither can there be one *purely of thinking*, nor one of *action alone* either"—and, it must be added: nor one *purely of believing*.

168 Sermon 52, DW 2:506 [*Meister Eckhart: The Essential Sermons*, 202].

169 Sermon 50, DW 2:454 [*Meister Eckhart: Sermons and Treatises*, 2:317]. Translation altered—Trans.

170 Sermon 48, DW 2:420–21 [*Meister Eckhart: The Essential Sermons*, 198].

171 Sermon 71, DW 3:224 [*Meister Eckhart: Teacher and Preacher*, 323].

172 Sermon 36a, DW 2:189–91 [*Meister Eckhart: Sermons and Treatises*, 1:275].

173 Sermon 80, DW 3:380 [*Meister Eckhart: Teacher and Preacher*, 332].

174 Sermon 17, DW 1:285 [*Meister Eckhart: Sermons and Treatises*, 1:172]. Translation altered—Trans.

175 Sermon 77, DW 3:337 [*Meister Eckhart: Sermons and Treatises*, 2:38].

176 Sermon 71, DW 3:221–22 [*Meister Eckhart: Teacher and Preacher*, 322].

177 Sermon 53, DW 2:732–33 [*Meister Eckhart: The Essential Sermons*, 203–4].

178 Sermon 20b, DW 1:510 [*The Complete Works of Meister Eckhart*, 198].

179 Sermon 36a, DW 2:190 [*Meister Eckhart: Sermons and Treatises*, 1:275].

180 Commentary on Genesis, §299, OLME 1:636.

181 Commentary on Genesis, §300, OLME 1:639.

182 Sermon 17, DW 1:284 [*Meister Eckhart: Sermons and Treatises*, 1:172].

183 Aristotle, *Metaphysics*, Λ.7.1072b25 [*The Complete Works of Aristotle*, 2:1695]. Translation altered—Trans.

184 Meister Eckhart, Latin Sermon 29, in *Meister Eckhart: Teacher and Preacher*, 225.

185 Sermon 76, DW 3:323 [*Meister Eckhart: Teacher and Preacher*, 329].

186 Sermon 34, DW 2:167 [*Meister Eckhart: Sermons and Treatises*, 1:208].

187 Translation altered—Trans.

188 Translation altered—Trans.

189 *Meister Eckhart: Parisian Questions and Prologues*, trans. Armand A. Maurer (Toronto: Pontifical Institute of Medieval Studies, 1974), 48. Translation altered—Trans.

190 Compare Mugler, *Dictionnaire historique de la terminologie optique des Grecs*, 45–46.

191 Meister Eckhart, Sermon 36a, DW 2:191 [*Meister Eckhart: Sermons and Treatises*, 1:275].

192 Henry Suso, *The Exemplar, with Two German Sermons*, trans. and ed. Frank Tobin (New York: Paulist Press, 1989), 319. Translation altered—Trans.

193 Suso, *The Exemplar, with Two German Sermons*, 309. Translation altered—Trans.

194 In the precise sense that Jean-Luc Marion understands this term: "In its ambiguity, denomination bears the twofold function of saying (affirming negatively) and undoing this say-

ing of the name. It concerns a form of speech that no longer says something about something (or a name of someone) but which denies all relevance to predication, rejects the nominative function of names, and suspends the rule of truth's two values" (*In Excess: Studies of Saturated Phenomena*, trans. Robyn Horner [New York: Fordham University Press, 2002], 139).

195 *Meister Eckhart: Parisian Questions and Prologues*, 49.

196 Sermon 1, DW 1:19 [*Meister Eckhart: Teacher and Preacher*, 243]. Translation altered—Trans.

197 Sermon 67, DW 3:133 [*Meister Eckhart: Sermons and Treatises*, 2:175].

198 Sermon 9, DW 1:150 [*Meister Eckhart: Teacher and Preacher*, 257]. Translation altered—Trans.

199 Sermon 13, DW 1:216 [*The Complete Mystical Works of Meister Eckhart*, 160].

200 Sermon 52, DW 2:497 [*Meister Eckhart: The Essential Sermons*, 201].

201 Sermon 71, DW 3:228 [*Meister Eckhart: Teacher and Preacher*, 324].

202 Sermon 83, DW 3:443 [*Meister Eckhart: The Essential Sermons*, 207].

203 Sermon 82, DW 3:431 [*Meister Eckhart: Sermons and Treatises*, 2:115].

204 Sermon 9, DW 1:145 [*Meister Eckhart: Teacher and Preacher*, 256].

205 Angelus Silesius, *The Cherubinic Wanderer*, trans. Maria Shrady (New York: Paulist Press, 1986), 54 and 44. Compare Heidegger, GA 10:53 and following [*The Principle of Reason*, 35 and following]. Translation altered—Trans.

206 Meister Eckhart, Sermon 26, DW 2:27 [*Meister Eckhart: Sermons and Treatises*, 1:98].

207 Sermon 41, DW 2:289 [*Meister Eckhart: Sermons and Treatises*, 2:2].

208 Sermon 83, DW 3:586 [*Meister Eckhart: The Essential Sermons*, 208].

209 Sermon 41, DW 2:288 [*Meister Eckhart: Sermons and Treatises*, 2:2].

210 Sermon 67, DW 3:131 [*Meister Eckhart: Sermons and Treatises*, 2:174]. Translation altered—Trans.

211 Sermon 52, DW 2:502 [*Meister Eckhart: The Essential Sermons*, 202].

212 Sermon 12, DW 1:194 [*Meister Eckhart: Teacher and Preacher*, 268]. Translation altered—Trans.

213 Sermon 52, DW 2:493 [*Meister Eckhart: The Essential Sermons*, 200]. Translation altered—Trans.

214 Sermon 80, DW 3:378 [*Meister Eckhart: Teacher and Preacher*, 332].

215 Sermon 29, DW 2:84 [*Meister Eckhart: Teacher and Preacher*, 289].

216 Sermon 101, DW 4.1:351 [*Meister Eckhart: Sermons and Treatises*, 1:5]. Translation altered—Trans.

217 *Counsels on Discernment*, DW 5:293 [*Meister Eckhart: The Essential Sermons*, 281]. Translation altered—Trans.

218 Sermon 42, DW 2:309 [*Meister Eckhart: Sermons and Treatises*, 2:238]. Translation altered—Trans.

219 Sermon 42, DW 2:308 [*Meister Eckhart: Sermons & Treatises*, 2:238].

220 Sermon 83, DW 3:586 [*Meister Eckhart: The Essential Sermons*, 208].

221 Sermon 73, DW 3:266 [*Meister Eckhart: Sermons and Treatises*, 2:196].

222 Sermon 1, DW 1:14 [*Meister Eckhart: Teacher and Preacher*, 242].

223 Translation altered—Trans.

224 Sermon 28, DW 2:68 [*Meister Eckhart: Sermons and Treatises*, 1:145].

225 Sermon 67, DW 3:134 [*Meister Eckhart: Sermons and Treatises*, 2:175].

226 Sermon 14, DW 1:235 [*Meister Eckhart: Teacher and Preacher*, 273]. Translation altered—Trans.

227 *On Detachment*, DW 5:423 [*Meister Eckhart: The Essential Sermons*, 291].

228 Sermon 101, DW 4.1:360 [*Meister Eckhart: Sermons and Treatises*, 1:8] (where Eckhart translates Pseudo-Dionysius the Areopagite, *Mystical Theology* 1.1; PG 3:998–99).

229 Sermon 48, DW 2:420 [*Meister Eckhart: The Essential Sermons*, 198].

230 Sermon 83, DW 3:586 [*Meister Eckhart: The Essential Sermons*, 208].

231 Sermon 52, DW 2:488, 492–93, and 504 [*Meister Eckhart: The Essential Sermons*, 199–203].

232 Sermon 10, DW 1:161 [*Meister Eckhart: Teacher and Preacher*, 261].

233 Sermon 2, DW 1:27 [*Meister Eckhart: The Essential Sermons*, 178].

234 Sermon 47, DW 2:401–2 [*Meister Eckhart: Sermons and Treatises*, 1:183].

235 Sermon 78, DW 3:356 [*Meister Eckhart: Sermons and Treatises*, 1:212]. Translation altered—Trans.

236 Sermon 102, DW 4.1:424 [*Meister Eckhart: Sermons and Treatises*, 1:22]. Translation altered—Trans.

237 Sermon 47, DW 2:400 [*Meister Eckhart: Sermons and Treatises*, 1:182].

238 *Counsels on Discernment*, §21, DW 5:278–79 [*Meister Eckhart: The Essential Sermons*, 275].

239 Sermon 57, DW 2:604 [*The Complete Mystical Works of Meister Eckhart*, 170].

240 Sermon 2, DW 1:28 [*Meister Eckhart: The Essential Sermons*, 178].

241 Sermon 47, DW 2:402–3 [*Meister Eckhart: Sermons & Treatises*, 1:183].

242 Sermon 20b, DW 1:510 [*The Complete Mystical Works of Meister Eckhart*, 197].

243 Sermon 66, DW 3:113 [*Meister Eckhart: Sermons and Treatises*, 2:91].

244 Sermon 65, DW 3:97 [*Meister Eckhart: Sermons and Treatises*, 1:50].

245 Sermon 41, DW 2:287 [*Meister Eckhart: Sermons and Treatises*, 2:2].

246 Sermon 4, DW 1:73–74 [*Meister Eckhart: Teacher and Preacher*, 251].

247 Sermon 69, DW 3:163 [*Meister Eckhart: Teacher and Preacher*, 312]. Compare also Angelus Silesius, *The Cherubinic Wanderer*: "I know that, without me, the life of God were lost" (trans. Willard R. Trask, 13); "God's love means me alone, it is for me He burns, / He dies of sheer dismay if I for Him not yearn" (trans. Maria Shrady, 73). Far from playing a heretic, Eckhart reflects here on the very mystery of Christian Revelation (that of God made man out of love for them, who did not recognize him, and in that way killed him). Thus is uncovered the possibility whose efficacy will be thought by Nietzsche: "God is dead! *And we have killed him!*" (Posthumous fragments [1881], 14 [26], KSA 9:632). Nietzsche's word is not a simple reformulation of what Hölderlin or Heine had already seen, it is the resolution of the enigma of the death of God, which identifies its nature (a murder) and its perpetrators—us, humans. But in doing so, Nietzsche states nothing new, he brings to language the oldest, he breaks the prohibition and says for the first time "the word that has always been implicitly spoken within the metaphysically determined history of the West. [. . .] Nietzsche's word gives the destiny of two millennia of Western history" (Heidegger, GA 5:213 [*Off the Beaten Track*, 160]), that is, the teleology of the onto-logical tautology of which Parmenides is the prophet.

248 Sermon 80, DW 3:385 [*Meister Eckhart: Teacher and Preacher*, 333]. Translation altered—Trans.

249 Sermon 20b, DW 1:345 [*The Complete Mystical Works of Meister Eckhart*, 197].

250 Sermon 33, DW 2:152 [*Meister Eckhart: Sermons and Treatises*, 2:241].

251 Sermon 54a, DW 2:561.

252 Translation altered—Trans.

253 Sermon 81, DW 3:396–97 [*The Complete Mystical Works of Meister Eckhart*, 323].

254 Translation altered—Trans.

255 Translation altered—Trans.

256 It is important to reject the journalistic cliché according to which Christianity is a "religion of the Book." The question is that of the mediation through which God is revealed to humans: Christianity states that this mediation is the singular person of Jesus of Nazareth, in his life of flesh, from birth to death under Pontius Pilate. Christianity is not a religion of the Book, it is the religion of Christ. The New Testament is not a book (understood as an organic whole),

it is a file, which at the end of the second century gathered the most reliable testimonies concerning the life of Jesus: it gives four different versions of it, thus lays bare the impossibility of a book saying this life, and these are the last words of the last Evangelist: "But there are also many other things that Jesus did; if every one of them were written down, I suppose that the world itself could not contain the books that would be written" (Jn 21:25). The expression "religion of the Book" comes from the Qur'an, which introduced the notion of "people of the Book," and Islam is in fact the one and only "religion of the Book," which states that a book is capable of gathering in itself the fullness of Revelation and can thus totalize the truth (for example, Qur'an 5:48: "And We have revealed to you, [O Muhammad], the Book in truth"). As for Judaism, it is the religion of the Law.

257 Meister Eckhart, Sermon 90, DW 4.1:59.

258 Sermon 72, DW 3:245 [*Meister Eckhart: Sermons and Treatises*, 2:326].

259 Heidegger, GA 39:201 [*Hölderlin's Hymns: "Germania" and "The Rhine,"* 183].

260 GA 5:27–28 [*Off the Beaten Track*, 20–21].

261 Meister Eckhart, Sermon 35, DW 2:180 [*Meister Eckhart: Sermons and Treatises*, 1:249]. The vocabulary of the Son, the Father, and the Trinity transgresses metaphysics just as much as the vocabulary of the Earth, the Sky, and the Fourfold (*Geviert*) developed by Heidegger to open an "other thinking," and that is how it must be received: not as a dogmatics, but as a poetics (which Heidegger expressly denies, seeing in metaphysical logic the common ground of the "Atomic Energy Commission" and Christianity's "doctrine of the Trinity"; GA 8:207 [*What Is Called Thinking?*, 204]).

262 Heidegger, GA 39:240–41 [*Hölderlin's Hymns: "Germania" and "The Rhine,"* 218–19].

263 Meister Eckhart, Sermon 47, DW 2:397 [*Meister Eckhart: Sermons and Treatises*, 1:182].

264 Sermon 15, DW 1:253 [*Meister Eckhart: The Essential Sermons*, 192].

265 Sermon 40, DW 2:276 [*Meister Eckhart: Teacher and Preacher*, 301].

266 Heidegger, GA 55:365 [*Heraclitus*, 273].

267 Meister Eckhart, Sermon 7, DW 1:123 [*Meister Eckhart: Teacher and Preacher*, 254].

268 Sermon 1, DW 1:19 [*Meister Eckhart: Teacher and Preacher*, 243]. God's dependence with respect to the creature affirmed by Meister Eckhart can be reformulated in this way. Revelation is the springing-forth of a source, but this source depends on the environment where it flows out: if it springs up in the middle of the desert, and there is neither river nor stream, the water immediately disappears in the sands and the source dies. It is because "*the desert grows*" that "*God is dead*," and Nietzsche only thinks the one as long as he thinks the other (KSA 4:380 and 14 [*Thus Spoke Zarathustra*, 248 and 5]).

269 Sermon 11, DW 1:180 [*Meister Eckhart: Sermons and Treatises*, 2:158]. Translation altered—Trans.

270 *The Book of Divine Consolation*, DW 5:42 [*Meister Eckhart: The Essential Sermons*, 227].

271 Sermon 29, DW 2:84 [*Meister Eckhart: Teacher and Preacher*, 289]. Translation altered—Trans. Eckhart transforms the substantive *Geist* (spirit) into a verb (*geisten*), which we translate with "exhale," remembering that "spirit," "exhale," "inhale," "aspirate," and "sigh" [*esprit, expirer, inspirer, aspirer, soupirer*] derive from the same Latin root *spirare*, "to blow or to breathe." It can also be noted that in dying on the Cross (Mk 15:37; Lk 23:46) Jesus "breathed his last" (ἐξέπνευσεν, where the root πνεῦμα, "breath," is found), which can be interpreted as the very gift of the spirit.

272 Heidegger, GA 65:369 [*Contributions to Philosophy (Of the Event)*, 291–92]. Translation altered—Trans.

273 GA 60:151–52 [*The Phenomenology of Religious Life*, 107–8]. Translation altered—Trans.

274 GA 4:55 [*Elucidations of Hölderlin's Poetry*, 77].

275 GA 39:72 [*Hölderlin's Hymns: "Germania" and "The Rhine,"* 66].

276 GA 4:39 [*Elucidations of Hölderlin's Poetry*, 57].

277 GA 39:74 [*Hölderlin's Hymns: "Germania" and "The Rhine,"* 67].

278 GA 6.2:188 and 194 [*Nietzsche*, 4:156 and 162]. Translation altered—Trans.

279 This peril finds its completed form in capitalism, where the community is atomized by its aim of the "money fetish" (Marx, MEW 23:108 [*Capital*, 187]), which was autonomized in the "*automatic fetish*" of Capital (MEW 26.3:447 [CW 32:451, *Theories of Surplus Value*]). If with Alfred Sohn-Rethel (*Warenform und Denkform* [Frankfurt/Main: Suhrkamp, 1978]) we recognize in money, as the objectification and reification of essance manifested in the dialectic of exchange, the transcendental object of the social synthesis, then it is possible to see in Christ the transcendental subject of the Christian community, and that is why there is a radical antagonism between Christ and Capital: "You cannot serve God and Mammon" (Lk 16:13), Mammon being an Aramaic term to designate money insofar as it is the object of an idolatrous cult. Marx himself defined the epoch of Capital as "these times of Mammon-worship" (MEW 13:203 [CW 16:191, "The State of British Manufactures," *New York Daily Tribune*, March 15, 1859]). Compare also Pope Benedict XVI (*Jesus of Nazareth: From the Baptism in the Jordan to the Transfiguration*, trans. Adrian J. Walker [New York: Doubleday, 2007], 98): "As we witness the abuse of economic power, as we witness the cruelties of a capitalism that degrades man to the level of merchandise, we have also realized the perils of wealth, and we have gained a new appreciation of what Jesus meant when he warned of riches, of the man-destroying divinity Mammon, which grips large parts of the world in a cruel stranglehold."

280 Translation altered—Trans.

281 Translation altered—Trans.

282 Translation altered—Trans.

283 Heidegger, GA 39:111 [*Hölderlin's Hymns: "Germania" and "The Rhine,"* 101].

284 This fact also remains a historiological enigma: against all expectations, what should have been only a lamentable and pathetic failure (in the epoch when Tiberius, *cæsar imperator* and *pontifex maximus*, establishes imperial power over the whole known world, a marginal figure roams an outlying province of the empire to preach love; he is beaten up by henchmen from the legion, then executed) becomes the zero point of universal history; in an epoch when the Roman senate approves the apotheosis of the emperor, attributing to him a divine essence and the title of *divi filius*, it is he who is "exalted" (Phil 2:9), recognized as *deus verus ex deo vero*, and becomes Christ Pantocrator.

285 Parmenides, *Poem*, fragment DK B VIII, 17–18 [*Early Greek Philosophy*, 5:45]. Translation altered—Trans.

286 Meister Eckhart, Sermon 67, DW 3:134 [*Meister Eckhart: Sermons and Treatises*, 2:175].

287 Sermon 47, DW 2:397 [*Meister Eckhart: Sermons and Treatises*, 1:181].

288 Sermon 21, DW 1:514 [*Meister Eckhart: Teacher and Preacher*, 281].

289 Sermon 47, DW 2:401 [*Meister Eckhart: Sermons and Treatises*, 1:183].

290 Sermon 48, DW 2:420 [*Meister Eckhart: The Essential Sermons*, 198].

291 Sermon 90, DW 4.1:59. There is in fact no immediate confrontation with the originary abyss, which is why to Philip's request: "show us [δεῖζον] the Father" (Jn 14:8), Christ responds: "If you know me, you will know my Father also," which means that the relation to the originary requires the mediation of "the way" without which "no one comes to the Father" (Jn 14:6). The impossibility of this immediate relation to the divine vastness is essential to Revelation,

since to the same question: "Show me your glory"—which the Greek of the Septuagint renders with the same verb: "δεῖζον"—YHWH responds: "no one shall see my Face and live" (Ex 33:18–20), which means not only that death alone is such a face-to-Face, but also that only this withdrawal and this withholding, this ab-stention, give the leeway for life (which is the play space of mourning: tragedy).

292 GA 39:189–90 [*Hölderlin's Hymns: "Germania" and "The Rhine,"* 173].

293 Hölderlin, "The Only One," lines 48–55, GSA 2.1:154, and fragment from the third version, GSA 2.1:164.

294 "Bread and Wine," lines 144, 155–56, and 146; GSA 2.1:94–95 [*Friedrich Hölderlin: Selected Poems and Fragments*, 159].

295 "Patmos (fragments of the later version)," line 169, GSA 2.1:182 [*Friedrich Hölderlin: Selected Poems and Fragments*, 249]. In his interpretation of the transformation of water into wine and of the presentation of Christ as the "true vine" (Jn 2:1–11 and 15:1–10), Benedict XVI emphasizes that it is possible to "see shining through the Cana story the mystery of the Logos and of his cosmic liturgy, which fundamentally transforms the myth of Dionysus, and yet also brings it to its hidden truth" (*Jesus of Nazareth*, 254).

296 Nietzsche, Posthumous fragments (1880–81), 6 [357], KSA 9:287–88.

297 Posthumous fragments (1884), 27 [60], KSA 11:289 [*The Will to Power*, trans. Walter Kaufmann and R.J. Hollingdale, ed. Walter Kaufmann (New York: Vintage Books, 1967), 513]. Nietzsche often insists on the essential relation between our time and Christianity: "Our nineteenth century has finally reached the conditions required to understand something that for nineteen centuries was misunderstood—Christianity . . . We were unspeakably far from that loving and scrupulous neutrality—a state of sympathy and cultivation of the spirit—we were in a shameful way, at all times of the church, selfishly blind, importunate, insolent, always with the expression of the most servile devotion" (1887–88), 11 [358], KSA 13:157; "Christianity is still possible at any time . . . It is not tied to any of the impudent dogmas that have adorned themselves with its name [. . .] it has absolutely no need of metaphysics" (1887–88), 11 [365], KSA 13:162 [*The Will to Power*, 124–25]; "Our age is in a certain sense ripe [. . .] Therefore a Christianity is possible, but without the absurd dogmas" (1887–88), 11 [366], KSA 13:163 [*The Will to Power*, 138].

298 Heidegger, GA 8:112 [*What Is Called Thinking?*, 69–70]. Translation altered—Trans.

299 Translation altered—Trans.

300 Augustine of Hippo, *City of God*, trans. George E. McCracken (Cambridge, MA: Harvard University Press, 1957), 1:139. In French, "sacred history" is "*l'histoire saint*," which aligns more appropriately with Vioulac's distinction between *le sacré* and *le saint*, "the sacred" and "the holy"—Trans.

301 In the sense that John Paul II was able to say (during his trip to Poland in June 1979) that Auschwitz was the "Golgotha of the modern world," in *Documentation catholique*, no. 1767, p. 632.

302 As Jean-Marie Lustiger said: "Whether we like it or not, the mystery of the election of Israel is at the center of the Shoah" (*Auschwitz-Birkenau. Que l'innommable ne reste pas innommé* [Paris: Criterion, 1990], 30).

303 Levinas, *Entre Nous: On Thinking-of-the-Other* (New York: Columbia University Press, 1998), 97.

304 Hans Jonas, "The Concept of God after Auschwitz: A Jewish Voice," *Journal of Religion* 67, no. 1 (January 1987): 10.

305 Jonas, "The Concept of God after Auschwitz," 2.

306 Jonas, "The Concept of God after Auschwitz," 11.

307 Jonas, "The Concept of God after Auschwitz," 4.

308 Jonas, "The Concept of God after Auschwitz," 4.

309 Jonas, "The Concept of God after Auschwitz," 8.

310 Jonas, "The Concept of God after Auschwitz," 10.

311 Jonas, "The Concept of God after Auschwitz," 8.

312 Jonas, "The Concept of God after Auschwitz," 6. Jonas specifies that this coextension of divine suffering with the whole time of creation distinguishes it from the suffering of the Christian God, which is limited in time: but as Catherine Chalier notes (in Hans Jonas, *Le concept de Dieu après Auschwitz. Une voix juive* [Paris: Rivages, 1994], 41–42), this interpretation is open to discussion, notably from Pascal ("Jesus will be in agony until the end of the world," *Pensées*, Laf. §919/Br. §553 [*Pensées*, 289]).

313 Jonas, "The Concept of God after Auschwitz," 5.

314 Jonas, "The Concept of God after Auschwitz," 4.

315 Jonas, "The Concept of God after Auschwitz," 5.

316 Jonas, "The Concept of God after Auschwitz," 12. Religious life is therefore no longer *submission* to a threatening power, but *gratitude* for what has been given, once and for all, through this consent to impotence. Henceforth, it is no longer up to God to save us, but rather up to us to save God: to safeguard him.

317 Jonas, "The Concept of God after Auschwitz," 3.

318 Jonas, "The Concept of God after Auschwitz," 5.

319 On this point, Hans Jonas comes closer to Ernst Bloch (*The Principle of Hope*, trans. Neville Plaice, Stephen Plaice, and Paul Knight [Cambridge, MA: MIT Press, 1995], 3:1236), who translates Ex 3:14: "I will be who I will be," and says that Revelation "places even at the threshold of the Yahweh phenomenon a god of the end of days, with futurum as an attribute of Being" (1236). Bloch thus conceives an Exodus-God, whose exile is the history of humanity, a God who unfolds his essance as the search for his own promised Land, and whose very essance is messianism.

320 Translation altered—Trans.

321 Thus, by thinking the German catastrophe, Hans Jonas recovers the thought of kenosis that Dietrich Bonhoeffer had developed in his theological letters, written in 1944 from the prison where his resistance to Nazism had led him: "The same God who is with us is the God who forsakes us [. . .] God consents to be pushed out of the world and onto the cross; God is weak and powerless in the world and in precisely this way, and only so, is at our side and helps us" (*Letters and Papers from Prison*, 478–79). Hans Urs von Balthasar developed a similar thought of kenosis, which conceives of it not as a one-time event, but as the eternal essance of the deity where the Father is nothing other than this pure self-giving in the Son. He thus defines "the Father's self-utterance in the generation of the Son [as] an initial 'kenosis' within the Godhead that underpins all subsequent kenosis. [. . .] The Father must not be thought to exist 'prior' to this self-surrender (in an Arian sense): he *is* this movement of self-giving that holds nothing back" (*Theo-Drama: Theological Dramatic Theory*, vol. 4: *The Action*, trans. Graham Harrison [San Francisco: Ignatius Press, 1994], 323).

322 According to Aristotle, *Physics* IV.6.213b22.

323 According to the well-known expression of Étienne Gilson, *Introduction to Christian Philosophy*, trans. Armand Maurer (Toronto: Pontifical Institute of Mediaeval Studies, 1993), 24–26.

324 Hans Jonas, "The Concept of God after Auschwitz," 4.

325 Translation altered—Trans.

326 Hölderlin, "As on a holiday . . . ," lines 57–58; GSA 2.1:119 [*Friedrich Hölderlin: Selected Poems and Fragments*, 177].

327 Translation altered—Trans.

328 In the precise phenomenological sense that Jean-Luc Marion understands this term: "That the phenomenon accedes to its visibility only by way of a givenness; that in order to rise into appearing it must cross a distance (an "elsewhere") that separates it and therefore must (sur) render itself there (in the sense of abandoning and moving itself); that this arising is unfolded according to an immanent axis with which the I must fall into alignment if it is to receive an appearing—all that defines one of the essential characteristics of the given phenomenon, its anamorphosis" (*Being Given*, 123).

329 The extreme divestment of the deity in its kenosis is indeed inseparable from a certain sadness, as Hölderlin had emphasized: "when will people recognize that the highest power is in its expression also the most modest and that the divine, when it makes itself manifest, can never be without a certain sadness and humility?" (Letter to his brother, November 28, 1798, GSA 6.1:294 [*Essays and Letters*, 111]). Sadness highlights the paradoxical insufficiency of the totality to satisfy finitude, but it is also a hypersensitivity that allows otherwise imperceptible realities to be detected: compare Heidegger, *Aus der Erfahrung des Denkens*, GA 13:79: "Who, as long as he avoids sadness, could ever be touched by an invigorating breeze?" Thus, boredom must be radicalized by sadness in the direction of melancholy: if boredom is the experience of pure time, melancholy overcomes it toward Eternity, and it is the enormity of Eternity that the melancholic endures, who is saddened by the transience and ephemerality of all things, and lives the infinite pain of the tear between time and Eternity. Compare some developments on this point in Romano Guardini, *De la mélancholie* (Paris: Seuil, 1992), 34 and 57–59.

330 Heidegger, GA 40:66 [*Introduction to Metaphysics*, 67–68].

331 Rimbaud, "Cities [II]," in *Illuminations*, 79. Translation altered—Trans.

332 Hegel, *Lectures on the Philosophy of World History: Introduction*, trans. H. B. Nisbet (New York: Cambridge University Press, 1975), 43.

333 Compare Hans Urs von Balthasar (*A Theology of History* [San Francisco: Ignatius Press, 1994], 24–25): "In Jesus Christ, the Logos is no longer the realm of ideas, values and laws which governs and gives meaning to history, but is himself history. [. . .] The facts are not only a phenomenal analogy for a doctrine lying behind them and abstractable from them (as Alexandrian theology still held to a certain extent); they are, grasped in their depth and totality, the meaning itself. [. . .] The value of the historical pole of human existence is thus heightened by the historical character of Christ's revelation and to some extent liberated from its un-just imprisonment within an unhistorical philosophy of essences [. . .] Contemporary religious existential philosophy has, indeed, gone a step beyond the Platonic scheme of thought."

334 Hölderlin, "Apriority of the individual," in *Cahier de l'Herne Hölderlin*, 111.

335 Translation altered—Trans.

336 Pascal, *Pensées*, Laf. §308 / Br. §793 [*Pensées*, 95].

337 Nietzsche himself tried to clarify: "I have never desecrated the holy name of love" (1885–87), 1 [216], KSA 12:58 [*Writings from the Late Notebooks*, trans. Kate Sturge, ed. Rüdiger Bittner (Cambridge: Cambridge University Press, 2003), 65]. He thus defined the way out of nihilism: "We must have a *goal* that would allow us to love one another! All other goals are worth destroying!" (Posthumous fragments [1882–84], 4 [75], KSA 10:135), and even said: "A Hebrew by the name of Jesus was, until now, the one who best knew how to love" ([1882–84], 4, [154], KSA 10:159).

338 Nietzsche emphasized the subversive dimension of Jesus's preaching: "I don't see what the

insurrection instigated by Jesus was against: if it was not against the Jewish Church—Church in the exact sense that we understand the word—it was an insurrection against the 'good and righteous,' against the 'saints of Israel,' against the hierarchy of society [. . .] it was lack of faith in 'higher men' in the ecclesiastical sense, which here led to indignation, an assassination attempt on everyone who is a priest or theologian. [. . .] This holy anarchist incited the lowly people, the outcasts and 'sinners' in opposition to the 'ruling class' in a language that even today would lead one to Siberia" (Posthumous fragments [1887–88], 11 [280], KSA 13:106–7).

339 Posthumous fragments (1887–88), 11 [336], KSA 13:144. Nietzsche's passionate conflict with Christ comes precisely from his lucidity with respect to the eschatological event proper to Western modernity, which had led him to *himself* take on the task of recapitulation: "Our pre-eminence: we live in the age of *comparison*, we can check the calculation as never before: we are the self-consciousness of history in general. [. . .] At bottom, we scholars are the ones who best fulfil the teachings of Christ today" ([1887–88], 11 [374], KSA 13:167 [*Writings from the Late Notebooks*, 236]). His final collapse then comes from his personal identification with Dionysus, with the Crucified, and with God (compare letters to Cosima Wagner, January 3, 1889, and to Jakob Burckhardt, January 6, 1889, KGB 3.5:573 and 578 [*Selected Letters of Friedrich Nietzsche*, 346–48]).

340 Translation altered—Trans.

341 Irenaeus of Lyons, *Against Heresies*, in *The Ante-Nicene Fathers*, ed. Rev. Alexander Roberts, D.D. and James Donaldson, LL.D. (Grand Rapids, MI: WM. B. Eerdmans, 1981), 1:455 and 446 (= PG 7:860 and 838). Greek text reconstituted. Translation altered—Trans.

342 Translation altered—Trans.

343 Hölderlin, "Patmos," lines 99 and 117–19; GSA 2.1:168 [*Friedrich Hölderlin: Selected Poems and Fragments*, 235 and 237].

344 As Paul Ricoeur was the first to emphasize, Heidegger "systematically eluded the confrontation with the block of Hebraic thought. He happened to think from the Gospels and from Christian theology, but always by avoiding the Hebraic cluster, which is the absolute stranger in relation to Greek discourse. [. . .] Does not the task of rethinking the Christian tradition by a "step back" demand that one recognize the radically Hebraic dimension of Christianity, which is first rooted in Judaism, and only afterwards in the Greek tradition? Why reflect only on Hölderlin, and not on the Psalms or Jeremiah?" (*Heidegger et la question de Dieu* [Paris: PUF-Quadrige, 2009], 37).

345 Heidegger, GA 65:4, 406, 405, 400, 403, and 399, respectively [*Contributions to Philosophy (Of the Event)*, 6, 322, 321, 317, 319, and 316].

346 Hölderlin, "The Only One" (fragment of the third version), GSA 2.1:169.

347 "Patmos," lines 137–40; GSA 2.1:169 [*Friedrich Hölderlin: Selected Poems and Fragments*, 237].

348 "Reconciler . . . ," line 73, GSA 2.1:132, and first draft, lines 8 and 10–11, GSA 2.2:699.

349 "The Only One" (fragment of the third version), GSA 2.1:163, and first version, line 33, GSA 2.1:154 [*Friedrich Hölderlin: Selected Poems and Fragments*, 221].

350 "Patmos," lines 147–48; GSA 2.1:169 [*Friedrich Hölderlin: Selected Poems and Fragments*, 237–39].

351 "Bread and Wine," lines 147–48; GSA 2.1:94 [*Friedrich Hölderlin: Selected Poems and Fragments*, 159]. Translation altered—Trans.

352 "Patmos," lines 109–11; GSA 2.1:168 [*Friedrich Hölderlin: Selected Poems and Fragments*, 235–37].

353 "Bread and Wine," lines 127–30; GSA 2.1:94 [*Friedrich Hölderlin: Selected Poems and Fragments*, 157]. Compare Jean-François Marquet ("Hölderlin, le retour des dieux," in *Miroirs de l'identité*

[Paris: Cerf, 2009], 284): "Such will be the basic ambiguity of Christianity: its God is a hidden God, unknown, but to this nocturnal monotheism, unrelated to the immanentist monotheism of Asia, is juxtaposed the inescapable memory of a concrete personality gone forever. With this in mind, the Christian era is a period properly without Gods, made of memories and premonitions under a storm-heavy sky."

354 Heidegger, GA 70:15 and 11.

355 GA 65:400 and 399 [*Contributions to Philosophy (Of the Event)*, 317 and 316].

356 GA 70:24.

357 Christian hope has nothing to do with waiting, within a linear and objective chronology, for an event liable to happen one of these days, it is eschatological tension, that is, opening to what exceeds history itself. Compare Heidegger, GA 60:102 and 114 [*The Phenomenology of Religious Life*, 71–72 and 81]: "The structure of Christian hope, which in truth is the relational sense of Parousia, is radically different from all expectation. [. . .] To the Christian, only his τὸ νῦν of the complex of enactment in which he really stands is to be decisive, but not the anticipation of a special event that is futurally situated in temporality."

358 Rimbaud, "Genie," in *Illuminations*, 163–65. Translation altered—Trans.

EPILOGUE

1 Mallarmé, "The Tomb of Edgar Allan Poe," in *Collected Poems and Other Verse*, trans. E. H. Blackmore and A. M. Blackmore (New York: Oxford University Press, 2006), 71.

2 A character from Hergé's *The Adventures of Tintin*—Trans.

3 A study published in July 2012 in the journal *Nature* under the title "*Approaching a State-Shift in Earth's Biosphere*," and signed by twenty-two researchers belonging to some fifteen international scientific institutions, foresees an "abrupt and irreversible shift" of the biosphere over the course of the twenty-first century, such that it would call into question the habitability of the earth in the short term; a report from the World Bank from November 2012 comes to the same conclusions; in *Our Final Hour*, the English astrophysicist Martin Rees estimates humanity's chances of survival at the end of the twenty-first century at 50 percent. It is not a question here of passing judgment on the reliability of these predictive models, but simply of noticing that the eschatological horizon is imposed by science and technology.

4 This return to animality, consented to out of fatigue, for Nietzsche characterizes nihilism: "The sight of man now makes us tired—what is nihilism today if it is not *that*? . . . We are tired of *man*. [. . .] Has not man's self-deprecation, his *will* to self-deprecation, been unstoppably on the increase since Copernicus? Gone, alas, is his faith in his dignity, uniqueness, irreplaceableness in the rank-ordering of beings,—he has become *animal*, literally, unqualifiedly and unreservedly an animal, man who in his earlier faiths was almost God ('child of God', 'God-man') . . ." (KSA 5:278 and 404 [*On the Genealogy of Morality*, trans. Carol Diethe, ed. Keith Ansell-Pearson (Cambridge: Cambridge University Press, 2007), 25 and 115]). Translation slightly altered—Trans.

5 Compare Rimbaud, "Clearance," in *Illuminations*, 123.

6 Heidegger, GA 38:149 [*Logic as the Question concerning the Essence of Language*, 123].

7 GA 5:325 [*Off the Beaten Track*, 245].

8 GA 39:61 [*Hölderlin's Hymns: "Germania" and "The Rhine,"* 57]. Translation altered—Trans.

9 GA 5:85 [*Off the Beaten Track*, 64].

10 Hans Urs von Balthasar, *L'apocalypse*, trans. Jean-Pierre Fels (Ourscamp: Éditions du Serviteur, 2000), 40–41.

11 Von Balthasar, *L'apocalypse*, 58–59.
12 Heidegger, GA 5:372 [*Off the Beaten Track*, 281].
13 Rimbaud, *A Season in Hell*, in *Arthur Rimbaud: Complete Works*, 219.
14 Translation altered—Trans.
15 In English in the original—Trans.
16 Ernst Jünger, *Passage de la ligne*, 92–93.

List of Primary Sources

I. MARTIN HEIDEGGER

Works

GA *Gesamtausgabe*. Frankfurt am Main: Vittorio Klostermann, 1976–. [Listed by volume number, with English translation given in brackets following.]

GA 4 *Erläuterungen zu Hölderlins Dichtung*. 1936–68. Edited by Friedrich-Wilhelm von Hermann. Frankfurt am Main: Vittorio Klostermann, 1981.

- [*Elucidations of Hölderlin's Poetry*. Translated by Keith Hoeller. Amherst, MA: Humanity Books, 2000.]

GA 5 *Holzwege*. 1935–46. Edited by Friedrich-Wilhelm von Hermann. Frankfurt am Main: Vittorio Klostermann, 1977.

- [*Off the Beaten Track*. Edited and translated by Julian Young and Kenneth Haynes. New York: Cambridge University Press, 2002.]

GA 6.2 *Nietzsche II*. 1939–46. Edited by Brigitte Schillbach. Frankfurt am Main: Vittorio Klostermann, 1997.

- [*Nietzsche, Volumes 3 and 4*. Translated by Joan Stambaugh, David Farrell Krell, and Frank A. Capuzzi. Edited by David Farrell Krell. San Francisco: HarperSanFrancisco, 1991.]

GA 7 *Vorträge und Aufsätze*. 1936–53. Edited by Friedrich-Wilhelm von Hermann. Frankfurt am Main: Vittorio Klostermann, 2000.

- [*Early Greek Thinking*. Translated by David Farrell Krell and Frank A. Capuzzi. New York: Harper & Row, 1975.]
- [*The Question concerning Technology, and Other Essays*. Translated by William Lovitt. New York: Harper & Row, 1977.]
- [*The End of Philosophy*. Translated with an introduction by Joan Stambaugh. Chicago: University of Chicago Press, 2003.]
- [*Bremen and Freiburg Lectures*. Translated by Andrew J. Mitchell. Bloomington: Indiana University Press, 2012.]
- [*Poetry, Language, Thought*. Translated by Albert Hofstadter. New York: Harper & Row, 1971.]

GA 8 *Was Heisst Denken?* 1951–52. Edited by Paola Ludovika Coriando. Frankfurt am Main: Vittorio Klostermann, 2002.

- [*What Is Called Thinking?* Translated by J. Glenn Gray. New York: Harper & Row, 1968.]

GA 9 *Wegmarken*. 1919–61. Edited by Friedrich-Wilhelm von Hermann. Frankfurt am Main: Vittorio Klostermann, 1996.

- [*Pathmarks*. Edited by William McNeill. New York: Cambridge University Press, 1998.]

GA 10 *Der Satz vom Grund*. 1955–56. Edited by Petra Jaeger. Frankfurt am Main: Vittorio Klostermann, 1997.

- [*The Principle of Reason*. Translated by Reginald Lilly. Bloomington: Indiana University Press, 1991.]

GA 11 *Identität und Differenz*. 1955–57. Edited by Friedrich-Wilhelm von Hermann. Frankfurt am Main: Vittorio Klostermann, 2006.

- [*Identity and Difference*. Translated with an introduction by Joan Stambaugh. Chicago: University of Chicago Press, 2002.]

GA 12 *Unterwegs zur Sprache*. 1950–59. Edited by Friedrich-Wilhelm von Hermann. Frankfurt am Main: Vittorio Klostermann, 1985.

- [*On the Way to Language*. Translated by Peter D. Hertz. New York: Harper & Row, 1971.]

GA 13 *Aus der Erfahrung des Denkens*. 1919–76. Edited by Hermann Heidegger. Frankfurt am Main: Vittorio Klostermann, 1983.

GA 14 *Zur Sache des Denkens*. 1962–64. Edited by Friedrich-Wilhelm von Hermann. Frankfurt am Main: Vittorio Klostermann, 1996.

- [*On Time and Being*. Translated by Joan Stambaugh. New York: Harper & Row, 1972.]

GA 15 *Seminare*. 1951–73. Edited by Curd Ochwadt. Frankfurt am Main: Vittorio Klostermann, 1986.

- ["Zurich Seminar." Unpublished in English.]

GA 16 *Reden und andere Zeugnisse eines Lebensweges*. 1910–76. Edited by Hermann Heidegger. Frankfurt am Main: Vittorio Klostermann, 2000.

- [*Discourse on Thinking*. Translated by John M. Anderson and E. Hans Freund. New York: Harper & Row, 1966.]
- [*The Heidegger Reader*. Translated by Jerome Veith. Edited by Günter Figal. Bloomington: Indiana University Press, 2009.]

GA 20 *Prolegomena zur Geschichte des Zeitbegriffs*. Summer semester, 1925. Edited by Petra Jaeger. Frankfurt am Main: Vittorio Klostermann, 1979.

- [*History of the Concept of Time: Prolegomena*. Translated by Theodore Kisiel. Bloomington: Indiana University Press, 1985.]

GA 29/30 *Die Grundbegriffe der Metaphysik*. Winter semester, 1929–30. Edited by Friedrich-Wilhelm von Hermann. Frankfurt am Main: Vittorio Klostermann, 2004.

- [*Fundamental Concepts of Metaphysics: World, Finitude, and Solitude*. Translated by William McNeill and Nicholas Walker. Bloomington: Indiana University Press, 1995.]

GA 33 *Aristoteles: Metaphysik θ 1–3: Vom Wesen und Wirklichkeit der Kraft*. Summer semester, 1931. Edited by Heinrich Huni. Frankfurt am Main: Vittorio Klostermann, 1981.

- [*Aristotle's Metaphysics θ 1–3: On the Essence and Actuality of Force*. Translated by Walter Brogan and Peter Warnek. Bloomington: Indiana University Press, 1995.]

GA 34 *Vom Wesen der Wahrheit. Zu Platons Höhlengleichnis und Theätet*. Winter semester, 1931–32. Edited by Hermann Mörchen. 2d ed. Frankfurt am Main: Vittorio Klostermann, 1997.

- [*The Essence of Truth: On Plato's Cave Allegory and Theaetetus*. Translated by Ted Sadler. London: Continuum, 2002.]

GA 38 *Logik als die Frage nach dem Wesen der Sprache*. Summer semester, 1934. Edited by Günter Seubold. Frankfurt am Main: Vittorio Klostermann, 1998.

- [*Logic as the Question concerning the Essence of Language*. Translated by Wanda Torres Gregory and Yvonne Unna. Albany: State University of New York Press, 2009.]

GA 39 *Hölderlins Hymnen "Germanien" und "Der Rhein."* Winter semester, 1934–35. Edited by Susanne Ziegler. 3d ed. Frankfurt am Main: Vittorio Klostermann, 1999.

- [*Hölderlin's Hymns: "Germania" and "The Rhine."* Translated by William McNeill and Julia Ireland. Bloomington: Indiana University Press, 2014.]

GA 40 *Einführung in die Metaphysik*. Summer semester, 1935. Edited by Petra Jaeger. Frankfurt am Main: Vittorio Klostermann, 1983.

- [*Introduction to Metaphysics*. Translated by Gregory Fried and Richard Polt. New Haven, CT: Yale University Press, 2014.]

GA 41 *Die Frage nach dem Ding. Zu Kants Lehre von den transzendentalen Grundsätzen*. Winter semester, 1935–36. Edited by Petra Jaeger. Frankfurt am Main: Vittorio Klostermann, 1984.

- [*What Is a Thing?* Translated by W. B. Barton Jr. and Vera Deutsch. Chicago: Henry Regnery Company, 1967.]

GA 45 *Grundfragen der Philosophie. Ausgewählte "Probleme" der "Logik."* Winter semester, 1937–38. Edited by Friedrich-Wilhelm von Hermann. 2d ed. Frankfurt am Main: Vittorio Klostermann, 1992.

- [*Basic Questions of Philosophy: Selected Problems of Logic*. Translated by Richard Rojcewicz and André Schuwer. Bloomington: Indiana University Press, 1994.]

GA 50 *Einleitung in die Philosophie—Denken und Dichten*. Winter semester, 1944–45. Edited by Petra Jaeger. Frankfurt am Main: Vittorio Klostermann, 1990.

- [*Introduction to Philosophy—Thinking and Poetizing*. Translated by Phillip Jacques Braunstein. Bloomington: Indiana University Press, 2011.]

GA 51 *Grundbegriffe*. Summer semester, 1941. Edited by Petra Jaeger. Frankfurt am Main: Vittorio Klostermann, 1991.

- [*Basic Concepts*. Translated by Gary E. Aylesworth. Bloomington: Indiana University Press, 1993.]

GA 53 *Hölderlins Hymne "Der Ister."* Summer semester, 1942. Edited by Walter Biemel. Frankfurt am Main: Vittorio Klostermann, 1984.

- [*Hölderlin's Hymn "The Ister."* Translated by William McNeill and Julia Davis. Bloomington: Indiana University Press, 1996.]

GA 54 *Parmenides*. Winter semester, 1942–43. Edited by Manfred S. Frings. Frankfurt am Main: Vittorio Klostermann, 1982.

- [*Parmenides*. Translated by Andrew Schuwer and Richard Rojcewicz. Bloomington: Indiana University Press, 1992.]

GA 55 *Heraklit. 1. Der Anfang des abendländischen Denkens. 2. Logik. Heraklits Lehre vom Logos*. Summer semester, 1944. Edited by Manfred S. Frings. 2d ed. Frankfurt am Main: Vittorio Klostermann, 1987.

- [*Heraclitus: The Inception of Occidental Thinking and Logic: Heraclitus' Doctrine of the Logos*. Translated by S. Montgomery Ewegen and Julia Goesser Assaiante. London: Bloomsbury Academic, 2018.]

GA 60 *Phänomenologie des religiösen Lebens*. 1. *Einleitung in die Phänomenologie der Religion*. Winter semester, 1920–21. Edited by M. Jung and T. Regehly. 2. *Augustinus und der Neuplatonismus*. Summer semester, 1921. Edited by C. Straube. 3. *Die philosophischen Grundlagen der mittelalterlichen Mystik*. Prepared notes and introduction to an undelivered course, 1918–19. Edited by C. Strube. Frankfurt am Main: Vittorio Klostermann, 1995.

- [*The Phenomenology of Religious Life*. 1. Introduction to the Phenomenology of Religion. 2. Augustine and Neo-Platonism. 3. The Philosophical Foundations of Medieval Mysticism. Translated by Matthias Fritsch and Jennifer Anna Gosetti-Ferencei. Bloomington: Indiana University Press, 2004.]

GA 65 *Beiträge zur Philosophie (Vom Ereignis)*. 1936–38. Edited by Friedrich-Wilhelm von Hermann. 2d ed. Frankfurt am Main: Vittorio Klostermann, 1994.

- [*Contributions to Philosophy (Of the Event)*. Translated by Richard Rojcewicz and Daniela Vallega-Neu. Bloomington: Indiana University Press, 2012.]

GA 66 *Besinnung*. 1938–39. Edited by Friedrich-Wilhelm von Hermann. Frankfurt am Main: Vittorio Klostermann, 1997.

- [*Mindfulness*. Translated by Parvis Emad and Thomas Kalary. London: Continuum, 2006.]

GA 68 *Hegel*. 1938–42. Edited by Ingrid Schüßler. Frankfurt am Main: Vittorio Klostermann, 1993.

- [*Hegel*. Translated by Joseph Arel and Niels Feuerhahn. Bloomington: Indiana University Press, 2015.]

GA 69 *Die Geschichte des Seyns*. 1938–40. Edited by Peter Trawny. Frankfurt am Main: Vittorio Klostermann, 1998.

- [*The History of Beyng*. Translated by William McNeill and Jeffrey Powell. Bloomington: Indiana University Press, 2015.]

GA 70 *Über den Anfang*. 1941. Edited by Paola-Ludovika Coriando. Frankfurt am Main: Vittorio Klostermann, 2005.

GA 77 *Feldweg-Gespräche*. 1944–45. Edited by Ingrid Schüßler. Frankfurt am Main: Vittorio Klostermann, 1995.

- [*Country Path Conversations*. Translated by Bret W. Davis. Bloomington: Indiana University Press, 2010.]

GA 79 *Bremer und Freiburger Vorträge*. 1949–57. Edited by Petra Jaeger. 2d ed. Frankfurt am Main: Vittorio Klostermann, 2005.

- [*Bremen and Freiburg Lectures*. Translated by Andrew J. Mitchell. Bloomington: Indiana University Press, 2012.]
- [*Poetry, Language, Thought*. Translated by Albert Hofstadter. New York: Harper & Row, 1971.]

SZ *Sein und Zeit*. 1927. 17th ed. Tübingen: Max Niemeyer Verlag, 1993.

- [*Being and Time*. Translated by John Macquarrie and Edward Robinson. New York: Harper Press, 1962. Cited as BT.]

Correspondence

Heidegger, Martin, and Elisabeth Blochmann. *Briefwechsel, 1918–1969*. Edited by Joachim W. Storck. Marbach am Neckar: Deutsche Schillergesellschaft, 1989.

II. OTHER PRIMARY SOURCES

Church Fathers

PG *Patrologia Graeca*. Edited by J.-P. Migne. 161 vols. Paris: 1857–66. Vols. 3, 7, 47, 49.

René Descartes

AT *Oeuvres de Descartes*. Edited by Charles Adam and Paul Tannery. New presentation by Bernard Rochot and Pierre Costabel. 11 vols. Paris: Vrin/CNRS, 1964–74.

AT 2 *Correspondance: Mars 1638–Décembre 1639*. Edited by Charles Adam and Paul Tannery. Paris: Vrin/CNRS, 1969.

AT 6 *Discours de la méthode et Essais*. Edited by Charles Adam and Paul Tannery. Paris: Vrin/CNRS, 1965.

AT 7 *Meditationes de prima philosophia*. Edited by Charles Adam and Paul Tannery. Paris: Vrin/CNRS, 1964.

AT 9 *Méditations et principes*. Edited by Charles Adam and Paul Tannery. Paris: Vrin/CNRS, 1971.

[*The Philosophical Writings of Descartes*. 3 vols. Translated by John Cottingham, Robert Stoothoff, and Dugald Murdoch. Cambridge: Cambridge University Press, 1984–91.]

Meister Eckhart

DW *Die deutsche Werke: Predigten und Traktate*. Edited by Josef Quint. Stuttgart: Kohlhammer, 1936–2008.

DW 1 *Predigten 1–24*. Edited by Josef Quint. Stuttgart: Kohlhammer, 1958.

DW 2 *Predigten 25–59*. Edited by Josef Quint. Stuttgart: Kohlhammer, 1971.

DW 3 *Predigten 60–86*. Edited by Josef Quint. Stuttgart: Kohlhammer, 1976.

DW 4.1 *Predigten 87–105*. Edited by Georg Steer. Stuttgart: Kohlhammer, 2003.

DW 5 *Traktate*. Edited by Josef Quint. Stuttgart: Kohlhammer, 1963.

OLME *OEUVRES latines de Maître Eckhart*. Edited by Alain de Libera, Edouard Wéber, and Emilie Zum Brunn. Paris: Cerf, 1984–.

[*Meister Eckhart: The Essential Sermons, Commentaries, Treatises, and Defense*. Translated and edited by Edmund College and Bernard McGinn. New York: Paulist Press, 1981.]

[*Meister Eckhart: Teacher and Preacher*. Edited by Bernard McGinn, with Frank Tobin and Elvira Borgstadt. New York: Paulist Press, 1986.]

[*Meister Eckhart: Sermons and Treatises*. 3 vols. Translated and edited by M. O'C. Walshe. Shaftesbury, Dorset, UK: Element Books, 1987.]

[*Meister Eckhart: Parisian Questions and Prologues*. Translated by Armand A. Maurer. Toronto: Pontifical Institute of Medieval Studies, 1974.]

Friedrich Hölderlin

GSA *Sämtliche Werke. Grosse Stuttgarter Ausgabe*. Edited by Friedrich Beissner. Stuttgart: Kohlhammer, 1946.

GSA 2.1 *Gedichte nach 1800: Text*. Edited by Friedrich Beissner. Stuttgart: Kohlhammer, 1951.

GSA 3 *Hyperion, oder der Eremit in Griechenland*. Edited by Friedrich Beissner. Stuttgart: Kohlhammer, 1957.

GSA 4.1 *Der Tod des Empedokles. Aufsätze: Text und Erläuterungen*. Edited by Friedrich Beissner. Stuttgart: Kohlhammer, 1961.

GSA 5 *Übersetzungen*. Edited by Friedrich Beissner. Stuttgart: Kohlhammer, 1952.

GSA 6.1 *Briefe: Text*. Edited by Friedrich Beissner and Adolf Beck. Stuttgart: Kohlhammer, 1954.

[*Friedrich Hölderlin: Selected Poems and Fragments*. Translated by Michael Hamburger. Edited by Jeremy Adler. New York: Penguin Books, 1998.]

[*Friedrich Hölderlin: Essays and Letters.* Translated and edited by Jeremy Adler and Charlie Louth. New York: Penguin Books, 2009.]

[*Friedrich Hölderlin: Essays and Letters on Theory.* Translated by Thomas Pfau. Albany: State University of New York Press, 1988.]

[*Hyperion and Selected Poems.* Edited by Eric L. Santner. New York: Continuum, 1990.]

Edmund Husserl

HUA *Husserliana: Gesammelte Werke.* Edited by Rudolph Bernet and Ullrich Melle. The Hague: M. Nijhoff, 1950–.

HUA 27 *Aufsätze und Vorträge (1922–1937).* Edited by Thomas Nenon and Hans Rainer Sepp. Dordrecht: Kluwer, 1989.

Immanuel Kant

AK *Gesammelte Schriften (Akademie-Ausgabe).* Edited by Königlichen Preußischen Akademie der Wissenschaften. Berlin: Walter de Gruyter, 1902–.

AK 3 *Kritik der reinen Vernunft, 2. Auflage 1787.* Edited by Königlichen Preußischen Akademie der Wissenschaften. Berlin: Walter de Gruyter, 1968.

AK 6 *Die Religion innerhalb der Grenzen der bloßen Vernunft. Die Metaphysik der Sitten.* Edited by Königlichen Preußischen Akademie der Wissenschaften. Berlin: Walter de Gruyter, 1968.

[*Critique of Pure Reason.* Translated by Paul Guyer and Allen W. Wood. New York: Cambridge University Press, 1998.]

[*Religion and Rational Theology.* Translated by Allen Wood and George di Giovanni. Cambridge: Cambridge University Press, 1996.]

Karl Marx and Friedrich Engels

MEW *Marx Engels Werke.* Institut für Marxismus-Leninismus beim ZK der SED. Berlin: Dietz, 1956–.

MEW 7 *Karl Marx und Friedrich Engels: August 1849–Juni 1851.* Institut für Marxismus-Leninismus beim ZK der SED. Berlin: Dietz, 1960.

MEW 13 *Karl Marx und Friedrich Engels: Januar 1859–Februar 1860.* Institut für Marxismus-Leninismus beim ZK der SED. Berlin: Dietz, 1961.

MEW 23 *Karl Marx: Das Kapital.* Institut für Marxismus-Leninismus beim ZK der SED. Berlin: Dietz, 1962.

MEW 26.3 *Karl Marx: Theorien über den Mehrwert.* Institut für Marxismus-Leninismus beim ZK der SED. Berlin: Dietz, 1968.

[*Karl Marx, Friedrich Engels: Collected Works.* Translated and edited by Richard Dixon et al. New York: Continuum, 1975–2004. Cited as CW.]

[*Marx-Engels Collected Works, Volume 10: 1849–1851.* Edited by Hugh Rodwell et al. New York: International Publishers, 1978. Cited as CW 10.]

[*Marx-Engels Collected Works, Volume 16: 1858–1860.* Edited by Richard Dixon et al. New York: International Publishers, 1980. Cited as CW 16.]

[*Marx-Engels Collected Works, Volume 29: 1857–1861.* Edited by Tatyana Vasilyeva et al. New York: International Publishers, 1987. Cited as CW 29.]

[*Marx-Engels Collected Works, Volume 32: Karl Marx, 1861–1863*. Edited by Emile Burns et al. New York: International Publishers, 1989. Cited as CW 32.]

[*Capital: Volume 1*. Translated by Ben Fowkes. New York: Penguin Books, 1981.]

Friedrich Nietzsche

KGB *Briefwechsel: Kritische Gesamtausgabe*. Edited by Giorgio Colli and Mazzino Montinari. New York: Walter de Gruyter, 1975–2004.

KGB 3.5 *Briefe von Friedrich Nietzsche Januar 1887–Januar 1889*. Edited by Giorgio Colli and Mazzino Montinari. New York: Walter de Gruyter, 1984.

KGW *Werke: Kritische Gesamtausgabe*. Edited by Giorgio Colli and Mazzino Montinari. New York: Walter de Gruyter, 1975–2004.

KGW 1.2 *Nachgelassene Aufzeichnungen (Herbst 1858–Herbst 1862)*. Edited by Giorgio Colli and Mazzino Montinari. New York: Walter de Gruyter, 2000.

KSA *Sämtliche Werke: Kritische Studienausgabe*. Edited by Giorgio Colli and Mazzino Montinari. 15 vols. New York: Walter de Gruyter, 1980–.

KSA 3 *Morgenröte. Idyllen aus Messina. Die fröhliche Wissenschaft*. Edited by Giorgio Colli and Mazzino Montinari. 2d ed. New York: Walter de Gruyter, 1988.

KSA 4 *Also sprach Zarathustra*. Edited by Giorgio Colli and Mazzino Montinari. 2d ed. New York: Walter de Gruyter, 1988.

KSA 5 *Jenseits von Gut und Böse. Zur Genealogie der Morale*. Edited by Giorgio Colli and Mazzino Montinari. 2d ed. New York: Walter de Gruyter, 1988.

KSA 6 *Der Fall Wagner. Götzen-Dämmerung. Der Antichrist. Ecce homo. Dionysos-Dithyramben. Nietzsche contra Wagner*. Edited by Giorgio Colli and Mazzino Montinari. 2d ed. New York: Walter de Gruyter, 1988.

KSA 9 *Nachgelassene Fragmente 1880–1882*. Edited by Giorgio Colli and Mazzino Montinari. 2d ed. New York: Walter de Gruyter, 1988.

KSA 10 *Nachgelassene Fragmente 1882–1884*. Edited by Giorgio Colli and Mazzino Montinari. 2d ed. New York: Walter de Gruyter, 1988.

KSA 11 *Nachgelassene Fragmente 1884–1885*. Edited by Giorgio Colli and Mazzino Montinari. 2d ed. New York: Walter de Gruyter, 1988.

KSA 12 *Nachgelassene Fragmente 1885–1887*. Edited by Giorgio Colli and Mazzino Montinari. 2d ed. New York: Walter de Gruyter, 1988.

KSA 13 *Nachgelassene Fragmente 1887–1889*. Edited by Giorgio Colli and Mazzino Montinari. 2d ed. New York: Walter de Gruyter, 1988.

[*The Anti-Christ, Ecce Homo, Twilight of the Idols, and Other Writings*. Translated by Judith Norman. Edited by Aaron Ridley and Judith Norman. Cambridge: Cambridge University Press, 2005.]

[*Beyond Good and Evil: Prelude to a Philosophy of the Future*. Translated by Judith Norman. Edited by Rolf-Peter Horstmann and Judith Norman. Cambridge: Cambridge University Press, 2002.]

[*Daybreak: Thoughts on the Prejudices of Morality*. Translated by R. J. Hollingdale. Edited by Maudemarie Clark and Brian Leiter. Cambridge: Cambridge University Press, 1997.]

[*On the Genealogy of Morality*. Translated by Carol Diethe. Edited by Keith Ansell-Pearson. Cambridge: Cambridge University Press, 2007.]

[*Selected Letters of Friedrich Nietzsche*. Translated and edited by Christopher Middleton. Indianapolis: Hackett Publishing Co., 1996.]

[*Thus Spoke Zarathustra*. Translated by Adrian Del Caro. Edited by Adrian Del Caro and Robert B. Pippin. Cambridge: Cambridge University Pres, 2006.]

[*The Will to Power*. Translated by Walter Kaufmann and R. J. Hollingdale. Edited by Walter Kaufmann. New York: Vintage Books, 1967.]

Presocratics

DK *Die Fragmente der Vorsokratiker*. Edited by Hermann Diels and Walther Kranz. Berlin: Weidmann, 1934–37.

[*Early Greek Philosophy*. 9 vols. Translated and edited by André Laks and Glenn W. Most. Cambridge, MA: Harvard University Press, 2016.]

[*Early Greek Philosophy, Volume 2: Beginnings and Early Ionian Thinkers, Part 1*. Edited and translated by André Laks and Glenn W. Most. Cambridge, MA: Harvard University Press, 2016.]

[*Early Greek Philosophy, Volume 3: Early Ionian Thinkers, Part 2*. Edited and translated by André Laks and Glenn W. Most. Cambridge, MA: Harvard University Press, 2016.]

[*Early Greek Philosophy, Volume 5: Western Greek Thinkers, Part 2*. Edited and translated by André Laks and Glenn W. Most. Cambridge, MA: Harvard University Press, 2016.]

[*Early Greek Philosophy, Volume 6: Later Ionian and Athenian Thinkers, Part 1*. Edited and translated by André Laks and Glenn W. Most. Cambridge, MA: Harvard University Press, 2016.]

[*Early Greek Philosophy, Volume 7: Later Ionian and Athenian Thinkers, Part 2*. Edited and translated by André Laks and Glenn W. Most. Cambridge, MA: Harvard University Press, 2016.]

Index